Developing Content Area Literacy

We dedicate this book to . . .

Theresa Cicchelli

A dedicated teacher

A visionary leader

A supportive colleague

Most of all, a true friend

40 Strategies for Middle and Secondary Classrooms

Developing Content Area Literacy

Patricia A. Antonacci
Catherine M. O'Callaghan

Iona College

Los Angeles | London | New Delhi
Singapore | Washington DC

For information:

SAGE Publications, Inc.
2455 Teller Road
Thousand Oaks, California 91320
E-mail: order@sagepub.com

SAGE Publications Ltd.
1 Oliver's Yard
55 City Road
London EC1Y 1SP
United Kingdom

SAGE Publications India Pvt. Ltd.
B 1/I 1 Mohan Cooperative Industrial Area
Mathura Road, New Delhi 110 044
India

SAGE Publications Asia-Pacific Pte. Ltd.
33 Pekin Street #02-01
Far East Square
Singapore 048763

Printed in the United States of America

Library of Congress Cataloging-in-Publication Data

Antonacci, Patricia.
Developing content area literacy: 40 strategies for middle and secondary classrooms/Patricia A. Antonacci, Catherine M. O'Callaghan.
 p. cm.
Includes bibliographical references and index.
ISBN 978-1-4129-7283-3 (pbk.)

 1. Content area reading—United States. 2. Reading (Middle school)—United States. 3. Reading (Secondary)—United States. I. O'Callaghan, Catherine M. II. Title.

LB1050.455.A58 2011
428.4'0712—dc22   2009043901

Printed on acid-free paper

10   11   12   13   14   10   9   8   7   6   5   4   3   2   1

Acquiring Editor:	Diane McDaniel
Editorial Assistant:	Ashley Conlon
Production Editor:	Brittany Bauhaus
Copy Editor:	Heidi Unkrich
Proofreader:	Victoria Reed-Castro
Indexer:	Diggs Publication Services, Inc.
Typesetter:	C&M Digitals (P) Ltd.
Cover Designer:	Glenn Vogel
Marketing Manager:	Carmel Schrire

Contents

Section III. Narrative Text: Developing Comprehension for Narrative Text   83

11   Interactive Think-Alouds: Collaborative Interpretation of Text   90

12   Inference Strategy Guide: Facilitating Reading Between the Lines   94

13   Imagination Recreation: Deepening Understanding Through Creativity   99

Section VIII. Independent Learning: Promoting Strategies for Independence in Learning

243

36   Talking Around the Text: Using Dialogic Reading and Writing to Promote Independent Learners

249

37   Textbook Activity Guide (TAG): Developing Independence in Learning From the Textbook

257

Preface

BACKGROUND: ESTABLISHING THE PURPOSE

There is increasing concern for middle and high school students who do not or simply cannot read and write the required range of texts needed for academic achievement. Students and parents know the consequences of school failure, and teachers and school administrators continue to explore ways to increase students' proficiencies in reading and writing. This growing frustration is not new to education, although recently these apprehensions have been reawakened within the professional community causing the topic of adolescent literacy to appear once again on center stage. Alliance for Excellent Education (Heller & Greenleaf, 2007) is one of the policy groups that has called attention to the problem. They have reported that although gains have been made in reading achievement by younger students, progress for middle and high school students is static. While nationwide efforts to promote literacy learning have targeted beginning readers and writers, no such attempts have been made for middle and high school students. It is time to sustain those gains made by young students by investing in adolescent literacy instruction.

We cannot help recalling our own experiences as teachers with students who were frustrated as they struggled with reading their texts and who had greater problems when trying to use writing to represent their ideas from various content areas. Our current collaboration with classroom teachers in middle and high schools reveals their strong concerns over students' lack of preparation for "reading to learn" from the textbooks, related literature, and Web sites. Entering the classroom for field work and student teaching, our preservice schoolteachers are confused as they witness the literacy problems manifested by so many adolescent students they tutor and teach.

For the seasoned content area teacher and for those entering the teaching profession, there was a sense of uncertainty when we offered suggestions to help students read and write in their content area classrooms. Although they do believe that literacy is the cornerstone to all learning, many practicing and preservice teachers in content area classrooms also believe that it is not their responsibility to teach literacy to middle and high school students. This problem of adolescent literacy has a history indeed, and for so many reasons, it is still pervasive in our nation's schools today.

PURPOSE OF THE BOOK

The complex challenges related to advancing literacy for all middle and high school students have defined our purpose for writing this book. Fundamental to our purpose and supported by policy makers such as International Reading Association and the National Council for Teachers of English, we believe that literacy instruction is the responsibility of all classroom teachers in Grades K through 12 and it needs to be the foundation of each school's mission and curriculum. To ensure that the core components of reading and writing development would be addressed across the instructional strategies, we have consulted recent reviews of research on adolescent literacy that serve to inform policy including *Reading Next* (Biancarosa & Snow, 2006), *Writing Next* (Graham & Perin, 2007), and *Academic Literacy Instruction for Adolescents* (Torgesen et al., 2007). For example, conclusions from reviews of research reported by Torgesen emphasize that classroom teachers need to continue to develop adolescent students' literacy in the following six areas:

1. Fluency of text reading

2. Vocabulary, or the breadth and depth of knowledge about the meaning of words

3. Background, or prior knowledge related to content of text being read

4. Higher-level reasoning and thinking skills

5. Active and flexible use of reading strategies to enhance comprehension

6. Motivation and engagement for understanding and learning from text (pp. 10–11)

To further address and fulfill our major purpose for writing this book, we designed and formatted a set of instructional strategies that are user-friendly to teachers in content area classrooms and would be highly effective for developing readers and writers in middle and high school. To that end, we selected literacy strategies that could be integrated in content area lessons and presented them in an easy-to-follow format. We wanted teachers to use this book in their classrooms, to keep it on their desks as a reference guide for planning their instruction, and define it as *user-friendly*. Most important, we selected instructional strategies because they are grounded in research and proven to demonstrate best practice.

Like many instructors of courses for teaching reading and writing in content areas, we were looking for an easy-to-use handbook of instructional strategies. Therefore, we designed a practical guide of strategies organized around eight essential areas for developing content area literacy. As instructors we found it frustrating to use texts that claim to address the learning needs of diverse students but only explain the importance of meeting the needs of all students rather than providing concrete ways to modify instruction to reach that objective. Therefore, for each instructional strategy, we have specific ways to differentiate instruction for striving readers and writers as well as for English language learners (ELL).

OUR AUDIENCE

Our primary intention in writing *Developing Content Area Literacy: 40 Strategies for Middle and Secondary Classrooms* was to create an easy-to-use resource for literacy instruction by content area teachers at the middle and high school levels. Therefore, the book is meant as a practical reference for teaching. Instructors of preservice teachers may use the book as a secondary text within their courses. Some instructors may choose the book as their primary text for classes with students who have a background in literacy development. In any case, there is a wide audience for *Developing Content Area Literacy* including the following: (1) instructors at the undergraduate and graduate levels who teach content area literacy courses in teacher preparation secondary programs, (2) preservice and inservice content area teachers of middle and high school students who are enrolled in teacher preparation programs, (3) content area classroom teachers at the middle and high school levels, (4) districtwide and schoolwide curriculum trainers who provide professional development to teachers, (5) instructors at the graduate level teaching courses in literacy specialist and literacy coaching programs, (6) literacy coaches and reading specialists at the middle and high school levels, and (7) districtwide and building curriculum specialists and administrators.

How the Book May Be Used

- *Supplementary text:* Within the classroom, instructors may select *Developing Content Area Literacy* to supplement their course textbook. Used as a supplementary text, the book offers instructional strategies to which students may easily reference as they are reading and learning about each of the essential components of literacy for middle and high school students.

- *Primary text:* Instructors may select the book as their primary text since it contains essential categories for adolescent literacy development, each supported by a summary of research relevant to learning in each of the eight areas. Further, the book contains suggested professional resources as well as an extensive reference list facilitating students' access to additional source material.

- *Reference guide or handbook:* All teachers, preservice and inservice, would find *Developing Content Area Literacy* a useful reference in planning instruction. Literacy strategies are organized and presented for ease of use, thereby creating a desktop reference guide for the busy teacher when planning lessons.

Organizational Features of the Text

A major goal in writing and organizing *Developing Content Area Literacy* was to offer preservice and inservice teachers of adolescent students an easy-to-use book containing a range of evidence-based literacy instructional strategies that could be used across content area classrooms. To achieve our goal, we carefully organized and formatted the presentation of each instructional strategy as described below.

- *Components of literacy instruction:* We began by focusing on the five important components of literacy identified by the National Reading Panel (National Institute of Child Health and Human Development, 2000) and the No Child Left Behind Act of 2001. Guided by research and practice, we added three additional components that are critical to adolescent literacy and learning. Using evidence-based instruction and best practices, we have organized 40 instructional strategies around the following eight components of adolescent literacy learning:

1. Academic vocabulary
2. Reading fluency

3. Comprehension of narrative text

4. Comprehension of informational text

5. Comprehension of media and digital literacies

6. Developing critical thinking skills

7. Writing informational text

8. Developing independence in learning

- *Categorizing instructional strategies:* We have selected 40 of the most compelling strategies that support adolescent literacy development and organized them around eight essential categories. Although each of the instructional strategies that we have selected develops a wide range of literacy concepts and skills, we chose to use focus on each strategy to classify it into one of the eight essential categories. For example, the focus of the "Textbook Activity Guide (TAG)" strategy in Section 8 is on developing students' independence in learning as they read the textbook. However, when the TAG strategy is used, students sharpen their skills in skimming, reading and retelling, writing responses to reading, making predictions, collaborating or sharing responses with others, as well as developing self-monitoring strategies. Clearly, each of the literacy strategies has an instructional focus as they address a number of additional literacy skills.

- *Forty strategies:* Around each of the eight essential categories of literacy development, there are five instructional strategies for the advancing literacy skills at the middle and high school levels. The evidence-based strategies selected are supported by research and have been used by teachers in content area classrooms who judged them as best practices.

- *Step-by-step procedure:* Having taught for several years at all levels—elementary, middle, and high school—we cannot forget the abundant demands of teaching and the busy lives of classroom teachers. It takes time from teachers' already very busy schedules to read through textbooks on literacy instruction to find and select the appropriate literacy instructional strategy they can use within their content area classroom; therefore, we have provided a convenient method of organizing the 40 strategies. Additionally, each of the strategies is presented in an easy-to-follow, step-by-step procedure structured around reading and writing—before reading (writing), during reading (writing), and after reading (writing).

PEDAGOGICAL FEATURES OF THE TEXT

To achieve our purpose in providing a user-friendly book that would serve as a reference guide for busy content area teachers and provide effective teaching practices to support student learning, we offer the following distinguishing pedagogical features:

- *Research related strategies for literacy instruction:* Teachers need to make the most effective use of their instructional time with students. Therefore, in selecting strategies for literacy development, it is important to select those that are proven to be effective or embedded in scientifically based reading research (SBRR). Thus for each of the sections, we have provided the foundations for strategy selection.

- *Clear and concise description of each strategy:* To facilitate the teacher in planning instruction and to encourage the content area teacher to incorporate literacy within their lessons, we have begun with a clear description of the strategy. Each description is followed by a step-by-step procedure for its implementation.

- *Graphics:* To further support strategy use with students, graphics have been developed for most strategies. In many cases, the graphics provide a clear understanding to teachers of the instructional procedures. Many of the graphics may be copied for classroom use.

- *Use of technology:* The landscape for comprehending texts has been dramatically transformed and will continue to change. Technology has had a major impact in the way we understand. Within *Developing Content Area Literacy*, we offer a section on digital and media literacy as well as present ways to use technology as a tool for teaching literacy in the content areas.

- *Suggestions for differentiating instruction for the striving readers and writers*: Within each classroom, students perform at a range of levels in reading as well as writing. Therefore, to address this issue, we have included ways to differentiate instruction. For each instructional strategy, there are specific suggestions to modify instruction to meet the learning needs of the striving reader and writer.

- *Suggestions for modifying instruction for ELL students:* A large percentage of students in classrooms across the nation are learning to read and write in a second language as well as learning content knowledge in their second language. For ELL students to be successful in school, instructional strategies must be modified to meet their linguistic needs. Thus, for each instructional strategy presented, there are specific approaches to modify instruction for ELL students.

- *Applications of strategy instruction to content areas:* To demonstrate how each instructional strategy may be used within content area classrooms, an application to a content area is presented. Throughout the book, the reader will find a wide range of applications across different disciplines. For example, in addition to the more common subject areas such as English language arts, mathematics, and social studies, readers will find applications to visual arts, physics, earth science, agriculture, economics, health education, and physical education.

- *A strategy for assessing student learning:* To help our readers support student learning, an assessment tool to monitor students' literacy development is provided for each of the eight essential literacy areas. Rubrics have been used for the purpose of focusing on important areas of learning and using results to assist students. Students are also encouraged to engage in self-assessment of their own learning. Examples of self-assessments have been demonstrated for some areas of literacy. For example, in Section VIII "Independent Learning: Promoting Strategies for Independence in Learning," students use a self-assessment survey to account for their progress in becoming independent learners.

- *Reflective practice for teaching:* Effective teachers consistently look for ways to improve their teaching. Within each section, specific ways for reflecting on teaching and learning related to literacy areas are provided. Reflective practices may be used by students who are preparing for teaching and are engaged in field experiences and student teaching, or they may be used by practicing teachers for finding ways to further increase students' literacy development.

- *Margin notes: Tips for teaching:* At the beginning of each section of the book, we have offered "Tips for Teaching" related to that section on literacy development derived from current research and best practices. These three essential tips offer reminders to the reader for using effective instruction for developing literacy in adolescent students.

REFERENCES

Biancarosa, C., & Snow, C. E. (2006). *Reading next: A vision for action and research in middle and high school literacy* (pp. 12–20). A report to Carnegie Corporation of New York (2nd ed.). Washington, DC: Alliance for Excellent Education.

Graham, S., & Perin, D. (2007). *Writing next: Effective strategies to improve writing of adolescents in middle and high schools.* A report to Carnegie Corporation of New York. Washington, DC: Alliance for Excellent Education.

Heller, R., & Greenleaf, C. (2007). *Literacy instruction in the content areas: Getting to the core of middle and high school improvement.* Washington, DC: Alliance for Excellent Education.

National Institute of Child Health and Human Development. (2000). *Report of the National Reading Panel. Teaching children to read: An evidence-based assessment of the scientific research literature on reading and its implications for reading instruction* (NIH Publication No. 00-4769). Washington, DC: U.S. Government Printing Office.

Torgesen, J. K., Houston, D. D., Rissman, L. M., Decker, S. M., Roberts, G., Vaughn, S., et al. (2007). *Academic literacy instruction for adolescents: A guidance document from the Center on Instruction.* Portsmouth, NH: RMC Research Corporation, Center on Instruction.

Acknowledgments

We would like to acknowledge and express our sincere thanks to so many people who have contributed to our project. Our deep gratefulness is given to the team at SAGE Publications who have made such valuable contributions to our book from prospectus to publication. With special gratitude and deep appreciation, we wish to acknowledge Diane McDaniel, acquisitions editor, who was so generous with her time and positive support throughout the project. Her editorial comments and suggestions were invaluable, her caring support throughout the process was sustaining and motivating, her responses and feedback were instant, and her attention to detail was helpful and useful. Thank you, Diane! Two editorial assistants worked with us and both are exceptional. Leah Mori provided the initial help that we needed in navigating through and understanding the process. Ashley Conlon facilitated us through the development and completion of the final manuscript. Your immediate, clear, and accurate responses were so helpful.

Our reviewers provided important and valuable comments and suggestions that were so useful. We greatly appreciate the feedback that we received from our reviewers from prospectus to manuscript. We wish to thank each of the following:

Jordan M. Barkley, *Jacksonville State University*

Heriberto Godina, *University of Texas at El Paso*

John R. Haught, *Wright State University*

Betty Higgins, *Sam Houston State University*

Patricia Hoffman, *Minnesota State University–Mankato*

Lois E. Huffman, *North Carolina State University*

Jennifer McGregor, *Tarleton State University*

Scott R. Popplewell, *Ball State University*

Jill Raiguel, *Cal Poly Pomona*

Maurine Richardson, *University of South Dakota*

Linda Wedwick, *Illinois State University*

Setting Standards in the English Language Arts

Although we present these standards as a list, we want to emphasize that they are not distinct and separable; they are, in fact, interrelated and should be considered as a whole.

IRA/NCTE STANDARDS FOR THE ENGLISH LANGUAGE ARTS

1. Students read a wide range of print and nonprint texts to build an understanding of texts, of themselves, and of the cultures of the United States and the world; to acquire new information; to respond to the needs and demands of society and the workplace; and for personal fulfillment. Among these texts are fiction and nonfiction, classic, and contemporary works.

2. Students read a wide range of literature from many periods in many genres to build an understanding of the many dimensions (e.g., philosophical, ethical, aesthetic) of human experience.

3. Students apply a wide range of strategies to comprehend, interpret, evaluate, and appreciate texts. They draw on their prior experience, their interactions with other readers and writers, their knowledge of word meaning and of other texts, their word identification strategies, and their understanding of textual features (e.g., sound-letter correspondence, sentence structure, context, graphics).

4. Students adjust their use of spoken, written, and visual language (e.g., conventions, style, vocabulary) to communicate effectively with a variety of audiences and for different purposes.

5. Students employ a wide range of strategies as they write and use different writing process elements appropriately to communicate with different audiences for a variety of purposes.

6. Students apply knowledge of language structure, language conventions (e.g., spelling and punctuation), media techniques, figurative language, and genre to create, critique, and discuss print and nonprint texts.

7. Students conduct research on issues and interests by generating ideas and questions, and by posing problems. They gather, evaluate, and synthesize data from a variety of sources (e.g., print and nonprint texts, artifacts, people) to communicate their discoveries in ways that suit their purpose and audience.

8. Students use a variety of technological and informational resources (e.g., libraries, databases, computer networks, video) to gather and synthesize information and to create and communicate knowledge.

9. Students develop an understanding of and respect for diversity in language use, patterns, and dialects across cultures, ethnic groups, geographic regions, and social roles.

10. Students whose first language is not English make use of their first language to develop competency in the English language arts and to develop understanding of content across the curriculum.

11. Students participate as knowledgeable, reflective, creative, and critical members of a variety of literacy communities.

12. Students use spoken, written, and visual language to accomplish their own purposes (e.g., for learning, enjoyment, persuasion, and the exchange of information).

Reference

Source: Standards for the English Language Arts, by the International Reading Association and the National Council of Teachers of English, 1996. **Newark, DE: International Reading Association and Urbana, IL: National Council of Teachers of English.** Copyright 1996 by the International Reading Association and the National Council of Teachers of English. Reprinted with permission.

Introduction

Adolescent Literacy

The Need for Literacy
Instruction in Content Area Classrooms

Ask any content area teacher how well their students read and learn from their required textbooks. Their descriptions will match research that suggest that too many adolescent students are struggling to read and write at grade level and are experiencing difficulty in understanding their science, mathematics, and social studies textbooks as well as essential pieces of literature. Many adolescent students fit into what Carnine and Carnine (2004, p. 204) defined as the "new class" of students who struggle to read their required textbooks. The number of adolescent students who fall below basic proficiency levels for reading and writing is unacceptable.

This commentary on adolescent readers who are unsuccessful in understanding and learning from their required textbooks is confirmed by their performance scores on reading examinations. Recent results reported in *The Nation's Report Card: Reading 2007* show that 67% of fourth graders and 74% of eighth graders performed at the basic level of proficiency. Basic level denotes "partial mastery of prerequisite knowledge and skills that are fundamental for proficient work at each grade assessed" (National Assessment of Educational Progress of Grades 4 and 8, 2007). What this means is that more than half of the students entering the middle and secondary grades lack the skills required to read and learn from assigned texts within content area classrooms. Further research confirmed in the *Reading Next* report indicates that 8 million students from Grades 4 to 12 struggle to read at grade level (Biancarosa & Snow, 2006). Think about these students who come to school each day and struggle to learn the range of subjects in content area classrooms but are hindered by their lack of literacy skills. It is true that over the past decade resources have supported the development of literacy skills for children in primary grades. Several programs supported by No Child Left Behind laws have been successful in helping many students to learn to read on grade level by Grade 3. However, those basic skills in reading and writing that students in the primary grades have acquired are not sufficient for the complexity of texts that are required reading for middle and high school students. Students' literacy achievements in the primary grades provide the critical foundation for building more complex skills that are essential for success in middle and high school learning; however, instruction in reading and writing must continue throughout middle and high school to ensure success in content area classrooms. The responsibility to provide continuous and effective instruction in reading and writing skills to adolescent students belongs to each content area teacher. Without instruction in academic literacy, we cannot expect students' success in content area classrooms. Thus instruction for academic literacy needs to be part of the content curriculum taught by knowledgeable and effective classroom teachers.

LITERACY DEMANDS FOR ADOLESCENT LEARNERS

What are the literacy demands for adolescent students within school and beyond? Answering this question is relative to what we are preparing them to do beyond high school. When adolescent students graduate, will they be prepared to enter college or be a productive member of the workforce? With respect to their literacy skills, many graduates may not be ready for college or their desired career path. The current literacy demands for entrance into the workforce are rapidly changing. The economy is being redefined as one that is global, society is emerging as international and multicultural, and employment opportunities are defined by the age of technology and information. Authors of *Reading Next* (Biancarosa & Snow, 2006) cited research related to the demands for adolescent literacy. They forecasted dramatic increases in required literacy skills for all jobs, and the picture worsens for professional employment where the literacy demands are greater. Will our students be prepared to meet this rise in the literacy demands required for a changing workforce? Research answers these questions based on our current graduates who do not have the necessary reading and writing skills required for the workplace demands (Biancarosa & Snow, 2006; Graham & Perin, 2007).

As adolescent students move from class to class, each teacher requires reading and writing assignments that pertain to their specific content areas. This is a starting point for defining the demands of adolescent literacy. Content area literacy involves a range of skills for reading and writing texts related to specific academic disciplines. Influenced by advances in technology and demands of society, literacy requirements within the 21st-century middle and high school classrooms have moved forward as well. Content area requirements and expectations for adolescent students parallel these increased academic demands within society. In addition to reading and writing assignments from multiple textbooks, students are required to be computer literate as they use rapidly changing technology for learning. Such requirements include students' use of specific software programs in different content areas, their developing proficiencies in using technology for research and multimedia presentations, as well as a greater reliance on the Internet for learning. Dalton and Proctor (2008) called this a "changing landscape of text and comprehension." Helping students succeed in middle and high school by facilitating their development of academic literacies is not simple, but their achievements will be rewarding, resulting in preparing adolescents for the competitive workforce. Their success demanded for this 21st century can be attained only through effective and consistent content area instruction that integrates content literacy development. Effective literacy instruction for adolescent students occurs when content area teachers are knowledgeable about the nature of literacy development and possess the appropriate strategies to teach reading and writing within their disciplines.

WHAT CONTENT AREA TEACHERS NEED TO KNOW ABOUT ACADEMIC LITERACY LEARNING

THE NATURE OF COMPREHENSION

Teachers need to know that the process of comprehension is complex and that the comprehension process develops over time. Understanding the text is more than simply translating words into meanings. Readers are required to construct meaning by interacting with text. This constructive and interactive process is based on the reader, the text, and the context or the situation in which the reading occurs, all of which are major factors affecting the meaning constructed around the text. Let us first consider the *reader*: Readers bring to the text a range of differences including knowledge about the text, personal experiences related to the text, cognitive and metacognitive strategies for reading, and motivation to read as well as dispositions or attitudes toward reading. The second aspect affecting the comprehension process to consider is the *text*, each varying with the author's writing style, level of reading difficulty including vocabulary and sentence length, content knowledge, and the presentation of content that may or may not be supported by graphics. Finally, the *context* in which the text is being read weighs in on what the reader comprehends. Part of the context includes the goals or purposes for reading as well as the time and the place in which the reading occurs. Another aspect of the context that affects comprehension is the sociosituational context: The events that have occurred before or during the reading of the text will contribute to how the reader constructs meaning. For example, consider students who are assigned readings about flooding and its effects on the lives of the people as well as the land. At the time of the reading, there is a sudden storm and students are experiencing the same weather condition they are reading about. The context will affect the way they have interacted with the text. Thus the reader, the text, and the context each contains numerous factors that affect how and what the reader comprehends from the text.

COGNITIVE AND METACOGNITIVE STRATEGIES AFFECTING LITERACY AND LEARNING

Teachers need to know how cognitive and metacognitive strategies affect students' comprehension and learning from texts. Proficient readers use learning or cognitive strategies to help them comprehend text. Cognitive strategies are plans that readers may use to accomplish their purpose for reading. Strategies are often taught and develop over time through use. Some cognitive strategies are more complex than others, depending on the task. For example, beginner readers are taught to make predictions about the story by looking at the title and pictures clues. Whereas adolescent readers will be taught to predict the content by using more complex cues such as the title, subheadings, graphics and illustrations, as well as skimming and scanning a chapter to survey the text.

As students advance through the grades, they are expected to learn and develop effective cognitive strategies that facilitate their comprehension of text and their use of reading as a tool for learning. Adolescent students who are proficient in literacy and learning continue to develop and refine their strategies that include the following: (1) setting a purpose for reading and writing, (2) activating and using prior knowledge and experiences to understand the text or write by making connections, (3) previewing texts before reading, (4) asking questions before, during, and after reading and writing, (5) figuring out unknown words, (6) using the text structure and its features for understanding and learning, (7) using talk and writing to explore one's own understanding of specific topics, (8) categorizing strategies, (9) reviewing and recalling information from text and the like. As students learn to use literacy strategies, they become flexible in their strategy use by refining it to fit the specific goal of their reading. In addition to using effective cognitive strategies, skilled readers take advantage of metacognitive strategies. That is, they think about their own thinking. For example, students who employ metacognitive strategies will know when they do not comprehend a passage and will know what to do about it. Additional examples of metacognitive strategies include thinking about one's learning by asking questions, planning, checking, and monitoring (Gunning, 2005). Further, when good readers fail to comprehend part of the text, they stop to think about why they failed to understand a passage and proceed to use "fix-up" strategies for comprehending the passage.

SOCIAL DIMENSIONS OF LITERACY AND LEARNING

Teachers need to know that students' literacy development and their learning are influenced by their social cultures or the communities in which they live and interact. Students entering our classrooms come from a wide variety of ethnic, cultural, and socioeconomic backgrounds. Their cultures shape their identities and influence their goals and purposes for reading, writing, and learning. Consider some cultural differences that teachers need to know. Within some family backgrounds, discussion is prominent among members of the family where children are frequently asked, "What do you think?" When children state their opinions, they are regarded by their listeners. For other family backgrounds, children listen and rarely voice their opinion. Varying social backgrounds among students will affect their levels of active participation in class discussion because they use the rules for communication that they learned from their own backgrounds. Some students come from families who engage in a wide range of reading activities, and other families do not regard reading as a priority. The goals that family members have set for their children, often a result of the socioeconomic differences as well as parents' educational backgrounds, make up an additional factor that may affect students' literacy development. Some students come to school prepared to learn with clear and articulated goals and plans for academic success; for others, objectives for learning are ambiguous, and school fails to become their priority. Another aspect of cultural influence on students' learning relates to the way they view the world. Students' opinions, perspectives, and beliefs and values all influence their interpretation of their readings and how they construct meaning. Therefore, teachers need to examine the social and cultural dynamics of students within their classrooms to understand their literacy and learning development.

THE ROLE OF LANGUAGE IN LITERACY DEVELOPMENT

Teachers need to know that language is central in developing literacy and learning content knowledge. Vygotsky (1978) referred to language as a mental tool that mediates all forms of higher learning. For example, reflect on the science teacher who is explaining the application of the convection principle to the earth's atmosphere. The teacher must use language to clarify the concepts that are expressed in academic vocabulary and is needed for understanding the scientific principle. The lesson frequently includes discussion or dialogue, verbal directions given to the students regarding an assignment or an experiment to be performed, and readings from the textbook that contain passages, as well as visuals, all of which are components of language. Clearly, language is the tool that the teacher uses throughout the lesson and what Vygotsky referred to as the tool for higher order learning. Thus, for students to acquire the knowledge of the discipline, they must also learn the language accompanying that discipline.

Another aspect of language is the interrelatedness of language forms. Reading and writing are aspects or forms of language that are connected. This means that both are parallel and complementary processes where growth in one area of language supports growth in the other. For example, when teachers assign readings, students receive added value for their development in writing. The logic of this connection is clear. The more students read, the more apt they will learn content knowledge, academic vocabulary, the expressions of the disciplines, and structures associated with texts used within that content area. This principle of the reading-writing connection is rightly supported by two major reports on adolescent literacy, *Reading Next* (Biancarosa & Snow, 2006) and *Writing Next* (Graham & Perin, 2007). Research shows that reading and writing are complementary processes, each providing support to the other. However, research also confirms that readers and writers need to acquire the learning strategies for different language forms that will advance their literacy development. In other words, although students may engage in reading a wide range of informational text and use effective reading strategies to comprehend and learn from reading, it does not necessarily mean that they will use cognitive strategies employed by effective writers. For example, many adolescent students do not revise their writing, and some do not edit theirs. Such strategies for writing must be taught and monitored. Other students would benefit from direct instruction of strategies to help them summarize ideas for writing or present a series of facts logically for their readers to understand.

WHAT ARE THE DIMENSIONS OF ADOLESCENT LITERACY INSTRUCTION?

THE COMPONENTS OF LITERACY DEVELOPMENT

Teachers need to know that adolescent literacy development includes the following major components: vocabulary, fluency, comprehension of narrative and expository text, and writing. When content area teachers develop students' academic *vocabulary,* they are teaching content knowledge as well. Simply, words and concepts enjoy a close relationship; knowing that words are labels for conceptual knowledge will provide an incentive for teachers to integrate instruction of academic vocabulary within the lesson. Further, without robust academic vocabularies, students will find it very difficult to learn about content, to discuss it, to write about it, or to read for learning. Each discipline maintains an academic vocabulary, a body of technical words that represent the concepts and processes of that discipline. For students to be literate in that content, they need to have acquired its academic vocabulary. A second component of adolescent literacy is *fluency.* Proficient readers demonstrate fluent reading. They read with accuracy and speed, adjusting their reading rate when it is needed; their expressive reading and phrasing sound like a natural conversation. Dysfluency—a lack of fluent reading—is marked by slow-paced reading, word reading, improper phrasing, poor expressive reading, and inaccurate word identification. These oral reading behaviors are indicators of reading difficulty, and such reading interferes with comprehension. *Comprehension of narrative and informational text* is critical to reading to learn. Adolescent students are expected to read a wide range of text, including fiction that represent different time periods and varied cultures written by diverse authors. Informational books include their textbooks, as well as scientific texts, primary source materials, related informational literature, visuals such as diagrams and charts, and various resources accessed from the Internet. To learn from their readings, students must comprehend varied texts and synthesize the information. Without developing reading strategies and skills over the years, students will be unable to meet these requirements. *Writing* is the last major component in literacy learning. We tend to view writing as a means of communication. Yet it is also a tool for learning that frequently reveals to writers how much they know about a specific topic. Students are required to engage in narrative as well as informational writing. When students prefer reading fiction over nonfiction or informational text, they will probably show a preference for writing narrative. Adolescent students are required to engage in writing in content area classrooms. Just as reading tasks in varied subject areas differ, so do writing requirements. Teaching writing and offering a number of opportunities for writing within content classrooms will facilitate students' writing skills.

In addition to the five components of literacy that have been the foundation for reading and writing, we have included the following three areas that affect literacy development and learning in the content areas: (1) media and digital literacies, (2) critical thinking skills, and (3) independent learning. The new literacies that include *media and digital literacies* are part of our students' world; they have been born into digital and multimedia environments. Their use of technology tools for social networking are an important part of their world—they text their friends and families, engage in instant messaging, twitter and blog, and search the Internet for social Web sites such as Facebook, MySpace, and others. For many classes, students are forced to leave their digital world behind them when they enter the classroom. Teachers who require students to remain in a print-only learning environment often provide them with content that is limited to their textbooks. Electronic texts, sound, graphics, Web sites, videos, and the like may avail students to a wealth of information that goes beyond the printed textbook. Media and digital literacies need to be made available to students in their classrooms in ways to support content learning. Another aspect of literacy development encourages students to be literate thinkers. Within this age of information, it is important to develop strategies that go beyond collecting facts and reporting ideas. The development of students' *critical thinking skills* assists them in evaluating print and electronic texts for the accuracy of their information. Students are required to develop strategies for selecting appropriate Web sites for research. Finally, an important goal in all education is to develop skills and attitudes within our students to be lifelong learners. This requires that students develop and use strategies to become *independent learners*. Such strategies will help students learn from more difficult texts, print and electronic, and use discussion and journaling for learning. To achieve success in school and be ready to compete in the workplace, our students must develop the skills related to the essential components of academic literacy.

Effective Literacy Instruction to Support Adolescent Literacy

As school districts begin to respond to the need for programs that will guarantee continuing support for adolescent literacy development, policy makers are offering recommendations that will help improve content area reading and writing. Included in such plans for programmatic changes are proposals for improving literacy instruction in content area classrooms. For example, Biancarosa and Snow (2006) made recommendations for designing effective adolescent literacy programs. Within their 15 key elements are a number of suggestions for effective content area instruction. We have used their following suggestions in selecting the instructional strategies presented in this book: (1) direct and explicit instruction in reading comprehension, (2) effective instructional principles embedded in content, (3) motivated and self-directed learning (4) text-based collaborative learning, (5) strategic tutoring, (6) diverse texts, (7) intensive writing, (8) technology, and (9) ongoing assessment (pp. 12–20).

THE NEED TO SUPPORT LITERACY DEVELOPMENT FOR ALL STUDENTS

Teachers know that there are differences among the students within their classrooms and such differences may affect their performances. Two major factors that contribute to students' success in school are their literacy levels and language proficiencies. When many striving readers and writers as well as English language learners enter the middle and secondary classrooms, their literacy levels are at or below basic proficiency levels. With such low proficiency levels in reading, students are not prepared for either middle or secondary content area learning. Students who perform at such nominal levels of literacy are simply not on track for success.

> If students are to be truly prepared for college, work, and citizenship, they cannot settle for a modest level of proficiency in reading and writing . . . content area literacy instruction must be a cornerstone of any movement to build high-quality secondary schools. (Heller & Greenleaf, 2007, p. 1)

For all students, content area teachers need to provide instruction in literacy; for striving readers and writers additional support in literacy development is required. Adolescent students who experience difficulty reading will benefit from modifications in literacy instruction.

Teachers know that the diverse student population within classrooms across the nation continues to increase. Many students are ELL students and are frequently classified as *at risk* for literacy development and learning as well. As ELL students advance through the grades, they are expected to learn content from textbooks. To most students, textbooks are cognitively demanding for a number of reasons. First, the content is rarely connected to students' experiences and prior knowledge making the concepts and ideas difficult to understand. Secondly, the discipline has its own language that must be learned. Another contributing factor that makes textbooks difficult is their readability levels. Readability is often affected by sentence length. Indeed, authors of textbooks do not write in conversational language; rather, they use academic language that further frustrates ELL students (Vacca & Vacca, 2007). It is understandable why ELL students cannot read and understand most textbooks. Therefore, effective content area teachers work to overcome these challenges by providing literacy instruction to all students and differentiating lessons for the needs of ELL students.

REFERENCES

Biancarosa, C., & Snow, C. E. (2006). *Reading next: A vision for action and research in middle and high school literacy* (pp. 12–20). A report to Carnegie Corporation of New York (2nd ed.). Washington, DC: Alliance for Excellent Education.

Carnine, L., & Carnine, D. (2004). The interaction of reading skills and science content knowledge when teaching struggling secondary students. *Reading & Writing Quarterly, 20,* 203–218.

Dalton, B., & Proctor, C. P. (2008). The changing landscape of text and comprehension in the age of new literacies. In J. Coiro, M. Knobel, C. Lankshear, & D. Leu (Eds.), *Handbook of research on new literacies* (pp. 297–324). New York: Routledge.

8 DEVELOPING CONTENT AREA LITERACY

Graham, S., & Perin, D. (2007). *Writing next: Effective strategies to improve writing of adolescents in middle and high schools.* A report to Carnegie Corporation of New York. Washington, DC: Alliance for Excellent Education.

Gunning, T. G. (2005). *Creating literacy instruction for all students* (5th ed.). Boston: Allyn & Bacon.

Heller, R., & Greenleaf, C. (2007). *Literacy instruction in the content areas: Getting to the core of middle and high school improvement.* Washington, DC: Alliance for Excellent Education.

National Assessment of Educational Progress (NAEP) at Grades 4 and 8. (2007). *The Nation's Report Card: Reading 2007.* Retrieved November 9, 2009, from http://www.nces.ed.gov/nationsreportcard/pubs/main 2007/2007496.asp

Vacca, R. T., & Vacca, J. L. (2007). *Content area reading: Literacy and learning across the curriculum* (9th ed.). Boston: Allyn & Bacon.

Vygotsky, L. S. (1978). *Mind in society.* Cambridge, MA: Harvard University Press.

SECTION I

Academic Vocabulary

Developing Vocabulary for Learning in Content Areas

Words—so innocent and powerless as they are, as standing in a dictionary, how potent for good and evil, in the hands of one who knows how to combine them.

—Nathaniel Hawthorne

Turn to history to realize the significance of the word: Words have been used to cause wars; they have brought peace to warrior nations. Words have the power to persuade the most unconvincing believer. Woven into fine tapestries of artful stories, words have been known to outlive their authors. The potential of words will continue as they make their mark by those who learn to respect their power. But for those who hold little regard for words—the word will remain a powerless tool.

Successful adolescent students in content area classrooms share a common characteristic: They have rich academic vocabularies with words that serve them as potent tools for learning in content area classrooms. The purpose of Section I is to provide middle and secondary school teachers with instructional strategies and resources that will promote and strengthen their students' academic vocabularies within various disciplines of content area classrooms.

WHAT RESEARCH HAS TO SAY ON THE DEVELOPMENT OF ACADEMIC VOCABULARY

Over the years, researchers have accumulated a body of evidence that links students' word knowledge to their academic success. They have also demonstrated to educators that key to comprehending text is the reader's knowledge of the words on the printed page. Finally, to provide teachers with tools for helping students to understand and learn from text, research offers an effective framework for teaching vocabulary in content area classrooms. Why is vocabulary instruction at the heart of learning?

VOCABULARY, READING COMPREHENSION, AND SUCCESS IN SCHOOL

Success in school is dependent on academic achievement. For students in middle and secondary schools, the textbook remains an essential tool for student learning. Without their capacity to read and understand the required texts from various disciplines, students will experience failure. The influence of students' vocabulary knowledge on their comprehension of text has been demonstrated over time through a range of studies (Anderson & Nagy, 1991; Baker, Simmons, & Kame'enui, 1998; Beck, Perfetti, & McKeown, 1982; Cunningham & Stanovich, 1998; Davis, 1944; Nagy, 1988). The strong relationship between vocabulary and comprehension is apparent to teachers who know that students who do well on vocabulary tests also do well on tests that measure their reading comprehension. This strong reciprocal relationship between students' word knowledge and their understanding of text suggests that systematic vocabulary instruction is critical to students' understanding and learning from content area texts. However logical this appears, it is not always the case (Snow, 2002).

Why is academic vocabulary crucial to comprehension? In primary grades, children's vocabularies grow rapidly. Snow, Griffin, and Burns (2005) explained that young children having a "less extensive vocabulary may not have problems, but by the end of Grade 3, vocabulary limits take a toll on reading comprehension" (p. 30). As students move up into the intermediate grades, instruction shifts from an emphasis on literacy to science, mathematics, and social studies. Students are now expected to read and learn from textbooks replete with "content heavy" words. The transition from reading stories or narrative text in the primary grades to reading content area texts in the intermediate grades has created challenges for many students. Their drop in achievement levels is referred to as the "fourth-grade slump." Students' problems related to reading and learning from content area texts are at least in part associated with the spiraling number of unfamiliar concepts and words they must learn on a daily basis. Teachers are reminded that to help students build strong academic vocabularies that produce positive effects on their "comprehension, learners need to actively work with new words" (Beck, McKeown, & Kucan, 2008, p. 4).

Graves (2007) emphasized the fundamental and decisive role that vocabulary plays in schooling for all students including English language learners (ELL): "Learning English vocabulary is one of the most crucial tasks for English learners" (p. 13), for without knowledge of words specific to the domain, they may experience school failure. Success of ELL students is often predicted by their English vocabulary, even though they may have large vocabularies in their native language (Garcia, 1991). Clearly, students with limited vocabularies are likely to experience low achievement levels, not only in literacy, but in content area studies as well.

Word Learning

There are some of us who think that the process of learning all words is the same. This is not the case. Nagy and Scott (2000) explained the complexity of word knowledge. They demonstrated that most words are learned in stages. Words are different: Some words are learned quickly; others take a longer time; some have multiple meanings and are confusing; others are low-frequency words that we do not use or hear often; some words have many associations with other words, while others do not and are difficult to understand. As students progress through the grades, they must learn a wide range of words, with varying levels of complexity. Within the middle and secondary grades, the words have a greater level of difficulty. Many of these are specialized words associated with content learning and referred to as academic vocabulary.

Defining Academic Vocabulary

Our academic vocabularies consist of words that are quite different from those words we learned from our everyday interactions through recreational reading, watching movies and television, or just going about our daily work. Academic vocabulary refers to the words associated with the content knowledge. Within every discipline there is a specific set of words to represent its concepts and processes. These words are conceptually more complex than everyday language; therefore, they are more difficult to learn. A student's depth of word knowledge within a discipline, or academic vocabulary, relates to success in that subject (National Institute for Literacy, 2007). To learn specialized words, such as the vocabulary of science, students must know the content associated with the word (Armbruster, 1992; Graves & Penn, 1986).

Developing academic vocabularies that support content learning is no easy task. Bravo and Cervetti (2008) noted that the number of new terms or specialized words presented in textbooks is staggering, citing research where students were required to learn at least 3,500 new vocabulary words to comprehend their science book. Consider young adolescent students as they move to the middle and then advance to secondary grades. The vocabulary demands dramatically increase as students are required to read and learn from a wide range of content area textbooks. Such demands require constant growth in their academic vocabularies. To help adolescent students, content area teachers are called on to teach the vocabularies of their disciplines.

Teaching Academic Vocabulary

Knowing that words and learning words are quite different and that students are required to develop robust academic vocabularies for achieving in content areas, which words should teachers select for instruction? Beck et al. (2008) provided a word classification system for targeting words for effective teaching and learning. Their three-category system for words include the following: *Tier 1* words are those words that are in the spoken or oral language vocabularies of students or everyday language; *Tier 2* words are the "words that characterize written text—but are not so common in everyday language" (p. 7); and *Tier 3* words are described as more abstract in nature. To help students comprehend content area readings, it is important that the teacher selects the words that represent the concepts that are fundamental to understanding the text for instruction. Students would benefit most from direct instruction in Tier 2 words because they are essential to understanding and remembering the text.

A FRAMEWORK FOR TEACHING ACADEMIC VOCABULARY TO ADOLESCENT LEARNERS

Clearly, research has emphasized the role that vocabulary plays in understanding text and the need for teachers to teach academic vocabulary to all students. Although there is no quick fix or one magic approach in developing students' word knowledge, research does provide a framework that teachers may use for designing and implementing an effective vocabulary program within their classrooms. Fundamental principles of successful vocabulary programs are based on current research and include the following:

1. Provide systematic vocabulary instruction for all grades across the curriculum (Blachowicz, Fisher, Ogle, & Watts-Taffe, 2006; Manzo, Manzo, & Thomas, 2009).

2. Ensure that vocabulary instruction include the following: (a) frequent, varied, and extensive language experiences that offer opportunities for wide reading; (b) individual word instruction; (c) word-learning strategy instruction; and (d) the development of word consciousness (Graves, 2007, pp. 14–15).

3. Design vocabulary instruction that fosters a deep understanding of the words through instructional activities, reading selections, and goals that are tailored to the learners' needs (Watts & Graves, 1997).

4. Select content words for instruction that lead to students' understanding of the text (Beck et al., 2008; Gerston & Baker, 2000).

Tips on Teaching Academic Vocabulary

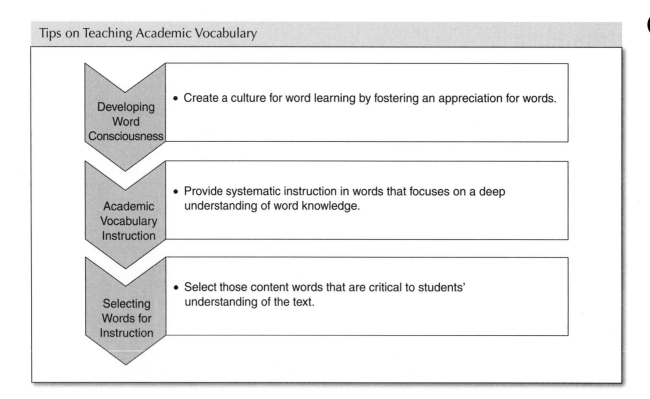

Developing Word Consciousness	• Create a culture for word learning by fostering an appreciation for words.
Academic Vocabulary Instruction	• Provide systematic instruction in words that focuses on a deep understanding of word knowledge.
Selecting Words for Instruction	• Select those content words that are critical to students' understanding of the text.

A STRATEGY FOR ASSESSING THE DEVELOPMENT OF ACADEMIC VOCABULARY

Assessment and evaluation of students' academic vocabulary is an integral part of teaching and student learning. Teachers in high-performance schools use the results of testing to adjust their instruction to improve student achievement (Langer, 2000). Moore and Hinchman (2006) have described how classroom assessment for adolescent learners can be effective in improving their achievement. Briefly, classroom assessment that supports student learning is ongoing, cyclical, focused, and involves students through self-assessment (pp. 154–155).

Classroom assessment that provides information to the teacher and students on their developing academic vocabulary is a valuable tool for the teacher in designing appropriate instruction and for the students in monitoring their own learning. The purpose of the rubric shown in Figure I.1, Rubric for Assessing Academic Vocabulary Development, is to guide teachers in their evaluation of students' development in word knowledge, word-learning strategies, and word consciousness as well as their use of academic vocabulary in comprehending text, classroom discussions, and assigned writing tasks. Teachers may use the form Figure I.2, Monitoring Academic Vocabulary Throughout the School Year throughout the school year to record each student's progress for the purpose of targeting students' special needs for additional help.

Figure I.1	Rubric for Assessing Academic Vocabulary Development			
Criteria	Beginning (0–1 Point)	Developing (2 Points)	Proficient (3 Points)	Exemplary (4 Points)
Word knowledge of content words	Demonstrates limited or no knowledge of content words and is unable to offer simple definitions	Provides simple definitions of content words; does not provide examples or nonexamples of the word	Provides complete definitions of content words and offers examples and nonexamples; is able to make some association to related words	Provides extensive definitions of content words with numerous examples and nonexamples; offers many associations to other related words; is able to compare and contrast content words through specific features of the words
Word learning strategies	Does not use context clues to determine unknown words	Attempts to use context clues to determine unknown words	Uses context clues with success to determine unknown words	Uses context clues with a high degree of success along with references to determine unknown words
Use of academic vocabulary to comprehend text	Demonstrates difficulty in comprehending text due to a lack of knowledge of content words	Comprehends most of the text as a result of some knowledge of content words	Comprehends the text as a result of knowledge of content words	Comprehends the text and makes reference to many of the content words in responding to the readings
Use of academic vocabulary in discussions	Rarely uses content words in class discussions	Uses some content words, often with a low to average degree of accuracy during class discussions	Uses a large number of content words with a moderate degree of accuracy during class discussions	Uses an extensive number of content words with a high degree of accuracy during class discussions
Use of academic vocabulary in writing assignments	Rarely uses content words in writing assignments	Uses some content words, often with a low to average degree of accuracy in writing assignments	Uses a large number of content words with a moderate degree of accuracy in writing assignments	Uses an extensive number of content words with a high degree of accuracy in writing assignments
Word consciousness	Does not demonstrate an interest in important or unusual words	Demonstrates some interest in important and unusual words	Demonstrates an interest in important and unusual words by recording them in a personal dictionary	Demonstrates a high interest in important and unusual words; looks up their meaning, and records them in a personal dictionary

Figure I.2	Monitoring Academic Vocabulary Throughout the School Year

STUDENT'S NAME _____ SCHOOL YEAR: _____ to _____

SUBJECT: _____ TEXT: _____

TEACHER: _____ PERIOD: _____ ROOM: _____

	Sept	Oct	Nov	Dec	Jan	Feb	Mar	Apr	May	COMMENTS
Word knowledge of content words										
Word learning strategies										
Use of academic vocabulary to comprehend text										
Use of academic vocabulary in discussions										
Use of academic vocabulary in writing tasks										
Word consciousness										

Directions: Using the rubric, monitor the student's development of academic vocabulary on each criterion with a rating of 1 to 4, noting changes in the student's growth. Use performance-based information of the student's progress to adjust instruction and practice in academic vocabulary.

Involving adolescent students in their own learning can be especially beneficial to their development. Shown in Figure I.3 is a Self-Assessment Scale of Academic Vocabulary that students may use to keep in touch with their own learning. Self-assessments become powerful tools for student growth when the teacher and student work together to set realistic goals for progress based on one's learning. Working with individual students, effective teachers focus on one or two areas at a time to help students.

| Figure 1.3 | Self-Assessment of Learning Academic Vocabulary |

HIGHEST PERFORMANCE	5	4	3	2	1	0	LOWEST PERFORMANCE
HOW CAN I IMPROVE?							

Directions: Think about your performance in learning new words and using them. For each item, rate how well you do. A rating of 5 indicates the highest performance and a rating of 0 shows the lowest performance. Then think about ways you might improve your performance, and write one way that you can increase your word knowledge in each of the areas.

LEARNING NEW CONTENT WORDS Highest Performance	5	4	3	2	1	0	*LEARNING NEW CONTENT WORDS* Lowest Performance
I have learned many new words and know their meanings very well.	**To improve, I will . . .**						I heard some new words and do not know their meanings.
LEARNING WORDS ON MY OWN	5	4	3	2	1	0	*LEARNING WORDS ON MY OWN*
When I come to a word in my textbook that I do not know, I try to get at the meaning of the word by using clues from the words around it and by how it is used in the sentence. Then I look it up when I am finished reading.	**To improve, I will . . .**						When I come to a new word in my textbook that I do not know, I skip it and continue reading. Eventually, I forget the word.
USING WORD KNOWLEDGE IN READING	5	4	3	2	1	0	*USING WORD KNOWLEDGE IN READING*
When I am reading my science text and come to a new word we just learned in class, I think about the meaning of the word to understand the readings in the text.	**To improve, I will . . .**						When I am reading my text and come to a new word that we have learned in class, I do not think about the meaning to understand the text.
USING WORD KNOWLEDGE IN DISCUSSIONS	5	4	3	2	1	0	*USING WORD KNOWLEDGE IN DISCUSSIONS*
I try to use words that I have learned in class discussions.	**To improve, I will . . .**						I do not attempt to use words that I have learned in class discussions.
USING WORD KNOWLEDGE IN WRITING	5	4	3	2	1	0	*USING WORD KNOWLEDGE IN WRITING*
In my assigned writing, I try to use words that I have learned. When I am not sure about whether I have used the words correctly, I will check my dictionary or glossary within the text.	**To improve, I will . . .**						In my assigned writing, I do not try to use words that I have learned.
INCREASING MY WORD POWER	5	4	3	2	1	0	*INCREASING MY WORD POWER*
I find a genuine interest in words, words that are challenging, words that I have never heard or seen in print, words that seem strange, words that are very long or very short. I write them down, find their meaning, and will try to use them.	**To improve, I will . . .**						I have no interest in learning new words.

REFLECTIVE PRACTICE ON TEACHING ACADEMIC VOCABULARY

Michael Graves has spent a number of years studying and teaching about vocabulary instruction. Within his research and practice, he focused on areas for building and strengthening students' vocabulary. His powerful four-part vocabulary program (Graves, 2007) may be translated into questions to help all teachers begin to reflect on how they support student learning through developing academic vocabulary within their classrooms.

- How do I provide *rich and varied language experiences* that support learning and using vocabulary?

- Do I spend time to *teach individual words?*

- What type of *word-learning strategies* have I taught to my students to help them increase their vocabularies?

- In what ways do I develop *word consciousness?* How does the culture of my classroom show a motivation and appreciation for word learning; in what ways do I support and encourage students in making a commitment to acquiring word knowledge, and do I share my own thirst for learning new words?

PROFESSIONAL RESOURCES

Allen, J. (1999). *Words, words, words: Teaching vocabulary in grades 4–12.* Portland, ME: Stenhouse.

Allen, J. (2007). *Inside words: Tools for teaching academic vocabulary, Grades 4–12.* Portland, ME: Stenhouse.

Fisher, D., & Frey, N. (2008). *Word wise and content rich: Five essential steps to teaching academic vocabulary.* Portsmouth, NH: Heinemann.

Harmon, J. M., Wood, K. D., & Hedrick, W. B. (2006). *Instruction strategies for teaching content vocabulary: Grades 4–12.* Westerville, OH: National Middle School Association and Newark, DE: International Reading Association.

Tompkins, G. E., & Blanchfield, C. (2008). *Teaching vocabulary: 50 creative strategies, Grades 6–12.* Upper Saddle River, NJ: Merrill/Prentice Hall.

REFERENCES

Anderson, R. C., & Nagy, W. E. (1991). Word meanings. In R. Barr, M. L. Kamil, P. B. Mosenthal, & P. D. Pearson (Eds.), *Handbook of reading research* (Vol. 2, pp. 690–724). Hillsdale, NJ: Lawrence Erlbaum.

Armbruster, B. B. (1992). Vocabulary in content area lessons. *The Reading Teacher, 45*(7), 550–551.

Baker, S. K., Simmons, D. C., & Kame'enui, E. J. (1998). Vocabulary acquisition: Research bases. In D. C. Simmons & E. J. Kame'enui (Eds.), *What reading research tells us about children with diverse learning needs* (pp. 183–218). Mahwah, NJ: Lawrence Erlbaum.

Beck, I. L., McKeown, M. G., & Kucan, L. (2008). *Creating robust vocabulary: Frequently asked questions and extended examples.* New York: Guilford Press.

Beck, I. L., Perfetti, C.A., & McKeown, M. G. (1982). The effects of long-term vocabulary instruction on lexical access and reading comprehension. *Journal of Educational Psychology, 74*(4), 506–521.

Blachowicz, C. L. Z., Fisher, P. J. L., Ogle, D., & Watts-Taffe, S. M. (2006). Vocabulary: Questions from the classroom. *Reading Research Quarterly, 41,* 524–539.

Bravo, M. A., & Cervetti, G. N. (2008). Teaching vocabulary through text and experience in content areas. In A. E. Farstrup & S. J. Samuels (Eds.), *What research has to say about vocabulary instruction* (pp. 130–149). Newark, DE: International Reading Association.

Cunningham, A. E., & Stanovich, K. E. (1998). What reading does for the mind. *American Educator, 22*(1 & 2), 8–15.

Davis, F. B. (1944). Fundamental factors in reading comprehension. *Psychometrika, 9,* 185–197.

Garcia, G. E. (1991). Factors influencing the English reading test performance of Spanish-speaking Hispanic children. *Reading Research Quarterly, 26,* 371–392.

Gerston, R., & Baker, S. (2000). What we know about effective instructional practices for English language learners. *Exceptional Children, 66,* 454–470.

Graves, M. F. (2007). Vocabulary instruction in the middle grades. *Voices from the Middle, 15*(1), 13–19.

Graves, M. F., & Penn, M. C. (1986). Costs and benefits of various methods of teaching vocabulary. *Journal of Reading, 29*(7), 596–602.

Langer, J. (2000). Excellence in English in middle and high school: How teachers' professional lives support student achievement. *American Educational Research Journal, 37*(2), 397–439.

Manzo, A. V., Manzo, U. C., & Thomas, M. M. (2009). *Content area literacy: A framework for reading based instruction* (5th ed.). Hoboken, NJ: Wiley.

Moore, D. W., & Hinchman, K. A. (2006). *Teaching adolescents who struggle with reading: Practical strategies.* Boston: Allyn & Bacon.

Nagy, W. E. (1988). *Teaching vocabulary to improve comprehension.* Newark, DE: International Reading Association.

Nagy, W. E., & Scott, J. A. (2000). Vocabulary processes. In M. Kamil, P. B. Mosenthal, P. D. Pearson, & R. Barr (Eds.), *Handbook of reading research* (Vol. 3, pp. 269–284). Hillsdale, NJ: Lawrence Erlbaum.

National Institute for Literacy. (2007). *What content-area teachers should know about adolescent literacy.* Washington, DC: National Institute of Child Health and Human Development.

Snow, C. E. (2002). *Reading for understanding: Toward an R&D program in reading comprehension.* Santa Monica, CA: RAND.

Snow, C., Griffin, P., & Burns, M. B. (Eds.). (2005). *Knowledge to support the teaching of reading: Preparing teachers for a changing world.* San Francisco: Jossey-Bass.

Watts, S., & Graves, M. F. (1997). Fostering students' understanding of challenging texts. *Middle School Journal, 29,* 45–51.

Strategy

1

Semantic Mapping

Developing Robust Academic Vocabularies

Semantic maps are graphic displays of word meanings that offer students a visual representation of how words and concepts are related through a network of organized knowledge (Heimlich & Pittelman, 1986). The real architects of word maps are the students who use their prior knowledge to deepen their understanding of the topic(s) that result in graphic representations of the relationships and associations of meanings or concepts to the target word (Schwartz & Raphael, 1985). The use of semantic maps as instructional tools provides students with a deepening understanding of words including their concept knowledge, relationships to other words, and multiple meanings.

The semantic mapping strategy is most effective when it is used before, during, and after reading and when the teacher serves as the guide or facilitator to the students who construct their own semantic maps. When semantic mapping is used as a prereading strategy, it helps to activate students' prior knowledge (Heimlich & Pittelman, 1986). Further, the teacher may use the students' prereading semantic maps to determine how much knowledge building is required before students read the text (Antonacci, 1988). When using semantic mapping as a postreading instructional strategy, teachers employ students' discussions to help them recall and organize information that they have learned from reading text as they make connections to words or concepts related to the topic. Fundamental to the success of the approach is the students' engagement in discussions of word concepts that focus on deepening their knowledge of the academic vocabulary related to content.

When semantic maps were first used to develop word knowledge, they all looked the same. Over the years, we have seen hybrids of the first maps that were used as teachers' purposes for using the graphics developed. For example, word maps may show associations with similar words; they may depict definitions and examples and nonexamples; they may map synonyms and antonyms of target words; they may present the hierarchical relationships to other words; or they may simply present free associations of words to the underlying meaning of the topic. Semantic maps are most effective when (a) they are used with teacher-guided discussion before, during, and after reading a text; (b) teachers select a few critical key words to be taught; and (c) students are actively engaged in constructing their word maps through participating in lively discussions on the conceptual nature of words.

IRA/NCTE Standards for the English Language Arts

3. Students apply a wide range of strategies to comprehend, interpret, evaluate, and appreciate texts. They draw on their prior experience, their interactions with other readers and writers, their knowledge of word meaning and of other texts, their word identification strategies, and their understanding of textual features (e.g., sound-letter correspondence, sentence structure, context, graphics).

12. Students use spoken, written, and visual language to accomplish their own purposes (e.g., for learning, enjoyment, persuasion, and the exchange of information).

Source: International Reading Association and National Council of Teachers of English (1996).

STEP-BY-STEP PROCEDURE

Using semantic maps requires full participation by students who are engaged during the teacher-directed discussion. Students will be required to use maps *before*, *during*, and *after* reading the text. Therefore, this step-by-step procedure is designed for using semantic maps as a strategy at different phases of reading informational or fiction text.

BEFORE READING

Prior to reading the text, the teacher examines the text to be read and carefully selects the key words to be learned (content or Tier 2 words) that are critical for understanding the text and the lesson.

1. The teacher introduces the selected content words using the semantic word map and guided discussion.

2. Using chart paper, the blackboard, or a software program with a graphics tool, draw or project the word map so that it is visible to the students. Write the topic or main concept in the center of the map.

3. Distribute semantic maps to the students.

4. Begin the prereading discussion that focuses on the content words. As students respond to concept-related questions, write the word and students' meanings and responses on the map and direct students to do the same.

5. When students fail to respond to the concept-related questions, the teacher should offer a contextual definition of the word that facilitates students' understanding of the text.

DURING READING

As students read, they use their semantic maps to add to the meaning of the words.

1. Before directing the students to read the assigned text, the teacher provides a quick review of the key words.

2. The teacher instructs students to add additional information from their readings to clarify the meanings of the key words. She encourages the students to note additional words that further explain the ideas from their readings.

3. As students read, the teacher reminds students to write down questions about words that need clarification.

AFTER READING

The teacher engages students in an extended discussion on their readings, focusing on the content words and their meanings.

1. The teacher directs the students to use their semantic maps during the discussion of their reading. She engages students in a discussion that further promotes and deepens their understanding of the content words by building on their conceptual knowledge.

2. As students discuss the reading and use the map as their guides, the teacher directs them to clarify the information that they gleaned from their readings.

3. The teacher guides the discussion with questions that will help students to further understand what they have read. As the students respond to the questions, the teacher notes their responses on the large semantic map as they take additional notes on their own maps.

With the variety of semantic maps that may be used to develop word knowledge, the teacher should select the semantic map that is most appropriate for the readings and content words for developing students' word knowledge around different disciplines. For example, the traditional semantic map helps to show relations among words, others are suitable for displaying examples and nonexamples of the word concept, and others may be used to encourage students to make a personal connection to the word. The graphics below are examples of three different types of semantic maps: Figure 1.1, Semantic Map: Using Word Relationships; Figure 1.2, Semantic Map: Synonyms, Antonyms, Examples, and Nonexamples; and Figure 1.3, Semantic Map: Word Connections.

DIFFERENTIATING INSTRUCTION FOR STRIVING READERS

Semantic mapping may be especially helpful in assisting striving readers and writers in developing their academic vocabularies that will lead to their comprehending content area text (Guastello, Beasley, & Sinatra, 2000; Sinatra, Stahl-Gemake, & Berg, 1984). Provide striving readers with additional scaffolding before and during reading. Before reading the text, the teacher should use expanded definitions of key words, definitions

Figure 1.1	Semantic Map: Using Word Relationships

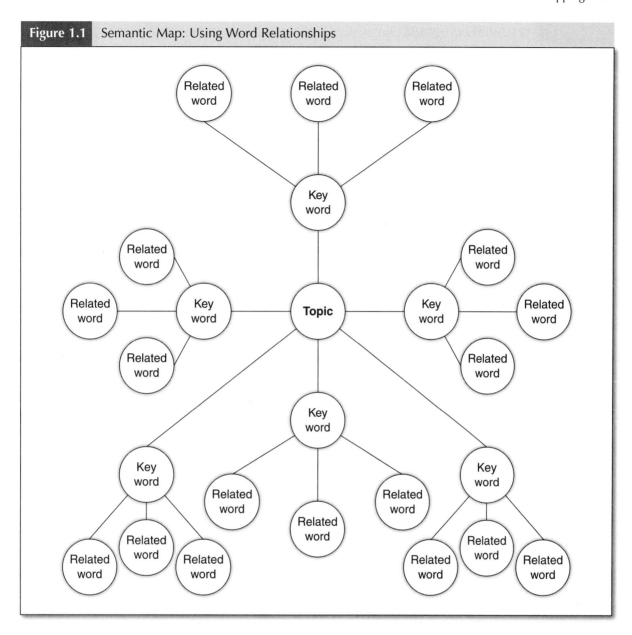

Figure 1.2	Semantic Map: Synonyms, Antonyms, Examples, and Nonexamples

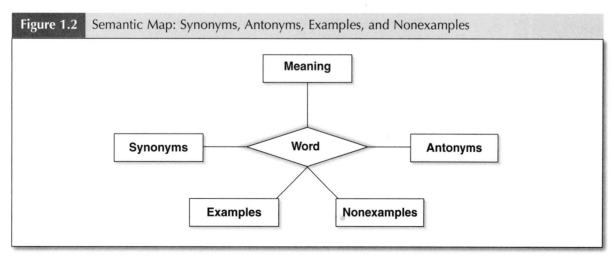

Figure 1.3	Semantic Map: Word Connections

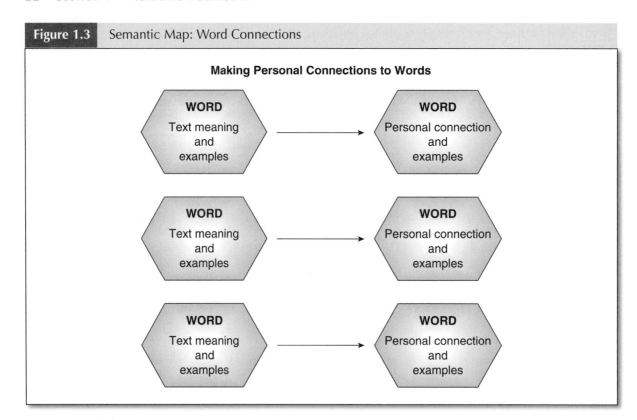

that are easier to understand, and those that relate to students' experiential vocabulary. Such definitions serve as scaffolds in helping low-achieving students comprehend content area textbooks. During reading, it is recommended that the teacher assists students who have difficulty in understanding the text and taking notes on their semantic maps.

CONSIDERING THE LANGUAGE NEEDS OF ELL STUDENTS

Source: International Reading Association and National Council of Teachers of English (1996).

IRA/NCTE Standards for the English Language Arts

10. Students whose first language is not English make use of their first language to develop competency in the English language arts and to develop understanding of content across the curriculum.

All students bring a wealth of experience to the classroom. The classroom teacher can tap the collective knowledge of her students and help them make specific connections of their personal experiences to the content. This is especially important for ELL students who are building their experiential word knowledge along with their academic vocabularies. For ELL students, building vocabulary by attaching new content words to a broader topic will facilitate their learning of content vocabulary (Au, 1993). Make the connection between students' prior knowledge, content knowledge, and the new key word(s). Encourage English language learners to provide the word from their native language that matches the key words on the semantic map. Two middle school teachers of ELL students, one in the math classroom and a second in social studies, reported that when they added a picture cue to each key word on the semantic maps, students found it easier to remember the words and their meanings.

AN APPLICATION FOR READING AND LEARNING IN THE MATHEMATICS CLASSROOM

In a mathematics class, the teacher prepared the students for an introductory lesson on triangles. The teacher began by introducing the names for four different triangles, showing the semantic map on an overhead projector depicted in Figure 1.4, Semantic Map: Before Reading, and gave copies to the students.

The teacher read the names of each of the triangles and asked the students if they knew the definition of each or could describe the properties of the triangles. Many students responded with the definition of the *right triangle*. The teacher wrote their responses in the appropriate box and continued. Because students did not know the remaining triangles, the teacher provided definitions for each triangle, wrote their meanings on the semantic map, and discussed the properties of the relationships among the triangles. As students read their text on the defining characteristics of triangles, they used their semantic maps to write the definitions, took notes, and drew the specific types of triangles. After students read their text, the teacher engaged them in a guided discussion for the purpose of expanding the initial definitions and clarifying any questions.

Figure 1.4	Semantic Map: Before Reading

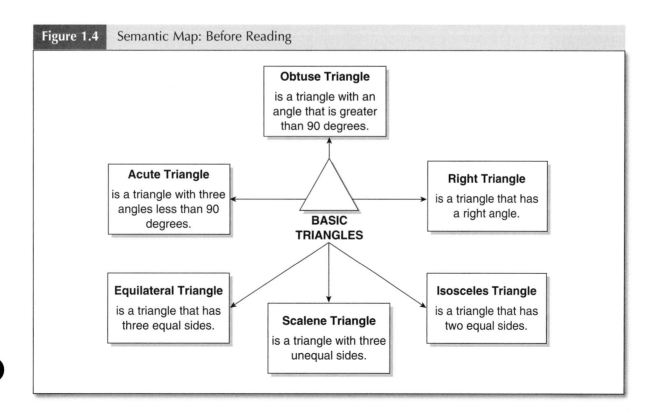

Students shared their definitions and comments and continued to take notes during the discussion while the teacher recorded their responses on the class semantic map. Figure 1.5, Semantic Map: After Reading, presents the development of word knowledge through reading and discussion.

Figure 1.5 Semantic Map: After Reading

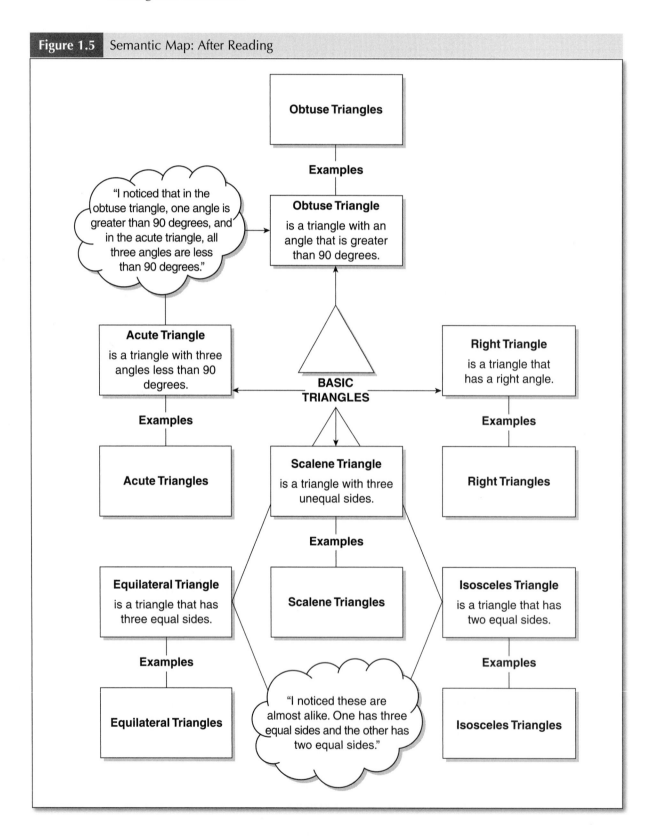

References

Antonacci, P. (1988). Comprehension strategies for special learners. In C. N. Hedley & J. Hicks (Eds.), *Reading for special learners* (pp. 155–176). Norwood, NJ: Ablex.

Au, K. H. (1993). *Literacy instruction in multicultural settings.* Fort Worth, TX: Harcourt Brace.

Guastello, E. F., Beasley, T. M., & Sinatra, R. C. (2000). Concept mapping effects on science content comprehension of low achieving inner-city seventh graders. *Remedial and Special Education, 21*(6), 356–364.

Heimlich, J. E., & Pittelman, S. D. (1986). *Semantic mapping: Classroom applications.* Newark: DE: International Reading Association.

International Reading Association and National Council of Teachers of English. (1996). *Standards for the English language arts.* Newark, DE: International Reading Association & Urbana, IL: National Council of Teachers of English.

Schwartz, R. M., & Raphael, T. E. (1985). Concept of definition: A key to improving students' vocabulary. *The Reading Teacher, 39,* 198–205.

Sinatra, R. C., Stahl-Gemake, J., & Berg, W. (1984). Improving reading comprehension of disabled readers through semantic mapping. *The Reading Teacher, 38*(1), 22–29.

Strategy 2

Vocabulary Self-Collection Strategy (VSS)

Promoting Word Consciousness

STRATEGY OVERVIEW

Teachers in content area classrooms know that robust academic vocabularies are required for students' success in learning content knowledge. They are also aware of the sheer volume of complex words across the disciplines that students need to know to support their learning. Therefore, strategies that promote students' word consciousness to support independent word learning are critical for their academic success.

The purpose of the vocabulary self-collection strategy (VSS) is to motivate students to learn new words by promoting a "long-term acquisition and development of the vocabulary of academic disciplines" with the goal of integrating "new content words into students' working vocabularies" (Ruddell, 2005, p. 166). As students develop word consciousness, or an interest in words, as well as the strategy for becoming a word collector, they will increase their academic vocabularies when confronted with unknown words from varied disciplines. The primary purpose of the VSS is to deepen students' understanding of words, promote their interest in new words, and offer them a strategy to identify and learn new and fascinating words.

Many educators have argued for the need to develop students' curiosity of new and interesting words. Graves's (2006, 2008) model of a long-term vocabulary program argues for the need for developing word consciousness as one of its critical components for teaching vocabulary that promises to lead to increased word knowledge. Briefly, word consciousness is having "an interest in and awareness of words" (Scott & Nagy, 2004, p. 202). With an expanding curiosity in words, students become motivated to learn new words on their own. This is especially useful for students in content area classrooms where they are expected to learn a wide range of technical and nontechnical words to understand the discipline (Harmon, Wood, & Hedrick, 2008). Ruddell and Shearer (2002) demonstrated that the VSS with middle school students has been an effective means for "increasing the depth and breadth of student vocabulary knowledge and for developing students' ability to be strategic, independent word learners" (p. 361).

Source: International Reading Association and National Council of Teachers of English (1996).

> ## IRA/NCTE Standards for the English Language Arts
>
> 3. Students apply a wide range of strategies to comprehend, interpret, evaluate, and appreciate texts. They draw on their prior experience, their interactions with other readers and writers, their knowledge of word meaning and of other texts, their word identification strategies, and their understanding of textual features (e.g., sound-letter correspondence, sentence structure, context, graphics).
> 12. Students use spoken, written, and visual language to accomplish their own purposes (e.g., for learning, enjoyment, persuasion, and the exchange of information).

STEP-BY-STEP PROCEDURE

The VSS is most effective when it is used with small groups of students working together. Fundamental to its success is the role that academic talk plays throughout this procedure as well as the teacher's own demonstrative interest in words. Briefly, the strategy consists of selecting, defining, finalizing, and using words (Tierney & Readence, 2005). The following procedure presents what the teacher and students do before, during, and after reading using the VSS in content area classrooms.

BEFORE READING

The teacher selects the reading that is appropriate for the topic that will be developed and decides on the words that students need to know to comprehend the text. Through modeling the process of using the VSS, the teacher demonstrates how to use the strategy.

1. The teacher reads the first paragraph aloud to the students.

2. The teacher then projects a copy of the reading on the screen and uses a think-aloud as a way of modeling how to select words that are important for understanding the reading. The teacher indicates her interest in a word that may result from her not knowing the word, or finding it difficult or interesting. She shares with the class the need to know something more about the word to understand the text.

3. The teacher then projects a graphic organizer that includes a box for the word, the reason for selecting the word, and the definition of the word as shown in Figure 2.1, Vocabulary Self-Collection Strategy Chart. She writes the word in the appropriate box, says the word, and asks the students why they think she chose this word as an important one for learning. She then writes the reason in the appropriate box. Finally, the teacher defines the word, writing the definition in the next box.

Figure 2.1	Vocabulary Self-Collection Strategy Chart	

Name: _____   Date: _____

Topic: _____   Pages: _____

WORD	REASON FOR SELECTION	DEFINITION

DURING READING

The teacher directs the students to read selected passages from the text and after reading the passages to do the following:

1. After reading, revisit the text and select at least five words that they think are important to their understanding of the readings or that they found interesting or challenging.

2. Complete the VSS Student Chart in Figure 2.1 that directs them to write the word, the reason for selecting the word, and a definition of the word if they know it.

AFTER READING

Students are divided into small groups that include students with varying reading abilities, ELL students, and those from different cultures. The groups will focus their discussions on the words they have selected and their reasons for choosing the words. Using their texts and completed VSS charts, each group is directed to do the following:

1. The group appoints one student to act as leader whose role is to keep the discussion moving as they focus their talk on the words they have selected.

2. Each student submits one word he or she has selected and provides the reason for choosing the word that becomes the focus of the discussion. The discussion may center on the word's meaning, the importance of the word in understanding the text, whether the members of the group selected the word, or another reason. The group then decides whether the word should be selected for the group chart.

3. The group leader uses the group chart to record the word, the reason it has been selected by the group, and the word's contextual definition. Each group limits the number of words included on the VSS chart to five.

4. Writing the contextual meaning of each word is the last step of using the VSS. Students then validate the meaning of each word through the use of the dictionary or the glossary that may be found in the text.

5. After the small-group discussion, the teacher brings the groups together for a class discussion. Each group leader reports to the class, providing the list of words selected by the small group. The teacher or student records the words on the VSS class chart, along with reasons for choosing the word and the contextual meanings.

6. The teacher may list additional words overlooked by students that are required for understanding the text. For words with a high-difficulty level that students do not understand, the teacher provides direct instruction, focusing on the words' contextual meanings.

Extensions of VSS

To extend the VSS, (a) students use personal dictionaries to add the words and meanings selected by the groups and the teacher. They are encouraged to add their own words whether they were considered as a key word needed to understand the text or simply a word of interest. Another extension of VSS includes (b) the use of selected words by the teacher to create a *thematic or topical word wall*. One way that students make the word their own is through frequent use and exposure to the word. The teacher makes reference to the words during class discussions and encourages students to use the words in their writing assignments, discussions, and projects.

DIFFERENTIATING INSTRUCTION FOR STRIVING READERS

Students who are struggling readers may benefit from working with a partner when first using the VSS. Asking students who have difficulty reading the text to select words that they think are important in understanding the text or are challenging may be overwhelming to struggling readers. To partner students with a proficient reader would provide a scaffold to less proficient reader(s) in learning the process of identifying key words or any word that is challenging and interesting. Through discussion, students articulate the reasons for selecting the words that lead to their understanding new words.

CONSIDERING THE LANGUAGE NEEDS OF ELL STUDENTS

Source: International Reading Association and National Council of Teachers of English (1996).

IRA/NCTE Standards for the English Language Arts

10. Students whose first language is not English make use of their first language to develop competency in the English language arts and to develop understanding of content across the curriculum.

Students who are learning the English language benefit from engaging in discussion about the meanings of words when talk is sheltered and collaborative. Therefore, when teachers form small groups for discussion, it is important that ELL students are placed with other students who are supportive of members of the group and accept their contributions. When recording key words on their VSS charts, they may use the native language word along with the English word.

AN APPLICATION FOR INSTRUCTION AND LEARNING IN THE BUSINESS LAW CLASSROOM

In an introductory business law class, students were introduced to the topic of *contracts*. The teacher directed the students to use the VSS to select important words from their readings that they needed to learn and to collect other words that were especially interesting and challenging. After students read the text, they reread the passages to find words they thought were important for knowing and understanding the text. Small-group discussions yielded the list of words found in Figure 2.2, Vocabulary Self-Collection Strategy Chart: Contracts.

Figure 2.2	Vocabulary Self-Collection Strategy Chart: Contracts

Class: *Period 3*		Date: *2/3/2007*
Topic: *An introduction to contracts*		Pages: *45–56*

WORD	REASON FOR SELECTION	DEFINITIONS
Contract	We will be reading about contracts. So this is an important word.	A contract is an agreement between two people.

Breach	This sounds like it has to do with not keeping the contract.	To breach a contract mean to break the promises made in the contract.
Executed contract	This is an important word because it has to do with carrying out the contract.	An executed contract is one that has been carried out by the parties that made an agreement.
Goods	This word sounds like it has to do with property that is part of a contract.	Goods are personal property that can be transported or moved.
Real property	This is a kind of property that must be part of an agreement.	Property that cannot be moved like a house or an acre of land.
Parties	Parties must be those who are part of the contract.	People who sign the agreement or the contract. They are part of the contract.
Informal contracts	These types of contracts will be studied.	They are types of contracts that are not formal. A lease for an apartment is an informal contract.

REFERENCES

Graves, M. F. (2006). *The vocabulary book: Learning and instruction.* Newark, DE: International Reading Association.

Graves, M. F. (2008). Instruction on individual words: One size does not fit all. In A. E. Farstrup & S. J. Samuels (Eds.), *What research has to say about vocabulary instruction* (pp. 56–79). Newark, DE: International Reading Association.

Harmon, J. M., Wood, K. D., & Hedrick, W. B. (2006). *Instruction strategies for teaching content vocabulary: Grades 4–12.* Westerville, OH: National Middle School Association and Newark, DE: International Reading Association.

International Reading Association and National Council of Teachers of English. (1996). *Standards for the English language arts.* Newark, DE: International Reading Association & Urbana, IL: National Council of Teachers of English.

Ruddell, M. R. (2005). *Teaching content reading and writing* (4th ed.). Hoboken, NJ: Wiley.

Ruddell, M. R., & Shearer, B. A. (2002). "Extraordinary," "tremendous," "exhilarating," "magnificent": Middle-school at-risk students become avid word learners with the vocabulary self-collection strategy (VSS). *Journal of Adolescent and Adult Literacy, 45,* 352–363.

Scott, J. A., & Nagy, W. E. (2004). Developing word consciousness. In J. F. Baumann & E. J. Kame'enui (Eds.), *Vocabulary instruction: Research to practice* (pp. 201–217). New York: Guilford.

Tierney, R. J., & Readence, J. E. (2005). *Reading strategies and practices: A compendium* (6th ed.). Boston: Allyn & Bacon.

Strategy
3

Contextual Redefinition

Using Clues as a Word-Learning Strategy

STRATEGY OVERVIEW

One of the primary goals of schooling is to create independent learners. This is also true for vocabulary instructional programs. "Showing learners how to construct meaning for unfamiliar words encountered during reading helps them develop strategies needed to monitor comprehension and increase their vocabularies " (Vacca & Vacca, 2007, p. 172). Word-learning strategies are especially important in the content area classrooms where each student is expected to read "like a scientist, historian, or mathematician" (Harmon, Wood, & Hedrick, 2008, p. 165). One of the most important strategies that will foster students' independence in word learning is becoming skilled at using context clues to unlock the meaning of unknown words (Graves, 2007, 2008).

To use context clues, students are directed to look for clues within the word and the sentence or surrounding sentences. Students use clues from meaningful word parts such as the base word, suffixes, or prefixes or from known words that surround the unknown word within the text. Teaching students to use context clues while they are reading will help them to infer meanings while they are reading, but the context alone does not lead to a deep understanding of the word. Additional tools, such as the dictionary and other references, are necessary to learn more complete meanings of words. Therefore, as an adjunct to this strategy, students should be encouraged to use context clues with other word-learning strategies. A systematic approach for using context clues along with the dictionary or the glossary is shown in Figure 3.1, Defining Unknown Words Using Context Clues.

Source: International Reading Association and National Council of Teachers of English (1996).

IRA/NCTE Standards for the English Language Arts

3. Students apply a wide range of strategies to comprehend, interpret, evaluate, and appreciate texts. They draw on their prior experience, their interactions with other readers and writers, their knowledge of word meaning and of other texts, their word identification strategies, and their understanding of textual features (e.g., sound-letter correspondence, sentence structure, context, graphics).

Figure 3.1 Defining Unknown Words Using Context Clues

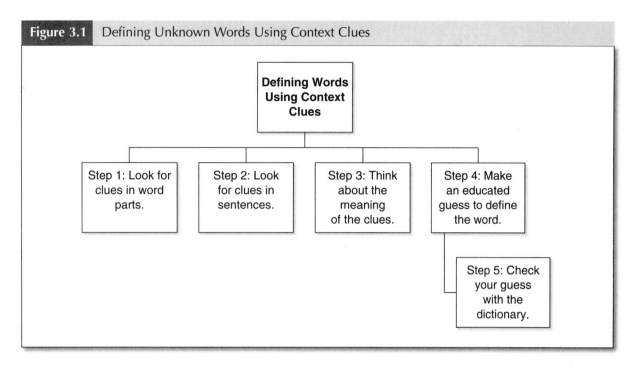

STEP-BY-STEP PROCEDURE

Tierney and Readence (2005, pp. 311–313) have provided a systematic approach for teaching students a word-learning strategy through the use of context clues and the dictionary. Their five-step strategy includes (1) selecting unfamiliar words, (2) writing a sentence, (3) presenting the words in isolation, (4) presenting the words in context, and (5) using the dictionary.

BEFORE READING

Prior to reading, the teacher demonstrates how to use word clues and sentence clues to assist students in unlocking the meaning of unknown words.

1. To teach the strategy, the teacher selects three key content words that are difficult yet central to understanding the text. She identifies the sentence or sentences from the text where the target words appear. To teach this strategy, it is important that the sentences that are used have multiple context clues that will help students guess the meaning of the word.

2. For students who are not familiar with using context clues, the teacher may consider using a think-aloud or modeling the process to demonstrate the strategy.

3. For each word, she uses the following procedure:

   a. The teacher provides an overview of the strategy and distributes copies of the graphic shown in Figure 3.2, Identifying the Meanings of Words Through Context Clues Chart, to students.

   b. The teacher presents the word to students, writing it on the chalkboard, carefully pronouncing it, and asking them to write each word on their charts in the column marked *words*.

   c. The teacher directs students to examine the word closely for word parts such as the base or root word, prefix, or suffix that may help them to discover the meaning of the word. Have students use the word parts to begin to guess the meaning of the word and write the word part and its meaning in the appropriate box on their chart. When students are unable to identify word parts, the teacher uses direct instruction, showing students how to recognize word parts that will offer meaningful clues.

d. The teacher writes a sentence on the chalkboard that is rich in context clues and asks the students to identify the clues within the sentence that may help them figure out the meaning of the target word. The teacher takes advantage of discussion and participation by the students to demonstrate how the use of context clues supports learning unfamiliar words. The students write the context clues in the appropriate column on their chart.

e. After studying the clues, the students guess the definition of the word and write it on their chart.

f. When students have used word parts and sentences as clues for arriving at the meaning of the target word, they employ their dictionary or the glossary in the text to identify the meaning of the word and write it on their chart.

Figure 3.2	Identifying the Meanings of Words Through the Context Clues Chart			
	Identify Context Clues and Meanings		*Combine the Clue Meanings*	*Check Your Meaning*
Words	**Step 1** **Word part**	**Step 2** **Surrounding**	**Step 3** **Clue meanings**	**Step 4** **Check your meaning with the dictionary**
				My word meaning: ✓ With dictionary definition:
				My word meaning: ✓ With dictionary definition:
				My word meaning: ✓ With dictionary definition:

DURING READING

The students read the text and practice their strategy for deriving meanings of words from word and text clues.

1. The teacher works with students who are having difficulty in identifying word and text clues.

2. The teacher conferences with students to assist them in using word and sentence clues guessing at the word meanings from context clues.

DIFFERENTIATING INSTRUCTION FOR STRIVING READERS

Proficient readers use a wide range of strategies in comprehending text including context clues to infer meaning from text. However, students who lack reading skills are not as capable in their use of context clues in making sense out of the text. To help struggling readers in developing efficient strategies for unlocking the meaning of words, it is important that teachers use more time modeling and scaffolding their attempts in using context clues (Scott, Nagy, & Flinspach, 2008). Create learning partners by pairing striving with average or advanced readers and provide them with a list of word parts and their meanings. Demonstrate to students how to use the meaning of word parts to discover the meaning of an unknown word. Allow time for the learning partners to practice together while monitoring their performance.

CONSIDERING THE LANGUAGE NEEDS OF ELL STUDENTS

IRA/NCTE Standards for the English Language Arts

10. Students whose first language is not English make use of their first language to develop competency in the English language arts and to develop understanding of content across the curriculum.

Source: International Reading Association and National Council of Teachers of English (1996).

Teaching ELL students word-learning strategies will equip them with essential tools toward developing vocabulary in their second language. When teaching the use of context clues in figuring out the meaning of an unknown word to ELL students, begin with words that are familiar to the students. Scaffold students' first attempts in identifying context clues through probing questions and selecting appropriate dictionary definitions.

AN APPLICATION FOR INSTRUCTION AND LEARNING IN THE BIOLOGY CLASSROOM

An eighth-grade class is beginning a unit on environmental science. Their opening reading includes description of the differences between an ecosystem and a biome. The teacher introduces the three key words and asks students for their meanings. Students take "wild guesses" in defining the key words. She then provides them with a strategy to unlock the meanings of unknown words through looking for clues in words and within the sentence or sentences surrounding the word, using the clues and their meanings to define the word, and checking their definition with the glossary in the text or the dictionary. Figure 3.3, Identifying the Meanings of Words Through the Context Clue Chart: Biology, illustrates how a group of students worked together to figure out the meanings of unknown words by applying the contextual clue strategy on the three target words from their textbook.

Figure 3. 3	Identifying the Meanings of Words Through the Context Clue Chart: Biology			
Words	*Identify Context Clues and Meanings*		*Combine the Clue Meanings*	*Check Your Meaning*
	Step 1 **Word part**	**Step 2** **Surrounding**	**Step 3** **Clue meanings**	**Step 4** **Check your meaning with the dictionary**
Ecologist	*eco*—has to do with the environment *ology*—the study of *ist*—person	The plant life and fish in the pond were being examined by the ecologist.	The person studying the environment, like the plants and fish in the pond.	My word meaning: someone studying the environment. ✓ My guess fits the meaning of the one in the glossary of the text.
Ecosystem	*eco*—has to do with the environment *system*—working together	The living things in an ecosystem work closely together. They are in balance like any good system.	All parts of the ecosystem are in balance working together.	My word meaning: things or parts in the environment that work together. ✓ My guess was almost the same as the dictionary meaning. The glossary included the ecological community to describe how they work together and said they were smaller than biomes.
Biome	*bio*—has to do with living organisms	The entire communities of living organisms that exist together in similar conditions.	Living organisms that live together.	My word meaning: large community of organisms that live together and share the same conditions. ✓ My guess was correct. I found out that ecosystems and biomes are almost alike. One main difference is that they differ in size.

REFERENCES

Graves, M. F. (2007). Vocabulary instruction in the middle grades. *Voices from the Middle, 15*(1), 13–19.

Graves, M. F. (2008). Instruction on individual words: One size does not fit all. In A. E. Farstrup & S. J. Samuels (Eds.), *What research has to say about vocabulary instruction* (pp. 56–79). Newark, DE: International Reading Association.

Harmon, J. M., Wood, K. D., & Hedrick, W. B. (2008). Vocabulary instruction in middle and secondary content classrooms: Understandings and direction from research. In A. E. Farstrup & S. J. Samuels (Eds.), *What research has to say about vocabulary instruction* (pp. 150–181). Newark, DE: International Reading Association.

International Reading Association and National Council of Teachers of English. (1996). *Standards for the English language arts*. Newark, DE: International Reading Association & Urbana, IL: National Council of Teachers of English.

Scott, J. A., Nagy, W. E., & Flinspach, S. L. (2008). More than merely words: Redefining vocabulary learning in a culturally and linguistically diverse society. In A. E. Farstrup & S. J. Samuels (Eds.), *What research has to say about vocabulary instruction* (pp. 182–210). Newark, DE: International Reading Association.

Tierney, R. J., & Readence, J. E. (2005). *Reading strategies and practices: A compendium* (6th ed.). Boston: Allyn & Bacon.

Vacca, R. T., & Vacca, J. L. (2007). *Content area reading: Literacy and learning across the curriculum* (9th ed.). Boston: Allyn & Bacon.

Strategy 4

Semantic Feature Analysis (SFA)

Comparing and Contrasting Features of Words

STRATEGY OVERVIEW

The primary purpose of the semantic feature analysis (SFA) strategy is to increase students' academic vocabulary. Through the use of categorization skills required by SFA, students are led to a deeper understanding of the key words as they examine the similarities and differences of related words through analyzing the features or characteristics of each word concept within the selected category (Tierney & Readence, 2005).

As students in content area classrooms advance, their requirement to learn from their texts augments. Therefore, they experience difficulty in acquiring knowledge through reading, and for many students, the challenge is overwhelming. Such "knowledge acquisition includes specific domain knowledge, such as categories, concepts, and processes" (Ruddell & Unrau, 2004, p. 1488). To comprehend and learn from text, it is essential that readers have acquired the conceptual understanding of the words that they read. SFA provides students with a strategy that helps to build their knowledge base through the development of related concepts or content words. For each word, students are required to examine its features and how words from a category may or may not share these features or characteristics. As students use SFA, they build conceptual knowledge of words and discover related words within a category, an important aspect of deepening their comprehension of the content words. Thus, SFA is a strategy that assists students in learning words within a category by examining their shared features and characteristics through the use of a matrix or a word grid (Brozo & Simpson, 2003).

Although SFA has been used to expand students' vocabulary outside a specific domain area, such as fictional literature, SFA is more appropriate to use as a vocabulary strategy in a content area around a given topic (Tierney & Readence, 2005). To optimize student learning when using SFA, consider the following recommendations for implementing the strategy:

1. Since SFA is considered a conceptual approach to word learning, it helps students connect the meanings of the new words to their prior knowledge (Herman & Dole, 1988).

2. Consider the students, the text, and the task when selecting the topic and related key words for vocabulary instruction.

3. Use an interactional approach to teaching the key words. Students' active participation in learning new academic vocabulary will guarantee better learning from text.

4. Guided by the content that is being studied as well as students' backgrounds, use small-group and whole-class discussion, questioning strategies, writing, and group sharing to facilitate students' understanding of the vocabulary.

IRA/NCTE Standards for the English Language Arts

3. Students apply a wide range of strategies to comprehend, interpret, evaluate, and appreciate texts. They draw on their prior experience, their interactions with other readers and writers, their knowledge of word meaning and of other texts, their word identification strategies, and their understanding of textual features (e.g., sound-letter correspondence, sentence structure, context, graphics).

12. Students use spoken, written, and visual language to accomplish their own purposes (e.g., for learning, enjoyment, persuasion, and the exchange of information).

Source: International Reading Association and National Council of Teachers of English (1996).

STEP-BY-STEP PROCEDURE

The SFA will be most successful when teachers use the strategy before, during, and after reading the text. Before students read the text, the teacher may select from various approaches such as questioning, a prewriting activity, or a think-pair-share activity to prepare students for reading the new word concepts in the text.

BEFORE READING

Prior to assigning students their readings, the teacher expands their understanding of the academic vocabulary required for comprehending and learning from the text. The following are the steps to follow before reading the text:

1. The teacher prepares by selecting the topic to be studied and the key words. After a careful reading of the students' text, the teacher selects only the related key words that belong to the category that are needed for understanding the text.

2. The teacher constructs a matrix, similar to the one in Figure 4.1, Semantic Feature Analysis Matrix, writing the topic or category name at the top and listing the selected key words to be studied in the first column. Along the top row, the teacher writes the major features or characteristics that belong to some or all of the categories that are to be discussed. The selected features are determined by the defining attributes of the words that will lead to an understanding of the word and the category and eventually a contextual definition.

3. The matrix will be used by the teacher for the guided discussion with the class. Therefore, a copy of the matrix may be projected using a transparency or the

computer. Copies of the blank matrix, as shown in Figure 4.1, Semantic Feature Analysis Matrix, are also distributed to the students.

4. The teacher introduces the topic of study by engaging the students in an active discussion that focuses on the key words needed to understand their reading. During the discussion, the teacher activates their prior knowledge through the use of questions and builds prerequisite knowledge needed to understand the content of the lesson as well as the readings. The focus of the discussion is on the comparison of the key words or concepts through examining their features and characteristics of the words.

5. When students' discussion of a word affirms that a feature is present, a check (✓) is recorded in the box that intersects with the word's row and the feature's column; for those words that do not possess the feature, a negative (−) sign is recorded.

Figure 4.1	Semantic Feature Analysis Matrix							
Key words	Features							Notes
								Comment and Definition

During Reading

During reading students work to confirm and develop their understanding of the concepts that they are learning.

1. As students read their text, they take notes on the key words that provide additional information related to their understanding of the word. Students use their notes to revise their responses on their matrix.

2. Students are directed to add words from their readings that they think belong to the category or are related to the topic.

After Reading

Remembering that lively discussions initiated by students promote engagement in learning, the teacher prepares for small-group discussions immediately after their reading and a whole-class discussion to follow.

1. The teacher provides for a 5-minute small-group discussion of the key words. Students are directed to focus on one key word they have revised or added to their matrix as a result of their readings. They provide the basis for their revision or addition of the new word by showing evidence from their readings.

2. The teacher continues the discussion around the key words with the whole class. The SFA prereading matrix is projected on the screen while the teacher asks probing questions to expand students' knowledge around each of the key words. She encourages students to revisit their text. The discussion may lead the students to

   • provide responses that were discussed in their small groups, giving additional features for the key words,

   • compare and contrast key words,

   • offer contextual definitions of the key words, and/or

   • include words from their readings that they believe belong to the topic or category, offering a reason for their new word and identifying the word's features.

Extensions of SFA

Following the whole-class discussion of the key words, the teacher may extend the activity to provide students with practice in using the new academic words. For example, a brief, on-demand writing assignment that requires the students to include the words in meaningful ways will offer extended practice. Further, having students add the words to their personal dictionaries with contextual meanings or adding the words to the classroom word wall provides a reference for later use.

Differentiating Instruction for Striving Readers

Without an understanding of academic vocabulary, students who are experiencing comprehension problems will not understand or learn from their textbooks. Researchers (Bos, Allen, & Scanlon, 1989) have found that SFA promotes academic vocabulary by readers with a learning disability as they benefited through increased word knowledge and improved reading comprehension. Additional studies (Bos & Anders, 1990) attribute improved academic vocabulary and reading comprehension to SFA, because it is an interactive approach that engages students in their own learning.

Teachers may use the SFA in a similar fashion as suggested with some modifications for students who are struggling readers. They may (a) divide the lesson into smaller parts, requiring a reduced number of pages with shorter word lists; (b) provide greater opportunities for students to engage in partnering for the purpose of clarifying and expanding word meanings; (c) present visuals for concepts that serve as cues for students' understanding and reminders of the features or attributes of the key words.

CONSIDERING THE LANGUAGE NEEDS OF ELL STUDENTS

Source: International Reading Association and National Council of Teachers of English (1996).

IRA/NCTE Standards for the English Language Arts

10. Students whose first language is not English make use of their first language to develop competency in the English language arts and to develop understanding of content across the curriculum.

Academic vocabulary has become an impediment for some students' success in content area classrooms. Bailey (2006) argued that for English language learners, it is especially true. One reason for the difficulty in acquiring and developing knowledge of words within the discipline is the nature of the words; academic vocabulary may be of abstract and have multiple meanings. Although research on specific strategy instruction of vocabulary learning for ELL students is limited, researchers Bos et al. (1989) found that with English language learners classified as students with special learning needs, the use of SFA to teach word knowledge had positive effects on vocabulary and reading comprehension. Among key ideas for effective ELL vocabulary instruction summarized from research, Helman (2008) suggested "vocabulary study built on students' background language such as with previews from home language and cognate identification" (p. 215). The SFA strategy may be modified for use with ELL students by translating the English key words into the home language of the students. Each key word would then appear on the matrix as a word in English and in the home language of the students. Further, the features or the characteristics of the category or topic should also be translated into the home language of the students.

AN APPLICATION FOR INSTRUCTION AND LEARNING IN THE HEALTH CLASSROOM

Students in the ninth grade were studying a unit on the importance and role of nutrition in maintaining a healthy lifestyle. Among the topics were the problems that confront teenagers related to sustaining a balanced diet; the role of vitamins, minerals, nutrients, and fat in the functioning of the body; and planning diets that support a healthy and active body. Using the SFA matrix, the teacher selected key words from the assigned readings. She conducted an extensive discussion that provided the introduction of the vocabulary prior to the students' reading of the text. The students used the matrix during and after reading to further develop their understanding of the key words within the readings. Figure 4.2, Semantic Feature Analysis Matrix: Nutrition, shows how the students completed the chart during and after reading the text.

Figure 4.2	Semantic Feature Analysis Matrix: Nutrition							
Key Words	Features							Notes
	Found in Foods	Found in Meat	Source of Nutrients	Aids in Body Functions	Eating Disorders	Necessary for Healthy Bodily Functioning	Components of Diets	Comment and Definitions
Calories	–	–	–	✓	–	✓	✓	As we move, work, sleep, etc., the body burns calories. They come from food.
Cholesterol	✓	✓	–	–	–	✓	✓	Found in blood. Come from different food products. Too much is not good.
Glucose	–	–	–	✓	–	✓	–	The body makes it.
Fats	✓	✓	✓	✓	–	✓	✓	There are different types of fat and not all fats are good for the body.
Fiber	✓	–	✓	✓	–	✓	✓	Fiber comes from certain foods, and it is very good for the body.
Anorexia	–	–	–	–	✓	–	–	Anorexia is an eating disorder where the person does not eat.
Minerals	✓	✓	✓	✓	–	✓	✓	Minerals are necessary to the body, and they come from food.
Vitamins	✓	✓	✓	✓	–	✓	✓	We can take vitamin pills but the best type comes from food. They are important for the body.
Bulimia	–	–	–	–	✓	–	–	Bulimia is an eating disorder where the person eats too much food and gets rid of it.

REFERENCES

Bailey, A. L. (2006). Teaching and assessing students learning English in school. In A. L. Bailey (Ed.), *The language demands of school: Putting academic English to the test* (pp. 1–26). New Haven, CT: Yale University Press.

Bos, C. S., Allen, A. A., & Scanlon, D. (1989). Vocabulary instruction and reading comprehension with bilingual learning disabled readers. *National Reading Conference, 38,* 173–179.

Bos, C. S., & Anders, P. L. (1990). Effects of interactive vocabulary instruction on vocabulary learning and reading comprehension of junior high school learning disabled students. *Learning Disability Quarterly, 13*(1), 31–42.

Brozo, W. G., & Simpson, M. L. (2003). *Readers, teachers, learners: Exploring literacy across the content areas.* Upper Saddle River, NJ: Merrill Prentice Hall.

Helman, L. (2008). English words needed: Creating research-based vocabulary instruction for English learners. In A. E. Farstrup & S. J. Samuels (Eds.), *What research has to say about vocabulary instruction* (pp. 211–237). Newark, DE: International Reading Association.

Herman, P. A., & Dole, J. (1988). Theory and practice in vocabulary learning and instruction. *Elementary School Journal, 89,* 43–54.

International Reading Association and National Council of Teachers of English. (1996). *Standards for the English language arts.* Newark, DE: International Reading Association & Urbana, IL: National Council of Teachers of English.

Ruddell, R. B., & Unrau, N. J. (2004). Reading as a meaning-construction process: The reader, the text, and the teacher. In R. B. Ruddell & N. J. Unrau (Eds.), *Theoretical models and processes of reading* (5th ed., pp. 1462–1521). Newark, DE: International Reading Association.

Tierney, R. J., & Readence, J. E. (2005). *Reading strategies and practices: A compendium* (6th ed.). Boston: Allyn & Bacon.

List-Group-Label (L-G-L)

Developing Conceptual Knowledge of Words

Strategy 5

List-group-label (Taba, 1967) strategy develops students' academic vocabulary by categorizing words into groups that relate to similar concepts. Through this process, students are required to activate their prior knowledge and engage in thinking about words in different ways. They connect their prior knowledge with new knowledge about words, thereby developing conceptual understandings useful for comprehending text.

Students begin brainstorming words associated with the topic, categorizing or grouping the words based on their similarities, and developing a label for each group of words that share related features. A number of variations of the strategy developed as a result of its use over time. For example, L-G-L was used as a minilesson before reading to help students make predictions about their text. Others (Boling & Evans, 2008; Massey & Heafner, 2004) have used the L-G-L strategy as a prereading strategy to assist students in activating their prior knowledge and making connections to the text. The L-G-L was also used as an assessment tool to determine students' word knowledge. Allen (2007) discussed how one teacher adapted L-G-L to assess students' prior knowledge of the related topics to be read as they were engaged in brainstorming words around the theme of the literature. L-G-L strategy was developed primarily for use in the social studies classroom. Since then it has been successfully applied in various content area classrooms such as science and the English language arts classroom.

Source: International Reading Association and National Council of Teachers of English (1996).

IRA/NCTE Standards for the English Language Arts

3. Students apply a wide range of strategies to comprehend, interpret, evaluate, and appreciate texts. They draw on their prior experience, their interactions with other readers and writers, their knowledge of word meaning and of other texts, their word identification strategies, and their understanding of textual features (e.g., sound-letter correspondence, sentence structure, context, graphics).
12. Students use spoken, written, and visual language to accomplish their own purposes (e.g., for learning, enjoyment, persuasion, and the exchange of information).

STEP-BY-STEP PROCEDURE

To engage students at deeper levels, the L-G-L strategy is used as a before-, during-, and after-reading strategy along with a writing component as an extension for using vocabulary words (Harmon, Wood, & Hedrick, 2006).

BEFORE READING

During this phase, the teacher prepares the students for reading by engaging them in a discussion on the topic to activate their prior knowledge related to key words or concepts within the readings.

1. Before using the L-G-L strategy, the teacher chooses the topic of study (assigned readings) and carefully selects the key words required for comprehending the discussion and the readings.

2. To motivate and engage students in learning about the topic, the teacher selects an appropriate technique, such as a short podcast, a 5-minute segment of a video, a series of pictures, or a brief reading. The teacher then introduces the topic by connecting it to the motivational procedure that she used to help students think about the topic.

3. The teacher directs the students to work in small groups to brainstorm a *list* of words or terms that are related to the topic.

4. Each group then shares their list of words, as the teacher pronounces each word and writes it on an overhead, the chalkboard, SMART board, or large chart paper. At this point, the teacher begins to assess how much vocabulary building may be required before reading the text. Do students have an adequate store of words related to the central topic?

5. The students are then directed to work in small groups for the purpose of *grouping* the lists of words or word phrases.
   a. When L-G-L is used for the first time, the teacher may need to demonstrate the grouping process to the class, showing them how certain words or phrases may be similar and placed in the same group.
   b. As students work in small groups, the teacher may monitor students' discussions and use guiding questions that will help them group the terms. Questions the teacher poses to the students that may help to group terms are: "What two words are alike?" "Can you find another word that may be similar?" "How are the words alike?"

6. After the small groups have completed the process of grouping the words, they are asked to *label* each group. The teacher may need to use a think-aloud approach to demonstrate how to label each group of words or phrases, asking the following questions aloud: "What makes this first set of words similar?" "What word or phrase can I use as a label that fits all of the words in this group?"

7. The teacher revisits the initial group of words, asking the students how they grouped and labeled the words. Students are expected to tell why the words were grouped together.

8. At this point, the teacher decides whether it is necessary to expand students' knowledge of the key words or to include additional key words for instruction that are required for their comprehension of the text.

During Reading

Before students read, the teacher reminds them that they will be reading about the topic that they have discussed and will encounter the key words that they grouped. To facilitate students' reading, the teacher will (a) encourage students to use stickies to jot down additional notes related to the concepts or key words that they grouped and labeled and (b) have students jot down unfamiliar words within their readings for further exploration.

After Reading

The teacher conducts a guided discussion with the class about their reading. Through posing questions about the reading, the students retell what they have read. Additionally, the class revisits the list of key words that they have grouped and labeled; the students then discuss each group of key word to do the following:

1. Confirm that each word belongs in the group and

2. Revise the group of words when necessary, adding or deleting words.

3. Revise the label for each group of words when necessary.

4. Develop other groups of words that were part of their readings related to the topic.

Extending L-G-L

One way that students acquire ownership of the content words that they have learned is to provide them with opportunities for using the key words. Such activities may be simple or elaborate depending on the topic of study. The teacher may ask the students to work in groups or work alone to do the following: (a) Have students create a poster that includes the key words to develop the ideas related to the topic and present it to the class, using the key words within their discussions or presentations. (b) Provide a prompt related to the topic of study and have students write a paragraph using the key words. (c) Using the key words, have students take notes in their learning logs on what they have learned from their readings and small- and large-group discussions. (d) Create word walls around the central concept or topic that is being studied, and have students add key words and new words along with contextual definitions to the word wall.

DIFFERENTIATING INSTRUCTION FOR STRIVING READERS

Strategies that employ classification and categorization skills are cognitively economical as students relate words they know to new words that are similar is some ways. This strategy is therefore especially helpful to the striving readers in expanding their academic vocabularies. One way to support students in content area classrooms in using the L-G-L is to have them partner with another student to complete the steps of the strategy. Additionally, providing students with useful prompts as they brainstorm the list of words and then group and label words will offer them the support they need.

CONSIDERING THE LANGUAGE NEEDS OF ELL STUDENTS

Source: International Reading Association and National Council of Teachers of English (1996).

IRA/NCTE Standards for the English Language Arts

10. Students whose first language is not English make use of their first language to develop competency in the English language arts and to develop understanding of content across the curriculum.

Students who are learning a second language have an especially difficult time in acquiring academic vocabulary. Researchers suggest that language-rich environments and strategies for developing word learning would benefit ELL students (Manzo, Manzo, & Thomas, 2009). The L-G-L strategy and follow-up activities offer English language learners the help they need to learn content area words. The teacher should consider the needs of ELL students when using L-G-L strategy by employing it as an assessment tool. When directing students to brainstorm words related to a specific topic, they may list words in their native language, which then will be translated for the students.

AN APPLICATION FOR INSTRUCTION AND LEARNING IN THE POLITICAL SCIENCE CLASSROOM

It is a presidential election year in the early month of October, and seniors in a political science class are reading newspapers and magazine articles, writing blogs, watching podcasts, and discussing various aspects of the election. The teacher is ready to introduce some of the rules and protocols that govern a national election. She directs students to brainstorm all of the words that they have heard and read about related to the election. Following the procedure for the L-G-L strategy, the teacher projects the words on an overhead as the students write them down. Students work in pairs or small groups and proceed with the next step. They find words that are similar in some way and group them. Finally, students label each group with a related word or phrase. After students have read their assigned readings from the text, the teacher conducts a discussion on the readings and key words. Their discussion moves from a retelling of the text to focus on how the key words have been grouped and labeled. Students contribute new words to the list and make revisions to their groups. This application of the L-G-L strategy to political science may be found in Figure 5.1, List-Group-Label Chart: The U.S. Presidential Election.

Figure 5.1	List-Group-Label Chart: The U.S. Presidential Election

Topic: The United States Presidential Election

Step 1 List Words

Republican	Democrat	Party favorite
Vote	Delegates	Voter registration
Democrat	Electors	Primaries
Electoral votes	Voter registration	Ballot
Absentee ballot	Nomination	Early voting
President	Party choice	Vice president
Independent	Planks	Constitutional
GOP	Incumbents	Popular votes
Demographics	Debates	Voting polls
Landside win	Libertarian	Platform
Republican	Voting patterns	Electoral college

Topic: The United States Presidential Election

Step 2 Group Words

President	Republican	Primaries	Vote	Exit polls
Vice President	Democrat	Republican	Voter registration	Landslide
Incumbents	Independent	Democrat	Ballot	Voting patterns
	Libertarian	Delegates	Absentee ballot	Demographics
	Constitutional	Nomination	Early voting	
	GOP	Party favorite	Electoral votes	
		Party choice	Popular votes	
			Landside win	
			Voting polls	

Topic: The United States Presidential Election

Step 3 Label Groups

Candidate	Party	Convention & Campaigns	Election	Election Results
President	Republican	Primaries	Vote	Exit polls
Vice President	Democrat	Republican	Voter registration	Voting patterns
Incumbents	Independent	Democrat	Ballot	Demographics
	Libertarian	Delegates	Absentee ballot	Landslide win
	GOP	Nomination	Early voting	Marginal win
		Party favorite	Electoral votes	
		Platform	Popular votes	
		Planks	Voting polls	
		Debates	Electors	
			Constitution & Rules for voting	

REFERENCES

Allen, J. (2007). *Inside words: Tools for teaching academic vocabulary, Grades 4–12*. Portland, ME: Stenhouse.

Boling, C. J., & Evans, W. H. (2008). Reading success in the secondary classroom. *Preventing School Failure, 52*(2), 59–66.

Harmon, J. M., Wood, K. D., & Hedrick, W. B. (2006). *Instruction strategies for teaching content vocabulary: Grades 4–12*. Westerville, OH: National Middle School Association and Newark, DE: International Reading Association.

International Reading Association and National Council of Teachers of English. (1996). *Standards for the English language arts*. Newark, DE: International Reading Association & Urbana, IL: National Council of Teachers of English.

Manzo, A. V., Manzo, U. C., & Thomas, M. M. (2009). *Content area literacy: A framework for reading based instruction* (5th ed.). Hoboken, NJ: Wiley.

Massey, D. D., & Heafner, T. L. (2004). Promoting reading comprehension in social studies. *Journal of Adolescent and Adult Literacy, 48*(1), 26–40.

Taba, H. (1967). *Teacher's handbook for elementary social studies*. Reading, MA: Addison-Wesley.

SECTION II

Reading Fluency

Developing Deep-Reading Fluency

Reading well is one of the great pleasures that solitude can afford you.

—Harold Bloom

When we read well it is not a task, it is pure enjoyment. Each book has the potential of offering a range of pleasures to its readers. Books allow them to travel in time and place without leaving their chairs. They present the history of the world by telling the personal stories of strangers allowing readers to become their friend or foe. With such confidence of true friendship during moments of loneliness, it is a good book that bestows its delightful gifts upon those who read well.

The purpose of Section II is to provide an understanding of the importance and need of achieving reading fluency by all students and ways to achieve it. Within this section, we argue for the need to teach fluency by providing (a) a more current definition of fluency, (b) a discussion of fluency as a developmental process, (c) a demonstration of how fluent reading leads to deeper comprehension of text, and (d) appropriate instructional strategies for the middle and secondary readers that promote advanced fluency in reading.

WHAT RESEARCH HAS TO SAY ABOUT THE DEVELOPMENT OF READING FLUENCY

Recently there has been an emphasis in reading fluency instruction (Cassidy & Cassidy, 2008); however, this has not always been the case. In his discussion on the history of reading fluency, Timothy Rasinski (2006) traced the changing position that fluency has taken in the

51

reading curriculum. For some time, reading fluency was not part of the reading program, even at the early stages of learning how to read. Once again instruction in reading fluency has been given a prominent role in reading programs in the elementary schools. The Report of the National Reading Panel (National Institute of Child Health and Human Development, 2000) has been a major influence on educators to emphasize the teaching of reading fluency to students. Such an emphasis is quite understandable since research points to fluency as one of the major areas in reading instruction that leads to proficiency in reading.

Although teaching reading fluency has received its rightful place in literacy programs for young children learning to read, it has not achieved such prominence for intermediate, middle, or secondary students. Yet current research suggests that attention to reading fluency at the middle and secondary levels would promote content area achievement for the average and struggling readers. What this means is that more than half of the students entering the middle and secondary grades lack the proficiencies and skills required to read and learn from assigned texts within content area classrooms (The Nation's Report Card: Reading 2007; Lee, Grigg, & Donahue, 2007). It is understandable that in a recent survey conducted by Cassidy, Garret, and Barrera (2006), 75% of the 25 literacy educators surveyed representing all areas of the country responded that fluency instruction for adolescent students is a "hot topic" and should remain a hot topic. Clearly, not all students advancing to the middle and secondary schools are fluent readers. Thus, the role of fluency instruction for adolescent students should be part of their instructional programs.

DEFINING READING FLUENCY FOR ADOLESCENT READING

Reading fluency is "the ability of readers to read quickly, effortlessly, and efficiently with good, meaningful expression" (Rasinski, 2003, p. 26). When you listen in on fluent readers, you hear words read with accuracy and confidence. Their phasing and expression mirror oral conversations. However, the same is not true for nonfluent readers. Striving readers pause before many of the words, they read slowly, and their phrasing and expression reflect a lack of comprehension. It stands to good reason that such labored reading is painful to nonfluent readers who then become reluctant readers.

Reading fluency is defined by reading behaviors and skills demonstrated by proficient readers. Such behaviors go beyond those only associated with oral reading such as accuracy of word recognition and reading rate. The current definitions of reading fluency include a comprehensive set of reading behaviors that are critical to reading proficiency (Chall, 1996; Ehri, 1995; Samuels, 2006; Topping, 2006). Such researchers view fluency as a set of developmental skills and behaviors that lead to strategic reading and are characterized as *deep fluency*. For example, Topping (2006) explained that as students further develop their ability to read, there is a need to become more strategic in acquiring a deeper understanding of text associated with deep fluency. Mature readers demonstrate deep fluency when they adjust their rate of reading and expression to the type of text. When students are faced with content area text that is difficult and contains unknown words, advanced readers will use multiple resources to comprehend the text. Depending on the text and the purpose for reading, they may slow down or read faster and use multiple resources to figure out unknown words. When readers have reached this stage of deep fluency, they are expected to go beyond comprehension to make personal responses to the reading, expand the meanings of the text, listen to their audience for their responses, and examine their own reading processes.

We view this growing body of research on reading fluency with a broad definition that incorporates the purpose of fluency development as well as the goal of all reading—the reader's comprehension of text. Without being fluent in their reading, students cannot expect to read for learning. They will fail to comprehend the required content area texts that are central to the middle and secondary school curriculum. Thus, for adolescent readers to achieve school success, fluency instruction needs to be part of the literacy and content curriculum.

A FRAMEWORK FOR TEACHING
READING FLUENCY TO ADOLESCENT STUDENTS

The importance of reading fluency in the development of proficient readers has been established by research. Too many students leaving fourth grade entering middle school and those leaving eighth grade entering secondary school are not reading at proficient levels. Yet the expectations for these students become increasingly more difficult as they are required to "read to learn." To ensure that all students progress toward the attainment of deep fluency levels when reading, it is important that instruction and assessment of reading fluency are included in the content area literacy program. The following framework for teaching reading fluency to adolescent students should include the following:

- Integrating comprehension

- Providing models of excellent fluent reading

- Utilizing students' reading fluency levels as a guide in selecting reading material

- Designing instruction to motivate and engage students in reading

- Providing opportunities within the classroom for daily independent reading and

- Monitoring the progress of reading fluency of all students

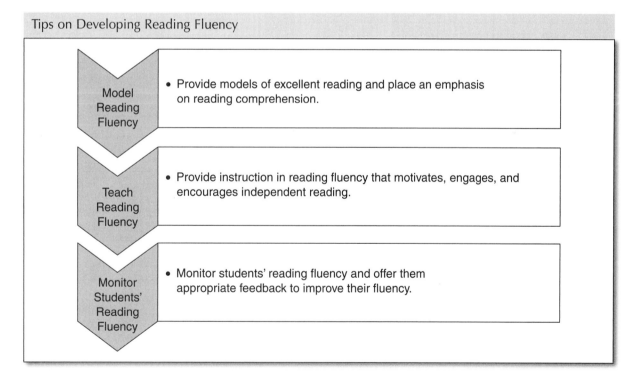

Tips on Developing Reading Fluency

Model Reading Fluency
- Provide models of excellent reading and place an emphasis on reading comprehension.

Teach Reading Fluency
- Provide instruction in reading fluency that motivates, engages, and encourages independent reading.

Monitor Students' Reading Fluency
- Monitor students' reading fluency and offer them appropriate feedback to improve their fluency.

A STRATEGY FOR ASSESSING READING FLUENCY DEVELOPMENT

Within this section, we have used the most effective criteria from current research related to developing reading fluency in adolescent students. Research demonstrates a strong correlation between fluent and proficient reading. Therefore, in evaluating reading fluency, it is important that the assessment tool be designed so that it measures the reading skills used for developing reading fluency. Fluency definitions comprise the following skills in oral reading: (a) accuracy for reading words, (b) appropriate pace for reading text, and (c) prosody or expression while reading that demonstrates a comprehension of text. The rubric shown in Figure II.1 Assessing Reading Fluency may be used to determine students' reading fluency levels and to monitor fluency in all students as well as striving readers and English language learning (ELL) students.

Figure II.1	Rubric for Assessing Oral Reading Fluency			
Reading Skill		*Striving (1)*	*Developing (2)*	*Advancing (3)*	*Proficient (4)*

Reading Skill		Striving (1)	Developing (2)	Advancing (3)	Proficient (4)
Word recognition	Accuracy in reading words	Reads grade-level texts with many errors; does not attempt to read more difficult text	Reads grade-level texts with some errors and makes numerous errors on more difficult texts	Reads grade-level texts accurately; makes some errors on more difficult texts	Reads texts with a wide range of difficulty levels accurately
Word-solving strategies		Does not employ word-solving strategies when encountering unknown words	Employs one or two word-solving strategies when encountering unknown words	Employs several word-solving strategies when encountering unknown words	Employs a range word-solving strategies when encountering unknown words, selecting the one that is appropriate for figuring out the word
Rate	Pace	Reads slowly and laboriously, hesitating at words and repeating some; demonstrates discomfort during reading	Reads at an uneven rate depending on the difficulty of the words; shows a lack of confidence	Reads at a normal rate, at times stops when confronted by more difficult words	Reads at a conversational rate, adjusting pace depending on the text and the audience
Expression	Prosody	Lacks expression while reading; uses a monotonous voice	Reads with some expression, but does not sound natural	Reads with expression, sounding natural for most of the reading; at times uses tone and stress to show an understanding of the text	Reads with a conversational-like expression, varying the tone and the stress to deliver the meaning of the text; engages the audience
Phrasing		Reads one word at a time in a hesitating manner, disregarding phases and punctuation	Reads with an unnatural phasing, failing to consider the syntax and punctuation as a guide	Reads with a moderate degree of phrasing; at times uses punctuation effectively	Reads with accurate phrasing, using punctuation and content of the text as a guide
Volume		Reads in an inaudible voice	Reads with an uneven volume	Reads with an appropriate volume	Reads with an effective volume, adjusting it to deliver meaning to the audience

REFLECTIVE PRACTICE ON TEACHING READING FLUENCY

Within the content area classrooms are a number of opportunities for teachers to promote and encourage fluent reading. Reflective teachers systematically monitor students' reading performances and use the results to adjust their teaching. Their goal is to improve students' reading fluency. For example, when a number of students are experiencing difficulty in pronouncing words or in accurate phrasing and expressive reading, the teacher uses specific strategies to target those difficulties. Additionally, striving readers and ELL students may perform at exceptionally low levels of reading fluency. For those students, the teacher will differentiate instruction to provide minilessons that focus on specific areas of fluency.

PROFESSIONAL RESOURCES

Flynn, R. M. (2007). *Dramatizing the content with curriculum-based readers theatre, grades 6–12.* Newark, DE: International Reading Association.

McEwan, E. K. (2007). *40 ways to support struggling readers in content classrooms, grades 6–12.* Thousand Oaks, CA: Corwin.

Wormeli, R. (2007). *Differentiation: From planning to practice, grades 6–12.* Portland, ME: Stenhouse.

REFERENCES

Cassidy, J., & Cassidy, D. (2008). What's hot, What's not. *Reading Today, 25*(4), 1, 10–11.

Cassidy, J., Garrett, S., Barrera, E. (2006). What's hot in adolescent literacy 1997–2006. *Journal of Adolescent and Adult Literacy, 50,* 30–36.

Chall, J. S. (1996). *Stages of reading development* (2nd ed.). Fort Worth, TX: Harcourt Brace.

Ehri, L. C. (1995). Phases of development in reading words by sight. *Journal of Research in Reading, 18,* 116–125.

Lee, J., Grigg, W. S., & Donahue, P. L. (2007). National Center for Educational Statistics: National Assessment of Educational Progress (NAEP): *The Nation's Report Card Reading 2007.* Washington, DC: U.S. Department of Education: Institute of Education Sciences.

National Institute of Child Health and Human Development. (2000). *Report of the National Reading Panel. Teaching Children to Read: Reports of the subgroups* (NIH Publication No. 00-4754). Washington, DC: Government Printing Office.

Rasinski, T. V. (2003). *The fluent reader: Oral reading strategies for building word recognition, fluency, and comprehension.* New York: Scholastic.

Rasinski, T. V. (2006). A brief history of reading fluency. In S. J. Samuels & A. E. Farstrup (Eds.), *What research has to say about fluency instruction* (pp. 4–22). Newark, DE: International Reading Association.

Samuels, S. J. (2006). Towards a model of reading fluency. In S. J. Samuels & A. E. Farstrup (Eds.), *What research has to say about fluency instruction* (pp. 24–46). Newark, DE: International Reading Association.

Topping, K. J. (2006). Building reading fluency: Cognitive, behavioral, and socioemotional factors and the role of peer-mediated learning. In S. J. Samuels & A. E. Farstrup (Eds.), *What research has to say about fluency instruction* (pp. 106–129). Newark, DE: International Reading Association.

Strategy 6

Readers Theatre

Increasing Fluency Through Student Engagement With Text

STRATEGY OVERVIEW

Readers Theatre is a powerful strategy for engaging students in reading for meaning as they focus on interpreting the text through its dramatization. Each student receives a part, rehearses it through several rereadings, and enacts the script for an audience that is performed through an oral reading. Repeated readings that are motivating to the students (Palumbo & Willcutt, 2006; Samuels, 2006) with the accompanying component of comprehension (Pikulski, 2006) will result in fluency development. Clearly, Readers Theatre includes the essentials that are supported by research related to successful fluency instruction.

Readers Theatre offers a wide range of benefits to all participants. Students develop components of language and literacy as they are engaged in interpretive readings of stories of content area texts. Oral communication skills are required as students must speak clearly so that their listeners understand their reading. When students reread their scripts, they improve their accuracy for word reading, pacing and phrasing of text, as well as expressive reading. Finally, as students work together while preparing to stage the text, their collaboration will lead them to discuss their parts to achieve appropriate dramatization of the text. Such engaged discussions foster students' deeper understanding of text (Martinez, Roser, & Strecker, 1999).

What types of scripts work well for Readers Theatre? Selecting a script is important, and it depends on the content area. Scripts for Readers Theatre may be selected from fiction or informational text. They may be stories written in narrative with a number of characters that contain much dialogue or stories with few characters and little dialogue. For content area disciplines such as science and mathematics, scripts may be written as expository text, developed for the purpose of helping students to learn academic vocabulary and an understanding of the related concepts. For fiction as well as nonfiction material, dialogue may be incorporated within the script bringing the textbook or story to life and providing deeper meanings to students as they work on text interpretations and dramatizations. Scripts have been written for many pieces of literature that are typically read by middle and secondary students, and such scripts may be purchased online. Teachers and students may write the scripts for use with Readers Theatre.

In Readers Theatre, there are no costumes or props. Members of the cast do not memorize their parts as in rehearsing for a play. Rather, they read their scripts with word accuracy, an appropriate reading rate, correct phrasing, and intonation and expression that will deliver the meaning to their audience. The emphasis is on fluent reading and not acting. Therefore, students know that they need to practice their scripts and read with word accuracy, correct phasing, and proper intonation to deliver meaning to their audience. Through repeated readings within a collaborative setting monitored by both peers and teacher, students will achieve fluent reading.

IRA/NCTE Standards for the English Language Arts

2. Students read a wide range of literature from many periods in many genres to build an understanding of the many dimensions (e.g., philosophical, ethical, aesthetic) of human experience.

3. Students apply a wide range of strategies to comprehend, interpret, evaluate, and appreciate texts. They draw on their prior experience, their interactions with other readers and writers, their knowledge of word meaning and of other texts, their word identification strategies, and their understanding of textual features (e.g., sound-letter correspondence, sentence structure, context, graphics).

4. Students adjust their use of spoken, written, and visual language (e.g., conventions, style, vocabulary) to communicate effectively with a variety of audiences and for different purposes.

Source: International Reading Association and National Council of Teachers of English (1996).

STEP-BY-STEP PROCEDURE

1. *Deciding on the script:* The teacher may choose the script for students, have students work together to select an appropriate script, or students may write their own scripts. Many scripts are available online and numerous books contain scripts for all grade levels and for a range of content areas. Passages within content area textbooks may be appropriate as scripts for Readers Theatre. Additionally, stories or parts of stories may be written into a script. Poetry is another type of script that works very well for Readers Theatre.

2. *Adapting the script:* Some teachers introduce Readers Theatre to students by first using a commercially prepared script so that they understand the purpose and process of the activity. Oftentimes the script is adapted for length or to include fewer or more students in the activity. The teacher or the students or both may work together to modify a script. Adaptation is especially required when using content area texts as scripts. Tierney and Readeance (2005, p. 251) explained how to adapt a script for a specific purpose and audience.

   a. Begin with a short script that has been written for the students. Show the students a model of the script, discussing how it is written with dialogue that expresses the characters' feelings, emotions, and moods.

   b. Have small groups of students adapt a book that they are reading. Assign each group to a small part of the book, and have them write a part of the script.

c. Adapting a part of the textbook to interpret content may be accomplished in a similar manner. To integrate drama in content, concepts such as oxygen or plants may be personified, becoming lifelike characters with emotions and feelings. In some instances, to portray a concept, characters are invented as in historical fiction.

3. *Ensuring comprehension—Introducing the script:* After the script has been selected, the teacher introduces it. Within the introduction there is an emphasis on comprehension of the story content and specific key words. Depending on the nature of the script, the introduction might include the following: (a) an overview of the story or the content, (b) explicit explanations of connections to the curriculum, (c) a descriptive analysis of the characters and their roles in the story or the content, (d) information on the key concepts related to the content, and (e) a discussion of the meanings and pronunciations of the academic vocabulary. The teacher provides the prerequisite background knowledge that students need to comprehend the text. Before the students begin to practice their scripts, the teacher ensures that they understand the content of the story or key concepts in the text.

4. *Modeling fluent reading of the script:* The teacher provides an opportunity to the students to hear what fluent reading sounds like. She selects parts of the script and reads them aloud at an appropriate pace, using accurate phasing and expression that will convey the meaning of the story or content. She may draw their attention to certain unfamiliar words and discuss their meaning and pronunciation or make connections to words students already know. She may also ask individual students to read like the character so that they understand the notion of interpretation and dramatization of the story content.

5. *Grouping students for learning and assigning roles:* This step is critical for optimizing learning through the use of Readers Theatre. Within the middle and secondary classrooms, there is a wide range of abilities among students, some of whom are highly fluent in reading, many are developing fluency, and a group of students are dysfluent or nonfluent in reading. The teacher should take into account the fluency skills that each student possesses when assigning roles. Further, mixing the abilities when grouping students will ensure that students who need assistance will receive it from more capable readers. In grouping students, it is important to consider the dynamics of students working together so as to avoid discipline problems.

6. *Practicing the script:* Provide ample time for students to practice their scripts, and encourage students to work collaboratively by reading, listening to each other, and offering advice and assistance when needed. Some teachers prefer structuring practice time in different ways. They may assign the reading and practicing of scripts as homework first then follow it up with group practice in class. Others set aside a block of time each day from the period for practice. The focus of the practice is how the reading should sound to portray the appropriate mood or feelings of the character, the poem, or the content of the text. This requires comprehension and interpretation of text that needs to be emphasized during practice.

7. *Casting the script:* The last step of Readers Theatre is important to the delivery of the script. Students are reminded that staging effects may assist the audience in understanding the story. Staging includes the visual aspects of the production that establishes the context of Readers Theatre. Examples of staging include where the performers sit or stand during the reading and the readers' body language such as posture, facial expressions, and gestures. Although props and costumes are not

necessary, some teachers and students choose to use them to provide a richer context. The focus is on the reading of the scripts with word accuracy, appropriate rate and tone, as well as expression. All of the characteristics of fluency help to deliver the meaning of the text to the audience.

DIFFERENTIATING INSTRUCTION FOR STRIVING READERS

Striving readers may need additional assistance in reading their assigned scripts to an audience. Carefully select appropriate scripts to match them with students' reading skill levels. Their scripts may be shorter, and vocabulary may be adjusted to their skill level as well. Striving readers will benefit from additional rereadings and peer assistance offered in a sheltered context. Scripts may include brief passages from important selections from the content area texts.

CONSIDERING THE LANGUAGE NEEDS OF ELL STUDENTS

IRA/NCTE Standards for the English Language Arts

10. Students whose first language is not English make use of their first language to develop competency in the English language arts and to develop understanding of content across the curriculum.

Source: International Reading Association and National Council of Teachers of English (1996).

ELL students will benefit from multiple approaches to fluency (Herrell & Jordan, 2006). It is critical that ELL students receive the benefit of clear articulation of the words from their script. Therefore, teachers should model fluent reading to all students, but ELL students especially benefit from such demonstrations (Kuhn & Stahl, 2003). Consider using shorter scripts that contain sentences with simple syntactical structure. When teachers are grouping students for Readers Theatre, pair ELL students with fluent readers who demonstrate excellent word articulation.

AN APPLICATION FOR INSTRUCTION AND LEARNING IN THE SOCIAL STUDIES CLASSROOM

Eighth-grade students in the social studies classroom were reading, discussing, and writing about the Lewis and Clark expedition. After reading from their textbook and literature as well as studying maps, the teacher directed the students to consult the Internet for additional sources. The teacher led them to the PBS Web site http://www.pbs.org/lewisandclark/archive/idx_jou.html where they consulted the archives and retrieved the journals of Lewis and Clark, a primary source of information. This particular Web site showed journal excerpts that were made for a documentary of the Lewis and Clark expedition.

1. The students skimmed the numerous excerpts of the journals that were taken from the journals of Captains Meriwether Lewis and William Clark, Sergeants Charles Floyd, Patrick Gass, and John Ordway, and Private Joseph Whitehouse that were used by Florentine Films to create *Lewis and Clark: The Journey of the Corps Discovery.*

2. The teacher directed the students to (a) search the Web site to find the short biographies of the members of the corps who made entries to the journal, (b) select the member that they liked the most, and (c) search the archives by the name of the member of the corps for at least 10 of his entries, which they would use for Readers Theatre.

3. When students downloaded the journal entries, the teacher explained that the documents were primary sources and that the journal entries were written by different people. She further explained that the entries were not edited, so there would be different spellings for one word, and the language spoken 200 years ago differs from our current language expressions.

4. The teacher then explained how their presentation would be conducted. Each student would read a short biography of the member of the corps who wrote the journal entries, select journal entries, and write their own statement of how the journal entries added to the understanding of the Lewis and Clark expedition.

5. Students practiced their presentations as the teacher monitored and assisted them in their readings. After practice, time was given to casting of the presentation, and the teacher explained that one or two visual effects that provided meaning to the presentations may help in their delivery. Although costumes were not necessary, the teacher encouraged effects such as body language, facial expressions, sitting, or standing that would contribute to their readings. Some students constructed artifacts to show as they read the journal entries.

REFERENCES

Herrell, A. L., & Jordan, M. (2006). *50 strategies for improving vocabulary, comprehension, and fluency: An active learning approach* (2nd ed.). Upper Saddle River, NJ: Merrill Prentice Hall.

International Reading Association and National Council of Teachers of English. (1996). *Standards for the English language arts.* Newark, DE: International Reading Association & Urbana, IL: National Council of Teachers of English.

Kuhn, M. R., & Stahl, S. A. (2003). Fluency: A review of developmental and remedial practices. *Journal of Educational Psychology, 95*(1), 3–21.

Martinez, M., Roser, N., & Strecker, S. (1999). I never thought I could be a star: A readers theatre ticket to fluency. *The Reading Teacher, 51,* 574–584.

Palumbo, T. J., & Willcutt, J. R. (2006). Perspectives on fluency: English language learners and students with dyslexia. In S. J. Samuels & A. E. Farstrup (Eds.), *What research has to say about fluency instruction* (pp. 159–178). Newark, DE: International Reading Association.

Pikulski, J. (2006). Fluency: A developmental and language perspective. In S. J. Samuels & A. E. Farstrup (Eds.), *What research has to say about fluency instruction* (pp. 70–93). Newark, DE: International Reading Association.

Samuels, S. J. (2006). Towards a model of reading fluency. In S. J. Samuels & A. E. Farstrup (Eds.), *What research has to say about fluency instruction* (pp. 24–46). Newark, DE: International Reading Association.

Tierney, R. J., & Readence, J. E. (2005). *Reading strategies and practices: A compendium* (6th ed.). Boston: Allyn & Bacon.

Strategy 7

Paired Reading

A Collaborative Approach for Developing Deep-Reading Fluency

The purpose for the *Paired Reading strategy* is to develop fluency in reading through collaboration with peers. Average and striving readers need opportunities and time to practice reading aloud while they receive appropriate feedback for developing different aspects of fluency. Further, students in the middle and secondary grades may be considered fluent readers on fiction or easier material and be nonfluent on more challenging textbooks.

For adolescent readers to be engaged, activities need to be purposeful, motivating, and related to content curriculum. Wood (1998) proposed Paired Reading be used with adolescent readers to increase their reading fluency. When students work in pairs, they offer assistance to one another. Allan and Miller (2005) suggested that during Paired Reading, one of the partners serve as the tutor. Such scaffolding is critical to students in building reading fluency because it provides the reader with immediate feedback.

The Paired Reading strategy for adolescent readers is supported by researchers who suggest that "students who read slowly or with difficulty should receive repeated opportunities to practice fluent reading orally with feedback from a more proficient reader—either a teacher or a peer" (Boardman, Vaughn, Wexler, Murray, & Kosanovich, 2008, p. 9).

IRA/NCTE Standards for the English Language Arts

3. Students apply a wide range of strategies to comprehend, interpret, evaluate, and appreciate texts. They draw on their prior experience, their interactions with other readers and writers, their knowledge of word meaning and of other texts, their word identification strategies, and their understanding of textual features (e.g., sound-letter correspondence, sentence structure, context, graphics).

Source: International Reading Association and National Council of Teachers of English (1996).

Step-by-Step Procedure

The teacher establishes the purpose for reading by providing an overview of the text and an explanation of the activity. Students work together in pairs as they read the material silently, talk about the question(s) and areas that they may have difficulty understanding, write a brief summary, and select the major parts of the text to read aloud. Each student takes a turn reading aloud and listening.

Before Reading

Prior to reading, the teacher prepares for engaging the students in the reading and discussions by doing the following:

1. The teacher carefully selects the material from the text for silent and oral reading.
2. Through discussion and direct instruction, the teacher develops the students' background knowledge related to the content and needed for understanding the text.
3. The teacher selects words in the text that students will find difficult and includes a brief vocabulary lesson.

During Reading

At this phase of reading, the students read silently.

1. The students begin by reading the assigned material from their text.
2. The teacher monitors students' reading, offering assistance to them when needed.

After Reading

During this phase, students work in pairs to discuss their readings, write brief summaries of what they have read, and select an important part of the text to read aloud to their partner.

1. After students have read the text, they engage in a student-led discussion by responding to the question(s) or prompts written on the board. Their dialogue is brief and its primary purpose is to clarify meanings. Students are encouraged to ask questions, retell parts of their text, and then respond to their readings through writing a summary statement that they share with their partners.
2. Students are then directed to select the text that represents the major ideas and engage in a Paired Reading. As one student reads aloud, the other listens and offers guidance or assistance when needed.
3. The teacher monitors students as they read aloud and helps those who need it.

Differentiating Instruction for Striving Readers

Striving readers need support while they are developing the skills related to reading fluency. Kuhn and Stahl (2003) found that while nonfluent readers listen to fluent readers model good reading, striving readers benefit from hearing words read with accuracy, expressive reading, correct phasing, and an appropriate reading pace. When Fuchs, Fuchs, and Kazdan (1999) used a peer-assisted model of reading that included reading aloud, summarization, and prediction activities with secondary students having reading problems, they found that students' achievement in reading fluency and comprehension increased. For nonfluent readers, Paired Reading will make a difference when it is used regularly. Further research supports such scaffolded instruction: Significant benefits for striving readers increased when they were given materials at their reading levels, heard models of fluent reading, and engaged in repeated readings (Valleley & Shriver, 2003).

CONSIDERING THE LANGUAGE NEEDS OF ELL STUDENTS

IRA/NCTE Standards for the English Language Arts

10. Students whose first language is not English make use of their first language to develop competency in the English language arts and to develop understanding of content across the curriculum.

Source: International Reading Association and National Council of Teachers of English (1996).

For developing reading fluency in ELL students, Reutzel and Cooter (2008) suggested the use of "choral reading, a tried and true method of instruction" (p. 174). In applying choral reading to Paired Reading with ELL students, the two or more students may read the passage together as one voice or the more fluent reader may read the passage first, followed by reading together with the partner who is an ELL student. Paired Reading for ELL students should occur in a sheltered environment. Carefully pair a fluent reader who has positive attitudes toward others with a nonfluent ELL student. Another important consideration for developing reading fluency is to select books that are appropriate for the readers on the basis of the linguistic, readability, and interest levels of the texts.

AN APPLICATION FOR INSTRUCTION AND LEARNING IN THE VISUAL ARTS CLASSROOM

High school students in a course in photography were studying the works of American photographers. The teacher presented the photographs of Walker Evans who has been called one of the finest photographers in the world. Within the discussion about his works, the teacher displayed the cover of the book *Something Perfect* on the whiteboard that illustrated Walker Evan's photograph, depicting a bare room, wooden floors, and walls with a simple bed and no accessories. The teacher asked, "What story does this picture tell you?" The students' responses centered on the impoverished room that did not have the bare necessities for any bedroom. The teacher opened the book to page 22 where the same photograph appeared along with the poem "Bed." The students listened to the Cynthia Rylant poem read by the teacher and interpreted it as one of beauty, love, sadness, and hope.

The teacher continued the discussion but focused on the book that contained Walker Evan's photographs each with the poet's interpretation. The teacher then provided background information of the photographs of the Great Depression and how Walker Evans was commissioned by the Farm Security Administration under President Franklin D. Roosevelt for the purpose of depicting the effects of the depression. The teacher explained that each photograph tells a story, and that Cynthia Rylant, poet and coauthor, captured the stories through poetry. Prior to their reading of the poems, the teacher further developed background knowledge of the Great Depression, describing the effects of this extreme circumstance on the lives of the people. She helped students to understand by making connections to the economic recession of 2008 that left many people homeless and with no jobs. The teacher then directed the students to do the following: (a) select one photograph and poem to read; (b) read the poem aloud to their partners, each taking a turn, reading aloud and listening to the words of interpretation; (c) continue to discuss the "story in the photograph" and the poetic interpretation and build on that story; (d) write a personal response in their journals and share them by reading them aloud to their partners.

As an extension of the class assignment, the teacher directed the students to use their understanding of photography to capture a story. After developing their photographs, students worked with them to write a story. They created a "photo-story presentation" putting the photographs and text together.

REFERENCES

Allan, K. K., & Miller, M. S. (2005). *Literacy and learning in the content areas: Strategies for middle and secondary school teachers.* New York: Houghton Mifflin.

Boardman, A. G., Vaughn, S., Wexler, J., Murray, C. S., & Kosanovich, M. (2008). *Effective instruction for adolescent struggling readers: A practice brief.* Portsmouth, NH: RMC Research Corporation, Center on Instruction.

Evans, W. (Photographs), & Rylant, C. (Poetry). (1994). *Something permanent.* New York: Harcourt Brace.

Fuchs, L. S., Fuchs, D., & Kazdan, S. (1999). Effects of peer-assisted learning strategies on high school students with serious reading problems. *Remedial and Special Education, 20*(5), 309–318.

International Reading Association and National Council of Teachers of English. (1996). *Standards for the English language arts.* Newark, DE: International Reading Association & Urbana, IL: National Council of Teachers of English.

Kuhn, M. R., & Stahl, S. A. (2003). Fluency: A review of developmental and remedial practices. *Journal of Educational Psychology, 95*(1), 3–21.

Reutzel, D. R., & Cooter, R. R. (2008). *Teaching children to read: The teacher makes the difference* (5th ed.). Upper Saddle River, NJ: Merrill Prentice Hall.

Valleley, R. J., & Shriver, M. D. (2003). An examination of the effects of repeated readings with secondary students. *Journal of Behavioral Education, 12*(1), 55–76.

Wood, K. D. (1998). Helping struggling readers read. *Middle School Journal, 29*(5), 67–70.

Audiobooks

Strategy 8

Modeling and Scaffolding Reading Fluency

As students advance to the middle and secondary grades, they are faced with increased expectations for reading. They are required to read a wide range of texts across the content areas that increase in difficulty level and in number. Yet many are not proficient readers, lacking the required fluency skills to keep up to such demands. Because of their lack of reading skills, these students fail to understand textbooks and literature that continues to build their background knowledge. Through the use of audio technologies, nonfluent readers may have access to young adult literature that will serve to enrich their lives and increase their knowledge required for understanding curriculum concepts. Literature for young adults by noted authors are available on tapes or CDs. The quality of the CDs is far superior to the tapes, and their use and access are becoming highly efficient. Students may download an audiobook from the CD or from a variety of sites on the Internet onto their iPods for easy access and listening. Schools and public libraries have an increasing number of audiobooks that students may use.

Listening to audiobooks offers a number of advantages to students. For one, they are motivated through listening to the high-quality delivery of literature that is often read by actors or the authors themselves. Such readings offer students the most effective models and demonstrations of fluent reading along with the motivation to engage in independent reading. In addition, students have the advantage of replaying the text when they feel that they did not understand part of it (Rickelman & Henk, 1990). Using audiobooks in reading instruction deepens the learning experience for students. O'Day (2002) found positive effects with students in an urban middle school who were struggling readers. When the teachers used audiobooks in their instruction, students demonstrated an increase in word recognition skills and text comprehension as well as an increased acquisition of English vocabulary. For students who are at the basic levels of reading proficiency, audiobooks scaffold their reading of difficult texts and provide excellent models of reading fluency.

Source: International Reading Association and National Council of Teachers of English (1996).

> ## IRA/NCTE Standards for the English Language Arts
>
> 1. Students read a wide range of print and nonprint texts to build an understanding of texts, of themselves, and of the cultures of the United States and the world; to acquire new information; to respond to the needs and demands of society and the workplace; and for personal fulfillment. Among these texts are fiction and nonfiction, classic, and contemporary works.
> 2. Students read a wide range of literature from many periods in many genres to build an understanding of the many dimensions (e.g., philosophical, ethical, aesthetic) of human experience.

STEP-BY-STEP PROCEDURE

Audiobooks of literature provide all students with the resources they need to develop related content knowledge of the required curriculum. Teachers have several instructional options for using audiobooks within the content classrooms. Instruction may be designed for whole group, small group, or individual uses.

BEFORE READING

The teacher prepares students for reading through selecting literature that is related to the content being taught. The teacher may use text sets or one piece of literature that is appropriate for the content being studied. A text set contains five or six books that relate to a theme or unit of study—for example, *survival, immigration, the Civil War, the Holocaust,* or *infectious diseases*. When text sets are used, members from each small group will read the same book from their text set, and one copy should be available for each member of the group. Prior to having the students engage in listening to text, the teacher uses the following procedure:

1. The teacher assigns students to small groups.

2. Whether the teacher uses one book for the whole class or a text set, the teacher engages students in book talks to introduce the literature.

3. Each group is given a choice of the book from the text set.

DURING READING

The students may listen to the book text during the allotted time. For reading or listening to a complete text, several days will be required. The teacher may choose to use the instructional period so that students listen for a short period of time such as a 20-minute block of time in class and read for 20 minutes outside of class, as part of a home assignment.

AFTER READING

1. The students respond to their reading, which may take place through discussions or journal writing.

   • When students are reading fiction, the teacher may request students to engage in response writing by using a writing prompt developed from a specific question that focuses on a selection of the text.

- If the text is informational, the students may be directed to use a learning log in which they respond to facts and make connections.
- For readings of historical fiction, students may be asked to respond to the character(s) and identify the facts, making connections to their content area texts.

2. After journal writing, students engage in a brief discussion. Using the print copy of the text, they select a passage from their readings that support their ideas to be read to the small group.

3. As each member of the group reads the short passage, the other students listen and offer support through their personal responses.

DIFFERENTIATING INSTRUCTION FOR STRIVING READERS

Audiobooks are exceptionally useful for students who are nonfluent or reluctant readers. Striving readers may be classified as special needs students who receive instruction in the general education classroom or the inclusion classroom as well as the resource room. In any case, the audiobook supports nonfluent readers in their development of content knowledge and academic language. However, the audiobook alone will not produce fluent readers. Clearly, students who are striving readers need repeated readings of text. Such rereadings produce greater positive effects especially when students receive feedback on their word recognition skills or coaching on phrasing and expressive reading. Although students may listen to good models of fluent reading through the use of audiobooks, they may not know how to apply the fluency skills to their own reading and would benefit from instruction and practice.

CONSIDERING THE LANGUAGE NEEDS OF ELL STUDENTS

IRA/NCTE Standards for the English Language Arts

10. Students whose first language is not English make use of their first language to develop competency in the English language arts and to develop understanding of content across the curriculum.

Source: International Reading Association and National Council of Teachers of English (1996).

In addition to offering models of reading fluency to ELL students, audiobooks provide demonstrations of effective use of the English language. To understand many of the new words, ELL students benefit from articulate speaking as well as language that is spoken slowly. Many CD and tape players allow for repetition of parts of the text as well as an adjustment of the reader's pace. Audiobooks may be slowed down when students feel that the content is delivered too fast, or part of the text may be repeated when students do not comprehend the text. This is especially helpful to ELL students who are listening to informational text and hearing the content expressed in English for the first time.

An Application for Instruction and Learning in the Integrated English Language Arts and Social Studies Classroom

In one middle school, English language arts and social studies are taught within one learning block. Teachers work together to integrate content and skills. For one lesson, they demonstrated how (a) biographies are written from primary sources, (b) writers can learn about people from primary sources (e.g., primary sources may show how people think, what they valued, and what they did within their lifetime), (c) to read primary sources to learn about Abraham Lincoln, and (d) to use the primary sources to write a biographical essay of Abraham Lincoln.

Before Reading

The teacher introduced the book *Voyages: Reminiscences of Abe Lincoln* by Neil Waldman (2009), author and illustrator. She explained that he wrote about and illustrated Lincoln's journeys up and down the Mississippi relying on primary sources from the documents found in *The Collected Works of Abraham Lincoln* (Basler, 1953) as well as others. One of the features of the book that the teacher emphasized is how the author has captured Abraham Lincoln's voice in telling the stories of his "life-changing voyages" along the Mississippi: Lincoln's own words are integrated within the author's writings to tell the story. To show the differences between the author's text and Lincoln's words, the author's text is in one color, and the Lincoln's writings appear in brown italics.

The teacher read the introduction aloud, "Following Lincoln's Words." The author explains how Lincoln's cousin's words clearly demonstrated how Abraham Lincoln's attitudes and feelings at the horror at the sight of slavery were shaping his values and attitudes. Using the projection system, the teacher then read the first chapter, "First Voyage," aloud to show how the author used primary source material to tell a small part of Lincoln's life.

During Reading

The teacher used the following three audiobooks that contain primary sources from the life of Abraham Lincoln: (1) *Abraham Lincoln* (Courtenay, 2008); (2) *The Gettysburg Address, the Emancipation Proclamation, Abraham Lincoln and Pericles* (Lincoln, 2007); and (3) *Lincoln's Prose: Major Works by a Great American Writer* (Lincoln, 2002). Students received an audiobook and a print copy of the book.

1. Students worked in small groups, with members reading the same book.

2. Students were asked to listen to one of the selected works of Lincoln.

After Reading

During this phase of reading, students worked together through discussion and rereading from primary sources to learn more about Abraham Lincoln. The teacher directed the students to use the primary source to answer the following questions:

1. What did this document reveal about Abraham Lincoln?

2. Students discussed the document focusing on the teacher-directed question.

3. During the discussion, students took notes on what they learned from the document about Lincoln's life.

4. Students shared with the class what the documents have revealed about the life of Abraham Lincoln.

REFERENCES

Basler, R. P. (Ed.). (1953). *The collected works of Abraham Lincoln.* Springfield, IL: Abraham Lincoln Association and New Brunswick, NJ: Rutgers University Press.

Courtenay, C. M. (2008). *Abraham Lincoln* [Recorded by Bob Barnes]. Sarasota, FL: CoolBeat Audiobooks.

International Reading Association and National Council of Teachers of English. (1996). *Standards for the English language arts.* Newark, DE: International Reading Association & Urbana, IL: National Council of Teachers of English.

Lincoln, A. (2002). *Lincoln's prose: Major works by a great American writer* [Recorded by George Vafiadis]. Falls Church, VA: InAudio/Sound Room.

Lincoln, A. (2007). *The Gettysburg address, the emancipation proclamation, Abraham Lincoln and Pericles* [Recorded by Deaver Brown]. Lexington, MA: Simply Magazine.

O'Day, P. S. (2002). *Reading while listening: Increasing access to print through the use of audio books.* Ann Arbor: UMI Microform 307753.

Rickelman, R. J., & Henk, W. A. (1990). Reading technology: Children's literature and audio/visual technologies. *The Reading Teacher, 43,* 682–684.

Waldman, N. (2009). *Voyages: Reminiscences of young Abe Lincoln.* Honesdale, PA: Calkins Creek.

Strategy 9

Radio Reading

An Authentic Approach for Developing Reading Fluency

STRATEGY OVERVIEW

Radio Reading is an instructional strategy that provides content area teachers with an authentic purpose for using oral reading with the students that motivates them to reread text for fluency. Radio Reading is appropriate for content area classrooms where students are engaged in reporting current events related to varied content areas.

Radio Reading integrates all forms of language to students who are radio announcers and the audience who listen and respond to the news broadcast (Tierney & Readence, 2005). As radio announcers, students are responsible to read the text and synthesize it, write a script for their audience, and read it aloud with accuracy and expression. The audience listens for understanding to the broadcast and is responsible for making comments and asking appropriate questions. Thus, all students have an opportunity of developing a range of language skills.

Radio Reading is an instructional strategy supported by research (Samuels, 2006). The strategy offers students the opportunity to develop reading fluency through repeated readings of text with its major goal being reading comprehension. Several suggestions have been made by Searfoss (1975) and Tierney and Readence (2005) for teachers to optimize instruction when using the strategy. Success will be achieved when the teacher (a) provides clear guidelines for students to follow, (b) selects the appropriate reading material for students, and (c) monitors and assists students throughout each phase of strategy implementation. To ensure success for all students, students should work in small groups in broadcasting the news or content. Collaborative groups will allow a supportive context to students as they practice reading their scripts. When teachers organize appropriate groupings and encourage peer-mediated assistance to students who need help with reading, problems that could arise during the performances are eliminated or at least minimized. Applications of Radio Reading to content area instruction are numerous. This strategy may be used on a weekly basis to broadcast the news in science, health, economics, political science, history, or mathematics. Within the arts or English language arts classrooms, it may be used as a broadcast for book reviews or other works of art.

Source: International Reading Association and National Council of Teachers of English (1996).

```
┌─────────────────────────────────────────────────────────────┐
│        IRA/NCTE Standards for the English Language Arts        │
│                                                                │
│  3. Students apply a wide range of strategies to comprehend,   │
│     interpret, evaluate, and appreciate texts. They draw on    │
│     their prior experience, their interactions with other      │
│     readers and writers, their knowledge of word meaning and   │
│     of other texts, their word identification strategies, and  │
│     their understanding of textual features (e.g., sound-letter │
│     correspondence, sentence structure, context, graphics).    │
│                                                                │
│  4. Students adjust their use of spoken, written, and visual   │
│     language (e.g., conventions, style, vocabulary) to         │
│     communicate effectively with a variety of audiences and    │
│     for different purposes.                                     │
└─────────────────────────────────────────────────────────────┘
```

STEP-BY-STEP PROCEDURE

BEFORE READING

The teacher provides the context and purpose for Radio Reading and selects appropriate material that is within students' reading levels. The length of the material should also be considered. Students need to read, synthesize the material, and write a short script, no longer than one page that may be read in 2 to 3 minutes.

1. *Grouping students:* If the teacher uses small groups of students, she should consider their attitudes, behaviors, and dispositions toward reading. The teacher organizes groups of two or three students with varying reading abilities, making sure that they can work collaboratively in reading, writing, and practicing their scripts. The teacher sets clear guidelines for the students to follow that include the purpose for reading and process of engaging in Radio Reading.

2. *Explaining Radio Reading:* The teacher explains the procedure for using Radio Reading in the classroom. Simply, students will read materials and then rewrite them into a script to be read to an audience. Within the discussion, the teacher emphasizes the importance of fluent reading to communicate with the audience as well as writing an accurate and interesting script. Although students work in small groups, they read their own text and write their own scripts; however, the material selected for each group will be related. Therefore, they will read their scripts as a group during its presentation.

3. *Preparing students for reading:* The teacher then prepares the students for reading. Before reading and writing, the teacher ensures that students make personal and text connections to the content of the text by offering a brief discussion and overview of the material to the class. At this point, the teacher may review some difficult words that students will encounter and use them as a springboard for discussion.

DURING READING

The teacher assigns students to small groups, provides students with parts of the text to read, and directs them to do the following:

1. Read the material silently for understanding, and identify the important parts of the text.

2. Using the main ideas, write a summary of the text that is approximately one page and will take 2 to 3 minutes to read. An alternative to rewriting the text into a script is to use the original text and divide it into parts for each student.

3. Take turns to read their summary aloud to their group. As the script is read, the listeners respond to its meaning, asking questions for clarification when the content is not clear.

4. Students practice reading aloud until they feel comfortable with meaning and understanding, word accuracy, pacing, and reading expression. The teacher monitors students' readings and assists them when needed.

After Reading: The Production

After students have read and discussed their parts, they perform together as a group to the whole class.

1. Depending on the nature of the readings and content, one of the students may provide a short introduction of the topic and introduce each student.

2. Each of the students reads the prepared script.

3. After their reading, the audience poses questions and responds with comments.

Differentiating Instruction for Striving Readers

Research is clear in identifying repeated readings as the most powerful tool for increasing the fluency levels of striving readers. Studies also show that at all grade levels, students who are striving readers will benefit from practicing on materials that are at their grade level. When too many unknown words are within the text, students cannot use strategies for figuring out unknown words, and they will not benefit from repeated readings to develop their reading fluency. Therefore, striving readers will benefit from Radio Reading because students must practice on the same text to perform for their audience; however, the texts that are assigned to them should be selected with care. The levels of the students' reading should match closely with the assigned text. Teacher feedback and assistance given to the student while practicing for reading aloud will be very beneficial.

Considering the Language Needs of ELL Students

Source: International Reading Association and National Council of Teachers of English (1996).

IRA/NCTE Standards for the English Language Arts

10. Students whose first language is not English make use of their first language to develop competency in the English language arts and to develop understanding of content across the curriculum.

Radio Reading includes repeated readings, collaborative and assisted learning, and a focus on comprehension of text, all of which are especially beneficial to ELL students; however, ELL students need extra time for practicing oral reading before performing to a large group of students. When selecting text for ELL students to read aloud, teachers need to take into consideration the students' reading and fluency levels as well as English language development. Additional support to ELL students may be given through monitoring their oral reading and providing them with individual assistance as well as time for practice in a sheltered environment.

AN APPLICATION FOR INSTRUCTION AND LEARNING IN THE ECONOMICS CLASSROOM

Twelfth-grade students in economics class are presented each day with the progress of the economy. Daily, they learn from media about how the White House plans to develop the economy. The teacher took advantage of the Web sites, newspaper articles, and podcasts to teach about the recession and the role that the government is playing to bring the country to economic prosperity. Many of the critical concepts in the economics curriculum were discussed each day on the news. Therefore, through the use of the Radio Reading strategy, students became involved in reporting on the current events related to economics.

BEFORE READING

Preparing students for reading is an important aspect of their performance. Within this aspect of the strategy, the teacher builds background knowledge that will assist students in developing fluency through the Radio Reading strategy.

1. The teacher spends time introducing students to the White House recovery plan by having them listen to a podcast of President Obama's introduction of the recovery plan delivered on January 24, 2009.

2. The students visit the official Web site of the *American Reinvestment and Recovery Act of 2009*, www.recovery.gov, to read various aspects of the recovery plan.

3. The teacher leads the students in a discussion on the economic recession and recovery plan to show how every aspect of life is affected by the economy.

DURING READING

The teacher explained Radio Reading to the students, telling them that they will be performing as journalists on "Greet the Press."

1. The teacher consulted the business section of several different newspapers over the course of a week and clipped out articles that relate to the recession, its status, its effects on various aspects of life, and the recovery or stimulus plan. For example, the teacher distributed the article "Leading Indicators Are Signaling the Recession's End" by Floyd Norris (2009) to one group and "Wealth Matters: Teaching the Entitled Young the Financial Facts of Life" by Paul Sullivan (2009) to a second group.

2. Students worked in small groups on one newspaper article, reading the article, identifying the central concepts, and discussing it. The group divided up the article, giving each member a part for reporting on. Each member rewrote their part of the article into a script. They practiced reading their scripts to their groups until they were ready for the production.

AFTER READING

Members of the group sat at the oval table ready for reporting. One member from the group was selected to introduce the topic and each reporter. Members of the group read their scripts and after reporting, the class posed questions to the group.

REFERENCES

International Reading Association and National Council of Teachers of English. (1996). *Standards for the English language arts.* Newark, DE: International Reading Association & Urbana, IL: National Council of Teachers of English.

Norris, F. (2009, July 25). Leading indicators are signaling the recession's end. *New York Times,* p. B3.

Samuels, S. J. (2006). Towards a model of reading fluency. In S. J. Samuels & A. E. Farstrup (Eds.), *What research has to say about fluency instruction* (pp. 24–46). Newark, DE: International Reading Association.

Searfoss, L. W. (1975). Radio reading. *The Reading Teacher, 29,* 295–296.

Sullivan, P. (2009, July 25). Wealth matters: Teaching the entitled young the financial facts of life. *New York Times,* p. B5.

Tierney, R. J., & Readence, J. E. (2005). *Reading strategies and practices: A compendium* (6th ed.). Boston: Allyn & Bacon.

Morphemic Analysis

Strategy 10

A Useful Resource for Becoming a Fluent Reader

STRATEGY OVERVIEW

The goal of all fluent reading is constructing meaning from text. During the course of the day, students in content area classrooms are expected to read from a range of textbooks that contain words they see for the first time. Fluent readers frequently will use one of their word-solving strategies when faced with unknown words. Such a strategy for figuring out the pronunciation and meaning of new and unknown words is a helpful resource that will assist in students' fluency development. Morphemic Analysis strategy is a valuable word-learning approach that fluent readers use to determine unknown words while they are reading. Briefly, readers analyze the word and examine it for word parts they may know. They then use these meaningful parts of the word to figure out the unknown word.

What do teachers need to know to use the Morphemic Analysis strategy? Morphemes are meaningful word parts that include root words, prefixes, or suffixes. Morphemes that are root words or base words may stand alone. Because root words do not need prefixes or suffixes, they are often referred to as *free morphemes*. Examples of free morphemes are *visit, port,* and *ship*. Bound morphemes include prefixes and suffixes—also referred to as affixes—that are attached to the beginning or ending of a root word. Examples of prefixes are *trans-, pre-, ex-* and examples of suffixes are *-ing, -ed,* and *-s*. Prefixes contribute to changes in the meanings of words, for example, adding *non-* to *negotiable* creates a change in the meaning of the word. Suffixes, on the other hand, change the parts of speech or functions of a word. For example, adding the suffix *-ness* to *happy* changes the root word *happy* from a verb to *happiness,* a noun.

How can Morphemic Analysis be useful to students? When students know the meaning and pronunciation of certain morphemes, they may use their knowledge when faced with an unknown word to help them figure out its pronunciation as well as determine its meaning. To help them employ morphemes to figure out a word, students need to know the following: (a) certain word parts are meaningful units, (b) meaningful parts or morphemes appear in many different words, and (c) proficient readers use their knowledge of morphemes to figure out unknown words. Therefore, knowing the meanings of

75

morphemes and using them for reading unknown words would be useful to all readers but especially nonfluent readers. Clearly, instruction in the use of meaningful word parts for identifying unknown words should include "the meanings of particular word parts and the strategy for when and why we use them" (Harmon, Wood, & Hedrick, 2008, p. 173).

Source: International Reading Association and National Council of Teachers of English (1996).

IRA/NCTE Standards for the English Language Arts

3. Students apply a wide range of strategies to comprehend, interpret, evaluate, and appreciate texts. They draw on their prior experience, their interactions with other readers and writers, their knowledge of word meaning and of other texts, their word identification strategies, and their understanding of textual features (e.g., sound-letter correspondence, sentence structure, context, graphics).

6. Students apply knowledge of language structure, language conventions (e.g., spelling and punctuation), media techniques, figurative language, and genre to create, critique, and discuss print and nonprint texts.

STEP-BY-STEP PROCEDURE

Direct teaching of the Morphemic Analysis strategy is important in helping students learn how to identify unknown words through the use of word parts or morphemes. The instructional strategy presented offers a systematic approach to learning morphemes and how to use them. The focus will be on learning roots and prefixes. Suffixes are word endings that change the structure of the word or part of speech, and most adolescence students are familiar with suffixes. Therefore, teachers of students at the secondary level may not need to use direct instruction in teaching suffixes.

ROOT WORDS, PREFIXES, AND SUFFIXES

In content areas such as science, mathematics, and social studies, students will be expected to read new words fluently. Many of these words contain similar roots and prefixes that students may know and can use to help them to figure out unknown words. Calling attention to roots, prefixes, and suffixes as well as their meanings and functions will benefit students as they try to figure out unknown words with similar word parts. Many adolescent students will be familiar with the more common prefixes and suffixes. However, for some disciplines the academic vocabulary contains Latin and Greek derivatives where direct instruction in prefixes would be beneficial in strengthening their academic vocabularies as well as developing reading fluency. The teacher needs to consider the level of the students and the academic vocabulary of the discipline when beginning to teach morphemic or structural analysis. Further, when teaching how to analyze words into root words, prefixes, and suffixes, begin with a limited number of words that are familiar to the students.

DIRECT INSTRUCTION OF MORPHEMIC ANALYSIS

Provide explicit instruction to help student figure out unknown words through the use of the Morphemic Analysis strategy. Demonstrations and modeling of structural or morphemic word analysis are very useful to all students. The teacher follows the steps below in teaching the strategy.

1. Begin by asking the students: "What do you do when you are reading and come to a word that you do not know?" Respond to their reading strategies, emphasizing the importance of using multiple word learning approaches to pronounce and understand words. Tell the students that the purpose of the strategy that they will learn is to use word parts within a word to figure out a word they do not know.

2. Demonstrate how words may be analyzed into their meaningful parts, root words and prefixes, and how each word part contributes to the meaning of the whole word. Use the graphic Figure 10.1, Analysis of a Word, during the explanation to help students understand breaking words into their parts.

3. Present a word with a root, prefix, and suffix that students already know, and ask them to highlight the prefix in each word. Use a graphic similar to 10.2, Analysis of the Word *Hemispheres*, to demonstrate how to take words apart to help them to say the words and to figure out their meanings.

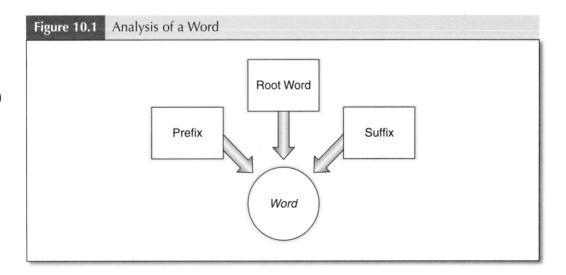

Figure 10.1   Analysis of a Word

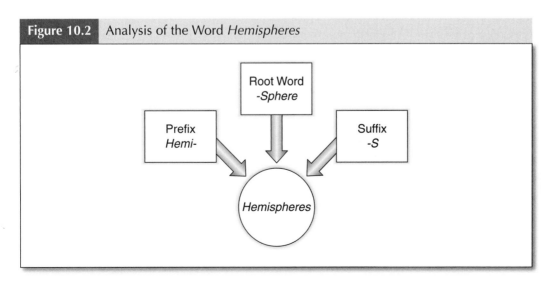

Figure 10.2   Analysis of the Word *Hemispheres*

4. Continue to demonstrate how words within their readings may be deconstructed into their meaningful parts. For each word, highlight and discuss the meaning of the root word and prefix and demonstrate how the prefix has changed the meaning of the root word. With middle school students and ELL students, the teacher may need to highlight and show how the suffix changes the word's function or part of speech.

5. Add the word and its meaning as well as the word's parts—root word, prefix, and suffix—and their meanings to a wall chart as a class reference. See Figure 10.3, Wall Chart: Word Parts and Their Meanings.

Figure 10.3	Wall Chart: Word Parts and Their Meanings			
Root Word	*Prefix*	*Suffix*	*Word*	*Meaning*
-port- to carry, deliver, ship	trans—across	-ed indicates the past tense of a word	transported	Goods have been delivered or shipped across an area.

Practice of the Morphemic Analysis Strategy

Have students work together on vocabulary words that they will be reading.

1. Provide practice by presenting words to students and telling them to find and highlight the root or base words and discuss their meanings.

2. Direct students to identify and highlight the prefix and the suffix, telling its meaning and function. Have students tell how adding the prefix and suffix changed the root word.

3. Encourage students to record new and challenging words, their word parts, and meanings on the wall chart.

DIFFERENTIATING INSTRUCTION FOR STRIVING READERS

Striving readers benefit from direct instruction on Morphemic Analysis and need more than one lesson. Additional instruction should begin with a review of the strategy and an application of words that students already know. Help students as they read independently, and encourage them to use Morphemic Analysis to figure out unknown words. As the students read, the teacher should monitor the process they use for solving unknown words and their success in word recognition, and the teacher should offer individual assistance based on their learning needs. Such additional support may be given to striving readers in the form of minilessons.

MINILESSONS

Students who are fluent readers learn how to analyze and deconstruct words that are unknown to them, and they use the word parts to figure out the word, guess at its meaning, and pronounce the word. For students who are not proficient in analyzing unknown words, additional instruction can make the difference. Such teaching may be in the form of minilessons that are short and given "on-the-spot" targeting the area of difficulty the student is experiencing. Minilessons are brief and are integrated into content instruction or are given to an individual student who gets stuck on words during reading. The teacher may offer a minilesson to students as they begin to read their texts. The teacher (a) reminds them of the steps in the strategy for analyzing the words; (b) directs their attention to the wall chart of roots, prefixes, and suffixes; and (c) reviews how to use word parts to figure out unknown words.

CONSIDERING THE LANGUAGE NEEDS OF ELL STUDENTS

IRA/NCTE Standards for the English Language Arts

10. Students whose first language is not English make use of their first language to develop competency in the English language arts and to develop understanding of content across the curriculum.

Source: International Reading Association and National Council of Teachers of English (1996).

When teaching Morphemic Analysis to ELL students, teachers may take advantage of cognates—words from two languages that have the same meaning or similar spelling patterns—when the cognate relates to the student's native language. Helman (2008) suggested that cognates are effective in teaching words to ELL students. However, students may need more scaffolding in making the relationship between the two. Hiebert and Lubliner (2008) found that 70% of the 570 words examined were English-Spanish cognates. Instruction in Morphemic Analysis of words, therefore, that includes the derivation of word parts, their meaning and pronunciation, and how the cognates relate to ELL students native language would be very beneficial. Further, ELL students gain from direct teaching of suffixes in words because even when they know how to say the word, they may not know how the suffix changes the function of the word. For example, the English language learner may know how to say the word *creation* but may not know how the suffix *-tion* changes the function of the root word *create*, from a verb to a noun. Therefore, teaching English language learners the role of suffixes within words assists their reading fluency as well as their language development.

An Application for Instruction and Learning in the Physics Classroom

Science is an excellent discipline for helping students to learn new words through Morphemic Analysis. Many of the words in science and mathematics have Greek and Latin prefixes and root words. Knowledge of these morphemes may be transferred across the disciplines when students have a strategy for figuring out unknown words using morphemes. Teachers use a variety of approaches to provide students with an understanding of using word parts to analyze unknown words.

One physics teacher provided a few lessons on Morphemic Analysis of words to unlock their meanings and pronounce the words. Throughout the year, she continued to add new root words and prefixes to the wall chart as they appeared in readings and lessons. When students studied states of matter and the atmosphere, the teacher presented the vocabulary essential to the lesson by demonstrating the analysis of the following words: *atmosphere, stratosphere, thermosphere, ionosphere, magnetosphere,* and *exosphere*. The teacher began by modeling how to identify the root word, saying it, and analyzing it for its meaning, then proceeding to the word's prefix, analyzing it in the same way, and finally putting the two word parts together to construct the meaning of the word.

The following is the process that the teacher uses in using explicit instruction through modeling to teach morphemic word analysis strategy:

1. Using the graphic in Figure 10.4, Finding the Root Word and Prefixes for Learning Words, the teacher selects one word from the vocabulary and writes it on the white board, pronounces it, identifies its root word, and highlights it.

2. The teacher then isolates the root word and pronounces it, explaining its meaning.

3. Using the same modeling process, the teacher identifies and highlights the prefix, pronounces and defines it.

4. The teacher goes back to the root word and discusses its meaning once again and the second time shows how the meaning of the root words is changed by adding a prefix.

5. The teacher asks the students to identify and highlight the root word, *sphere,* in each of the words.

6. The teacher leads a discussion on the meaning of the root word and its derivation from the Greek word *sphaira*.

7. The teacher writes the root word and its meaning on the wall chart and each of the words that contain the root word.

8. The teacher and students identify and highlight the prefixes in the words and discuss their meaning and derivation. Within the discussion, the teacher demonstrates how each prefix changed the meaning of the word when it was added to the root word. There are some words that when the prefixes are removed, the readers have difficulty identifying the root word.

9. The prefixes and their meanings are added to the wall chart similar to the one shown in Figure 10.3.

10. The teacher discusses the word and its meaning by bringing it back to the context of the text.

Figure 10.4	Finding the Root Word and Prefixes for Learning Words

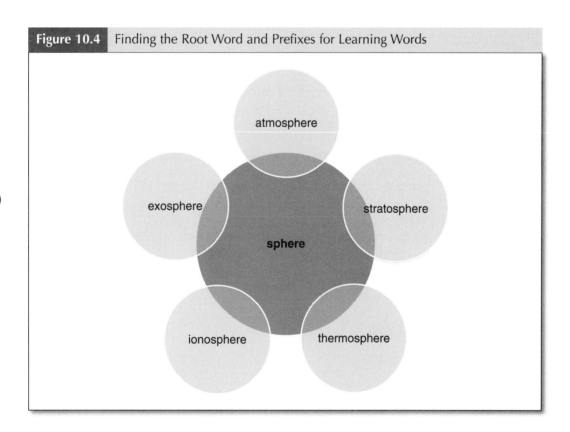

REFERENCES

Harmon, J. M., Wood, K. D., & Hedrick, W. B. (2008). *Instructional strategies for teaching content vocabulary: Grades 4–12*. Westerville, OH: National Middle School Association.

Helman, L. (2008). *Literacy development with English learners*. New York: Guilford Press.

Hiebert, E. H., & Lubliner, S. (2008). The nature, learning, and instruction of general academic vocabulary. In A. E. Farstrup & S. J. Samuels (Eds.), *What research has to say about vocabulary instruction* (pp. 106–129). Newark, DE: International Reading Association.

International Reading Association and National Council of Teachers of English. (1996). *Standards for the English language arts*. Newark, DE: International Reading Association & Urbana, IL: National Council of Teachers of English.

SECTION III

Narrative Text

Developing Comprehension for Narrative Text

The process of reading is not a half sleep, but in the highest sense, an exercise, a gymnast's struggle: that the reader is to do something for him or herself, must be on the alert, just construct indeed the poem, argument, history, metaphysical essay—the text furnishing the hints, the clue, the start, the framework.

—Walt Whitman

Finding yourself in the pages of a book enables the reader to explore worlds and ideas beyond time and place. The power of the imagination to envisage castle fortresses or jungle landscapes illuminates our everyday existence with thrilling adventures or calming interludes. Yet for many adolescents, the printed word evokes only fear or disdain as they struggle to make sense of tiny letters on a page.

WHAT RESEARCH HAS TO SAY ABOUT THE DEVELOPMENT OF COMPREHENSION OF NARRATIVE TEXT

How do students process text and monitor their understanding? Researchers have strived to find the answers to these puzzling questions for many decades. Due to their efforts, we now have scientific evidence that students need direct, explicit instruction in comprehension. It is also evident that students' engagement with text needs to be scaffolded before, during, and after reading. This section will provide the research framework for effective comprehension instruction of narrative text.

THE READER, THE TEXT, AND THE PROCESS

Today's global economy is creating jobs that demand a higher level of literacy where the ability to read and write critically is a minimum requirement for entry-level jobs (Heller & Greenleaf, 2007). Yet data from the 2007 National Assessment of Educational Progress in reading report that 69% of eighth-grade students fall below the proficient level in their ability to comprehend the meaning of text. Even more disturbing is that 26% of students read below the basic level. These statistics add to the sense of urgency for direct, explicit comprehension instruction for adolescent learners.

Comprehension is an active, internal process involving the reader, the text, and the activity of reading (RAND Reading Study Group, 2002). The readers bring their background knowledge, sociocultural context, as well as linguistic ability to the act of reading (Kamil, 2004). Factors regarding the reader such as level of word recognition, fluency, vocabulary knowledge, oral language abilities, metacognitive ability, and motivation to read impact the comprehension process (Snow & Biancarosa, 2003). For example, struggling readers attempting to read by engaging in "word-by-word" reading find it next to impossible to shift cognitive processing to comprehending text when they cannot decode.

The text is the second integral component of the comprehension process. The level of text difficulty and the students' depth of background knowledge regarding its topic are critical to successful engagement with text (Kamil, 2004). When a text is selected that is pertinent to students' lives, their motivation to engage with the text is increased (Wood, 2008). Diverse texts, representing a variety of difficulty levels and topics, enable readers to practice a myriad of comprehension strategies (Snow & Biancarosa, 2003). Struggling readers especially benefit when texts are selected that connect to their "out of school" literacies and their linguistic/cultural differences (Alvermann, 2004; Moore, Alvermann, & Hinchman, 2007).

The activity of reading needs a supportive, nonthreatening environment (Wood, 2008). Research indicates that effective readers take risks while engaging with text, setting goals before, during, and after reading. Effective readers query the text while reading and make predictions, recognizing how story genres impact understanding. They also consider the authors of their texts, their styles of writing, and how this impacts the main idea (Duke & Pearson, 2002). Struggling readers need to be shown models of how to engage in these metacognitive processes and how to solve problems while reading (Kamil et al., 2008). Teachers who carefully consider factors impacting the reader, the text, and the process of reading are setting the stage for successful engagement with text.

SCAFFOLDING ENGAGEMENT WITH TEXT

Research indicates that teaching explicit comprehension strategies before, during, and after reading leads to improved engagement and analysis of text (Snow & Biancarosa, 2003). In fact, a higher level of performance is attained when students are asked to apply comprehension strategies to challenging, content rich text (Alvermann, 2004). In 2000, the National Reading Panel stated that the most effective instruction in comprehension occurs when teachers scaffold the acquisition of comprehension strategies (National Institute of Child Health and Human Development, 2000). In this apprenticeship model, teachers explicitly model the strategy and provide guided practice and independent use of the strategy. According to the research, the most effective strategies are comprehension monitoring, summarization, graphic organizers, question generating and answering, as well as story structure (Kamil et al., 2008). Effective teachers also instruct their students to use multiple comprehension strategies to solve their problems while reading and encourage cooperative learning to engage students in supporting one another's engagement with text (Kamil, 2004).

READING, WRITING, AND TALKING ABOUT TEXT

When adolescent students read, write, and talk about stories, they experience multiple ways of thinking and evaluating text (Kamil et al., 2008). As students argue their interpretation of narrative text, they learn to use material from the text to support their perspective and learn to summarize points of view (RAND Reading Study Group, 2002).

Research indicates that students' understanding of text is most improved when discussions are structured to enable students to work collaboratively to critically analyze text by referring and using information from the text (Hirsch, 2003).

Productive discussions about text require careful planning by the teacher. Effective teachers carefully select stimulating texts that will engage students and provide multiple perspectives. They also provide students with discussion protocol formats so that questions probe responses to text and follow up with supporting arguments and summarizations of main ideas (Kamil et al., 2008). These participatory lesson formats facilitate engaged reading by adolescent students and increase their motivation for reading of narrative text (Alvermann, 2004). When students are motivated and engaged with text, the framework is set for improved comprehension.

A FRAMEWORK FOR TEACHING COMPREHENSION OF NARRATIVE TEXT TO ADOLESCENT LEARNERS

Research indicates that adolescent readers need direct, explicit instruction in how to use and apply comprehension strategies. When teachers model, provide guided practice and feedback as well as independent use of comprehension strategies, adolescent readers are provided with the tools they need to interact with text. The following suggestions provide the foundation for a comprehension strategy approach:

1. Effective comprehension strategy instruction uses diverse, challenging, content rich text that is pertinent to students' lives (Adams, 1998; Alvermann, 2004; Snow, 2002).

2. Research indicates that teaching explicit comprehension strategies before, during, and after reading improves students' engagement and understanding of text (RAND Reading Study Group, 2002).

3. In effective comprehension strategy instruction, (a) teachers select the most appropriate text to model the strategy, (b) show students how to apply the strategy to the text, (c) make sure the text is not too difficult for students, and (d) provide guided practice and discussion about use of the strategy.

4. Sustained, elaborate discussions about stories allow students to explore multiple perspectives and concepts about narrative text that support critical reflection and interpretation (Kamil, 2004).

5. Effective comprehension instruction teaches students to monitor their comprehension and to repair problems while they read text. Teachers that explicitly model this process through "think-alouds" provide adolescent readers with explicit demonstrations of processing difficult text (Kamil et al., 2008).

In this section, "Developing Comprehension of Narrative Text," five instructional strategies are presented for use in content area classrooms. The strategies are presented as guides for teachers of adolescent learners to adapt and use for their specific discipline and student profile.

Tips on Teaching Comprehension of Narrative Text

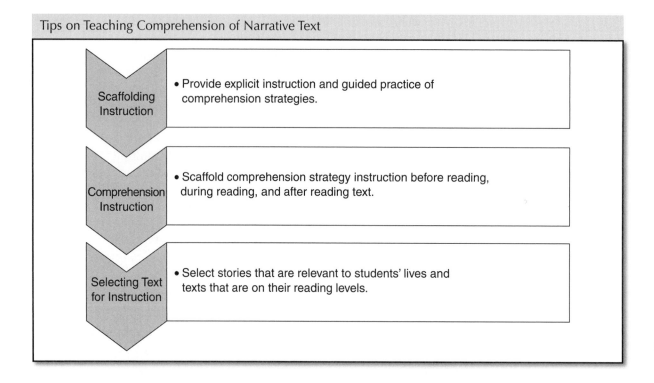

Scaffolding Instruction	• Provide explicit instruction and guided practice of comprehension strategies.
Comprehension Instruction	• Scaffold comprehension strategy instruction before reading, during reading, and after reading text.
Selecting Text for Instruction	• Select stories that are relevant to students' lives and texts that are on their reading levels.

A Strategy for Assessing Comprehension of Narrative Text

Assessment of adolescent learners' literacy practices has not garnered the research or resources given to early literacy. However during the last 10 years, researchers have ascertained the essential elements of effective assessment of adolescent literacy (Conley, 2008). To be effective, assessments must have the following elements:

- Define targets and goals being assessed
- Assess what has been actually taught and learned
- Provide adolescents with feedback to improve their literacy performance
- Communicate performance and growth

The performance-based assessment illustrated in Figure III.1, Assessment of Comprehension of Narrative Text, meets these essential elements. In Part A of the assessment instrument, the teacher uses the rubric provided to evaluate the students' mastery of comprehension strategies before, during, and after reading. In Part B, students use the comprehension strategy checklist to monitor their own performance while reading. After analyzing the assessment data, the teacher may use the assessment data to inform instructional practice and to further differentiate lessons for individual learners.

Figure III.1 Part A	Assessment of Comprehension of Narrative Text		
Comprehension Strategy	Developing	Target	Advanced
Identifies and describes story elements: characters, plot, setting	Student inadequately describes and identifies story elements.	Student thoroughly describes and identifies story elements.	Student uses prior knowledge to make inferences about story elements.
Makes predictions using prior knowledge, title, illustrations, or story description	Student inadequately makes predictions by using prior knowledge and book features.	Student adequately makes predictions by using prior knowledge and book features.	Student makes advanced predictions by using prior knowledge and book features.
Uses prior knowledge to construct meaning from text	Student does not use prior knowledge to construct meaning from text.	Student adequately uses prior knowledge to construct meaning from text.	Student makes text-to-self connections to construct meaning.
Elaborates on peers' responses to deepen their comprehension	Student inadequately uses peers' responses to deepen their comprehension.	Student adequately uses peers' responses to deepen their comprehension.	Student uses peers' responses to deepen their own comprehension at the advanced level.
Comments:			

Figure III.1 Part B	Self-Assessment of Strategies for Comprehending Narrative Text					
Directions: Rate your use of comprehension strategies while reading on a scale from 1–5. A score of 5 indicates that you *always* use the strategy and a score of 1 indicates that you *never* use it.						
I use prior knowledge to make predictions about characters, story events, and setting.		1	2	3	4	5
I make inferences about the story by using text information and my prior knowledge.		1	2	3	4	5
I identify and describe the characters, setting, and story events.		1	2	3	4	5
I use my discussions about the story with classmates to further my understanding of the story.		1	2	3	4	5
I use strategies such as visualization if I do not understand the story.		1	2	3	4	5
Summarize your areas of strengths and areas for improvement:						

REFLECTIVE PRACTICE ON TEACHING COMPREHENSION OF NARRATIVE TEXT

To promote comprehension of narrative text, ongoing data analysis and monitoring of adolescent readers' progress are critical. Additionally, the collaborative assessment conversations that take place between teachers and students are another essential component of data-driven instruction. When teachers and students have completed the Assessment of Comprehension of Narrative Text (see Figure III.1), they confer on the results and ponder the following questions:

- What strategies are you using to comprehend the difficult passages?
- What are your goals to improve your reading performance?
- What steps do you need to take to meet your goals?

As adolescent learners become partners in assessment conversations, they begin to internalize their performance goals and to self-monitor their progress. Collaborative, dialogic conversations regarding reading performance will help the teacher to analyze, reflect, and plan effective instruction.

PROFESSIONAL RESOURCES

Atwell, N. (2007). *The reading zone: How to help kids become skilled, passionate, habitual, critical readers.* New York: Scholastic.

Beers, K. (2002). *When kids can't read, what teachers can do: A guide for teachers 6–12.* Portsmouth, NH: Heinemann.

Harvey, S. (2007). *Strategies that work: Teaching comprehension for understanding and engagement.* Portland, ME: Stenhouse.

Tovani, C. (2000). *I read it, but I don't get it: Comprehension strategies for adolescent learners.* Portland, ME: Stenhouse.

REFERENCES

Adams, P. (1998). Imaginative recreation of literature: A critical examination from the perspective of the 90's. In W. Sawyer, K. Watson, & E. Gold (Eds.), *Reviewing English* (pp. 154–163). Sydney, Australia: St. Clair Press.

Alvermann, D. (2004). *Comprehension instruction: Ongoing through the middle and high school years.* Retrieved November 17, 2009, from http://www.ciera.org

Conley, M. (2008). Literacy assessment for adolescents: What's fair about it? In K. Hinchman & H. Sheridan-Thomas (Eds.), *Best practices in adolescent literacy instruction* (pp. 297–313). New York: Guilford Press.

Duke, N., & Pearson, P. D. (2002). Effective practices for developing reading comprehension. In A. E. Farstrup & S. J. Samuels (Eds.), *What research has to say about reading instruction* (pp. 205–243). Newark, DE: International Reading Association.

Heller, R., & Greenleaf, C. (2007). *Literacy instruction in the content areas: Getting to the core of middle and high school improvement.* Washington, DC: Alliance for Excellent Education.

Hirsch, E. D. (2003). Reading comprehension requires knowledge of words and the world. *American Educator,* pp. 10–29.

Kamil, M. (2004). *Reading for the 21st century: Adolescent literacy teaching and learning strategies.* Washington, DC: Alliance for Excellent Education.

Kamil, M. L., Borman, G. D., Dole, J., Kral, C. C., Salinger, T., & Torgesen, J. (2008). *Improving adolescent literacy: Effective classroom and intervention practices. A practice guide (NCEE #2008-4027).* Washington, DC: National Center for Education Evaluation and Regional Assistance, Institute of Education Sciences, U.S. Department of Education. Retrieved November 21, 2009, from http://ies.ed.gov/ncee/wwc

Moore, D., Alvermann, D., & Hinchman, K. (2007). Literacies in and out of school: A survey of U.S. youth. *The Reading Matrix, 7,* 6–10.

National Center for Education Statistics. (2007). *NAEP 2007 Reading Report Card: National and state highlights.* Washington, DC: National Center for Education Statistics.

National Institute of Child Health and Human Development, (2000). *Teaching children to read: An evidence-based assessment of the scientific literature on reading and its implications for reading instruction.* Washington, DC: Author.

RAND Reading Study Group. (2002). *Factors creating differences in reading comprehension.* New York: RAND.

Snow, C. (2002). *Reading for understanding.* New York: RAND.

Snow, C., & Biancarosa, G. (2003). *Adolescent literacy and the achievement gap: What do we know and where do we go from here?* New York: Carnegie.

Wood, E. (2008). Does feeling come first? How poetry can help readers broaden their understanding of metacognition. *Journal of Adolescent and Adult Literacy, 51,* 564–576.

Strategy 11

Interactive Think-Alouds

Collaborative Interpretation of Text

STRATEGY OVERVIEW

"You can read this text and I'll show you how" (Lapp, Fisher, & Grant, 2008, p. 372). Struggling adolescent readers are often at a loss when asked to make inferences or to analyze novels or short stories. Expert readers are aware of the myriad ways to construct inferences or make predictions; however, struggling readers need an explicit demonstration of the strategies necessary to comprehend narrative text (National Institute of Child Health and Human Development, 2000).

The *Interactive Think-Aloud* is a collaborative instructional activity where comprehension strategies to infer, predict, and analyze text are directly modeled by the teacher. As the teacher models how to infer or predict, the students are able to "eavesdrop" on the thinking process and to see invisible cognitive processes in action (Lapp et al., 2008). A critical component of the interactive read-aloud is the collaborative sharing of thinking processes by adolescent readers as they practice the think-aloud with a partner. As research indicates, discussion allows readers to learn about multiple ways of interpreting texts and how perspectives are formed (Kamil, 2004). The following step-by-step procedures describe how to implement the interactive think-aloud with adolescent readers.

Source: International Reading Association and National Council of Teachers of English (1996).

IRA/NCTE Standards for the English Language Arts

3. Students apply a wide range of strategies to comprehend, interpret, evaluate, and appreciate texts. They draw on their prior experience, their interactions with other readers and writers, their knowledge of word meaning and of other texts, their word identification strategies, and their understanding of textual features (e.g., sound-letter correspondence, sentence structure, context, graphics).

STEP-BY-STEP PROCEDURE

BEFORE READING

Before selecting a text to use for the demonstration, the teacher refers to assessment data from the previous lesson to ascertain which areas are providing difficulties for students. For example, if in prior lessons the students were unable to make inferences, the teacher selects a passage that lends itself to making inferences.

1. After analysis of the assessment data, the teacher sets a goal for the interactive read-aloud, which focuses on a comprehension skill such as making predictions or a strategy such as using text features.

2. The teacher selects a text to demonstrate the comprehension skill or strategy and additional passages for the students to read with a partner. The passages selected for the shared reading component should be "just right," which denotes a slightly challenging text but not too difficult for the students to read.

DURING READING

The teacher begins the interactive read-aloud by modeling the comprehension skill or strategy. Figure 11.1 illustrates the presentation by the teacher during the demonstration.

1. After the demonstration, the teacher discusses the strategy with the students. After the discussion, the teacher collaborates with the students to record on chart paper the strategies that were demonstrated during the think-aloud to infer or predict. The chart is posted in a prominent place to be used as a reference tool during the guided reading component.

2. Students are then given a partner to practice the interactive think-aloud. Each student takes turns reading the selected passage and saying aloud their strategies to infer or predict. During the guided practice component, the teacher circulates around the room to observe the dialogue and strategies used by the students. If the teacher observes that the text is too difficult for the students, an alternative passage on the same topic can be used. After each partner has read the text, they list the comprehension strategies they used on a Post-it note.

| Figure 11.1 | Interactive Think-Aloud Model |

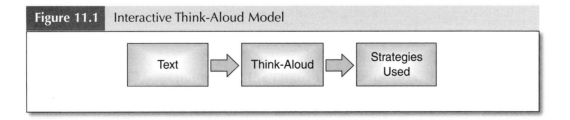

After Reading

After students have completed their interactive think-alouds, the teacher leads a debriefing session. Each partner team describes the strategies they listed on the Post-it note and how they learned from one other.

1. Any comprehension problems encountered during the interactive think-aloud session are used as "teachable moments." The teacher uses the difficulty to ask students to brainstorm ways to solve the comprehension problem. For example, if students had difficulty inferring, students can generate a list of ways they were able to use context, chapter headings, and illustrations to make an inference.

2. At the conclusion of the session, students record on the reference chart the top three comprehension strategies used during the interactive think-aloud. This remains in the classroom as a reference guide during independent reading until students have mastered the particular comprehension skill or strategy.

Differentiating Instruction for Striving Readers

Striving readers bring their anxiety regarding reading when they encounter text, and this can impede comprehension; therefore, it is critical to provide all adolescent readers, but especially striving readers, with choices of narrative texts to tackle. The text sets available for selection should include titles that speak to issues in their young lives or culture. When students are given choices and allowed a voice in their literacy selections, their engagement and motivation to read increases (Moje, 2006).

Striving readers also may require additional supports during the interactive think-aloud activity. For example, a comprehension strategy bookmark that includes the questions to consider before, during, and after reading would be helpful. As striving readers work with their reading partner, they can refer to the bookmark before reading the text with the following question prompts: (a) What is my purpose for reading? (b) What predictions can I make?

Considering the Language Needs of ELL Students

Source: International Reading Association and National Council of Teachers of English (1996).

IRA/NCTE Standards for the English Language Arts

10. Students whose first language is not English make use of their first language to develop competency in the English language arts and to develop understanding of content across the curriculum.

Similarly to striving readers, English language learners need additional layers of support during comprehension strategy instruction. Before engaging in the interactive read-aloud, the teacher can conduct a preassessment of English language learners' prior knowledge regarding the text topic or story setting. Based on assessment data, a small guided reading group can be formed to address gaps in their conceptual understandings. English language learners may need a book walk such as looking at the front and back covers of the text and reading the summary blurb. Such small efforts will provide the English language learners with a purpose for reading and help them to formulate questions. In addition, they may need to see visuals of the story setting or topic if the story events are set in a specific historical period. Content area teachers can assist English language learners with these additional supports by partnering them with a more advanced reader to do these activities prior to engaging in the interactive think-aloud.

AN APPLICATION FOR INSTRUCTION AND LEARNING IN THE SCIENCE CLASSROOM

Seventh graders have just completed a unit on women in science. The class is beginning to read *Something Out of Nothing: Marie Curie and Radium* by Carla Killough McClafferty (2006). The text uses photographs to tell Marie Curie's story in a narrative style. The teacher begins by asking students to define the term *think-aloud*. The teacher presents the chart illustrated in Figure 11.1 as she models the interactive think-aloud. As the teacher begins to read the text, she uses photos to discuss the culture of the time. "From the photos, I can tell that it is the early 1900s from the way she is dressed along with her hairstyle. I know right away she must have been unusual for her day." As the teacher comments, the students note her remarks in the second column. The teacher queries, 'What strategy did I just use there?' Students respond that the teacher made predictions using illustrations and note that in the final column. The teacher continues to model the interactive think-aloud strategy for the first class session. During the second class session, students use their charts to work with partners to complete their own interactive think-aloud. When students have completed the chapter assigned for that session, the teacher asks students to comment on how they used the strategy and to discuss any problems they encountered while reading.

REFERENCES

International Reading Association and National Council of Teachers of English. (1996). *Standards for the English language arts*. Newark, DE: International Reading Association & Urbana, IL: National Council of Teachers of English.

Kamil, M. (2004). *Reading for the 21st century: Adolescent literacy teaching and learning strategies*. Washington, DC: Alliance for Excellent Education.

Lapp, D., Fisher, D., & Grant, M. (2008). You can read this text—I'll show you how: Interactive comprehension instruction. *Journal of Adolescent and Adult Literacy, 51*, 372–384.

McClafferty, C. K. (2006). *Something out of nothing: Marie Curie and radium*. New York: Farrar, Straus, & Giroux.

Moje, E. B. (2006). Motivating text, motivating contexts, motivating adolescents: An examination of the role of motivation in adolescent literacy practices and development. *Perspectives, 32*, 10–14.

National Institute of Child Health and Human Development. (2000). *Report of the National Reading Panel: Teaching children to read*. Washington, DC: U.S. Department of Health and Human Services NIH Pub No. 00-4754.

Strategy 12

Inference Strategy Guide

Facilitating Reading Between the Lines

STRATEGY OVERVIEW

"Because each person's experiences are different, the art of inferring takes the reader beyond the text to a place only he or she can go" (Keene & Zimmermann, 2007, p. 145). The art of making an inference is especially difficult for struggling readers since the process is difficult to grasp. However, studies have shown that inexperienced readers can be taught how to make an inference when they are given explicit strategy instruction (Nokes, 2008). When proficient readers infer, they base their inference on evidence from the text. They also draw on their background knowledge to make reasonable predictions about the text. Proficient readers critically analyze text when they infer and reflect on their thought processes (Keene & Zimmermann, 2007; Nokes, 2008).

The *Inference Strategy Guide* is an explicit comprehension strategy for teaching struggling readers how to make an inference (Nokes, 2008; Serafini & Youngs, 2008; Sheridan-Thomas, 2008). The goal of the strategy is to make adolescent readers metacognitive as they engage in dialogue about their thought processes. As the teacher guides students in tapping their background knowledge, citing evidence from text, making text-to-text connections, the art of making an inference is made visible. The strategy is presented as a cyclical process since students refer back to the text or to their own prior knowledge to make an inference.

Source: International Reading Association and National Council of Teachers of English (1996).

IRA/NCTE Standards for the English Language Arts

3. Students apply a wide range of strategies to comprehend, interpret, evaluate, and appreciate texts. They draw on their prior experience, their interactions with other readers and writers, their knowledge of word meaning and of other texts, their word identification strategies, and their understanding of textual features (e.g., sound-letter correspondence, sentence structure, context, graphics).

12. Students use spoken, written, and visual language to accomplish their own purposes (e.g., for learning, enjoyment, persuasion, and the exchange of information).

STEP-BY-STEP PROCEDURE

BEFORE READING

The session begins with the teacher asking students, "What is an inference?" Student responses are written on a descriptive web. The teacher summarizes student responses and explains that the purpose of the making an inference strategy chart (Figure 12.1) is to improve the quality of their inferences.

1. Students are given the text and asked to examine the front and back covers of the text. The teacher leads the class in making predictions based on the illustrations on the cover or the blurb in the back of the text.

2. The teacher uses the predictions made to refer to the making an inference strategy chart.

The teacher uses the generic chart shown in Figure 12.1 to guide discussion and to list prompts such as "Use your background knowledge to make predictions about the plot, characters, or events," or "How did you use your background knowledge to infer about the characters, plot, or setting?" Student responses are recorded in the first circle entitled "In my head."

DURING READING

The teacher presents the making an inference strategy chart (Nokes, 2008; Serafini & Youngs, 2008) and explains how they will use it while reading.

1. Students silently read the first chapter and record their observations regarding the text in the second circle. In the third circle, students record their questions regarding the text or information they feel is missing from it.

2. Students are then given a partner to discuss their chart responses. Together they share their observations and questions. As they discuss their chart responses, partners decide the information sources for their notes. The following are categories of information:
   - Text (explicitly stated)
   - My own knowledge (in my head)

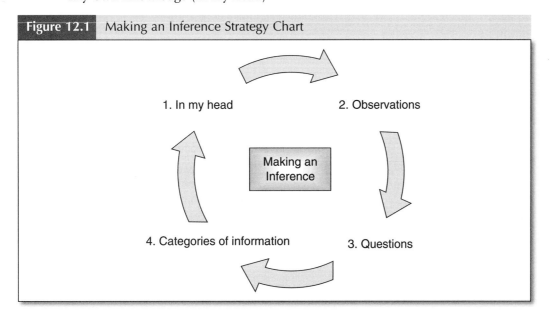

Figure 12.1 Making an Inference Strategy Chart

1. In my head

2. Observations

Making an Inference

4. Categories of information

3. Questions

- Text and me (combination of text and my knowledge)
- Investigate (may be several different places in text) (Raphael & Au, 2005)

3. After the dialogue, students collaborate to make inferences in the central circle. The final component of the discussion is to decide how their information sources helped them to make an inference and to report any problems they had with the process.

AFTER READING

The teacher refers to the making an inference strategy chart (Figure 12.2) to discuss the process with the students. Students are asked to give explicit examples of how they used their sources of information categories to make predictions or analyze characters.

1. The inferences made by students are listed on chart paper. Each pair of students has to cite evidence from the text to support their inference as they report out.

2. At the conclusion of the session, students record any problems they encountered while making inferences. The teacher leads a discussion on how to fix these processing problems before their next reading of the text.

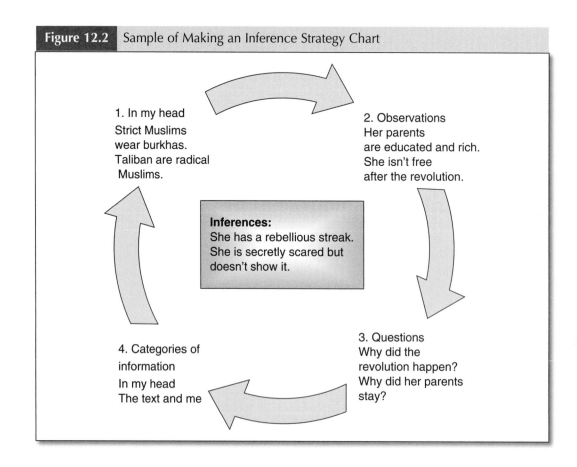

| **Figure 12.2** | Sample of Making an Inference Strategy Chart |

1. In my head
Strict Muslims wear burkhas. Taliban are radical Muslims.

2. Observations
Her parents are educated and rich. She isn't free after the revolution.

Inferences:
She has a rebellious streak.
She is secretly scared but doesn't show it.

3. Questions
Why did the revolution happen? Why did her parents stay?

4. Categories of information
In my head
The text and me

DIFFERENTIATING INSTRUCTION FOR STRIVING READERS

Disengagement with literacy is a primary problem facing teachers of striving readers. Due to their lack of confidence and anxiety regarding reading, the striving reader is often unmotivated to read. Research has shown that when teachers focus on the task with adolescent learners rather than performance goals, their engagement with literacy improves as well as their confidence in their ability to read (Guthrie & Davis, 2003). For example, a striving reader will not be able to make an inference if their background knowledge is inadequate. Therefore, an effective instructional strategy is to provide the "autonomy support" for the striving reader to acquire the necessary subject matter to make an inference. Autonomy support refers to the supportive framework that the teacher uses to provide the necessary context for the striving reader to complete the task successfully (Guthrie & Davis, 2003). For instance, teaching a thematic unit on the Middle East or the Muslim World would enable the striving reader to feel more confident as they approach the text *Persepolis*. Another supportive framework would be to provide multiple texts on the subject matter that are on their ability level. When adolescent striving readers engage in text that they can understand and discuss with peers, they are empowered to improve their self-confidence when approaching the task.

CONSIDERING THE LANGUAGE NEEDS OF ELL STUDENTS

IRA/NCTE Standards for the English Language Arts

10. Students whose first language is not English make use of their first language to develop competency in the English language arts and to develop understanding of content across the curriculum.

Source: International Reading Association and National Council of Teachers of English (1996).

Making an inference is especially difficult for English language learners. Similarly to striving readers, English language learners may not have the necessary background knowledge or vocabulary to "read between the lines." One method for differentiating this strategy for ELL students is through imagery. The guided imagery strategy (Boyd-Batstone, 2006) is an effective way to engage English language learners in critical thinking through imagery. As they engage in prereading, during reading, and postreading tasks, they keep an illustrated journal of their visualizations of key scenes while they read. The students are instructed to "imagine yourself in the scene. . . . What are you thinking? What are you feeling?" As they create their imagery for each phase of the reading process, it is critical that they discuss their work with a partner. The ELL students use their making an inference strategy chart to support their images with observations from the text and their background knowledge. As they engage in these discussions, the ability to read between the lines will increase as their content knowledge is enriched.

AN APPLICATION FOR INSTRUCTION AND LEARNING IN THE SOCIAL STUDIES CLASSROOM

It is the fall semester and ninth graders are completing a unit on the Middle East. Students are using the graphic novel *Persepolis* by Marjane Satrapi (2003) to discuss the Iranian revolution and the impact of radical Muslim culture on society in Iran. The teacher begins the session by asking students to brainstorm about the Iranian revolution based on their studies during the unit. Students skim the blurb and illustrations to record their prior knowledge in the "In my head" circle. As students read, they record their observations and questions in the appropriate areas on the chart. When they have completed reading the text, students meet with their reading partner to record inferences they made such as "She has a rebellious streak," or "She appears brave but is secretly scared." Partners record the categories of information they used to make those inferences on the chart. When students finish discussing the text, the teacher leads a debriefing session. As partners present their inferences, the teacher records them on chart paper along with text citations to defend their inferences.

REFERENCES

Boyd-Batstone, P. (2006). *Differentiated early literacy for English language learners*. Boston: Allyn & Bacon.

Guthrie, J., & Davis, M. (2003). Motivating struggling readers in middle school through an engagement model of classroom practice. *Reading and Writing Quarterly, 19*, 59–85.

International Reading Association and National Council of Teachers of English. (1996). *Standards for the English language arts*. Newark, DE: International Reading Association & Urbana, IL: National Council of Teachers of English.

Keene, E., & Zimmermann, S. (2007). *Mosaic of thought* (2nd ed.). Portsmouth, NH: Heinemann.

Nokes, J. (2008). The observation/inference chart: Improving students' abilities to make inferences while reading non-traditional texts. *Journal of Adolescent and Adult Literacy, 51*, 538–546.

Raphael, T., & Au, K. (2005). QAR: Enhancing comprehension and test taking across grade levels and contents. *The Reading Teacher, 59*, 206–221.

Satrapi, M. (2003). *Persepolis*. New York: Pantheon Books.

Serafini, F., & Youngs, S. (2008). *More advanced lessons in comprehension*. Portsmouth, NH: Heinemann.

Sheridan-Thomas, H. (2008). Assisting struggling readers with textbook comprehension. In K. Hinchman & H. Sheridan-Thomas (Eds.), *Best practices in adolescent literacy instruction* (pp. 164–185). New York: Guilford Press.

Imagination Recreation

Strategy 13

Deepening Understanding Through Creativity

Today's adolescent is a millennial learner who has never known a world where information cannot be accessed in multiple ways (Boyd & Thompson, 2008). It is by seeing, feeling, hearing, and viewing information in a social context that adolescent learners construct meaning (Love, 2005). The traditional theory of comprehension posited that meaning was constructed once and was static. In 2001, Kress and Van Leeuwen developed the multimodal communication theory that argued how multiple sources of information are used to construct meaning. They theorized that we make multiple meanings as we view text from different representations such as print, multimedia, audio, visual, and kinesthetic modes. Meaning is continually reshaped as we access different sources of information or collaborate with others.

Research indicates that proficient readers have always used sensory modes to comprehend text (Keene & Zimmermann, 2007). They purposefully create images while reading and adjust them while reading or discussing the text with peers. As proficient readers have realized, the use of sensory modes to connect to text enables the reader to process and retrieve information. The *Imaginative Recreation* strategy is one way to use multiple modes of accessing text with adolescent readers.

IRA/NCTE Standards for the English Language Arts

6. Students apply knowledge of language structure, language conventions (e.g., spelling and punctuation), media techniques, figurative language, and genre to create, critique, and discuss print and nonprint texts.

8. Students use a variety of technological and informational resources (e.g., libraries, databases, computer networks, video) to gather and synthesize information and to create and communicate knowledge.

Source: International Reading Association and National Council of Teachers of English (1996).

STEP-BY-STEP PROCEDURE

The Imagination Recreation strategy provides adolescent readers with multiple modes to interpret text. The teacher facilitates the process by carefully selecting text that students will appreciate and comprehend. The purpose of the strategy is to enable adolescent learners to draw on multiple ways of accessing text to deepen their understanding.

BEFORE READING

Before the session, the teacher decides on the form of recreating text that students will use in the strategy.

1. The teacher lists the choices on a chart with examples such as the following:
   - Change the setting or place of the story
   - Transform the short story into a newspaper article
   - Create a video based on the novel
   - Construct a map of the setting
2. The teacher presents the text and guides students through a prereading strategy of skimming the title, chapter headings, or book features to make predictions about the story.
3. Critical vocabulary words that might pose comprehension difficulties are presented in the context of a sentence and students discuss possible meanings.

DURING READING

While students engage in reading, they record their observations.

1. Students silently read the text and use Post it notes to jot down their story impressions, inferences, or questions.
2. When they are finished reading, students work in groups of three to discuss their interpretation of the text and to address any comprehension difficulties.

AFTER READING

The discussion groups continue to work together to choose the form they will use to recreate text. For example, if they are recreating the story as a video segment, they will first have to create a storyboard to plan their text.

1. As students work on their recreations, they decide collaboratively on roles, such as narrator, for group members to present their work.
2. At the conclusion of the session, students present their recreations for their peers. When all groups have presented, the teacher leads a discussion of how the projects illustrated their different interpretations of the text.

The Imagination Recreation strategy can be adapted in a number of ways to fit the needs of the adolescent learner. The teacher may choose to have students focus on switching the genre of the text from short story to poem or the medium from printed text to radio broadcast. Text can also be reconstructed from the antagonist's perspective.

Differentiating Instruction for Striving Readers

To successfully reconstruct text, adolescent learners must understand the concept of multiple representations of text. However, striving readers may lack clarity on this process. For example, teachers often assume that striving readers understand the directive to recreate text from another perspective. Yet often striving readers are unclear about the process of viewing an event from a different lens. An instructional strategy to prepare striving readers for perspective taking is to use photographs of historical events. As students view the photographs, the teacher leads a discussion of how the event is being viewed by the different people in the photograph (Boyd & Thompson, 2008). The students can extend the activity by creating speech bubbles, which display their thoughts as the event unfolds. This simple activity can facilitate the striving reader's conceptual understanding of perspective taking.

Considering the Language Needs of ELL Students

IRA/NCTE Standards for the English Language Arts

10. Students whose first language is not English make use of their first language to develop competency in the English language arts and to develop understanding of content across the curriculum.

Source: International Reading Association and National Council of Teachers of English (1996).

To recreate text, English language learners need to comprehend text at the literal level. Graphic organizers such as story maps are useful tools for enabling second language learners to visualize the main character, story events, setting, and main idea of the text. English language learners can use the graphic organizer to join in the group discussion on recreating the text. As they refer to their graphic organizer, they can offer ways to alter the setting, events of the story, or character perspective. If second language learners are struggling to comprehend at the literal level, the instructional strategy can be adapted further by partnering them with a slightly more advanced partner reader.

An Application for Instruction and Learning in the Social Studies Classroom

During the unit on empire building, 10th graders are eager to devour the fictional memoir of Napoleon Bonaparte during the Battle of the Nile. Before beginning the strategy, the teacher leads the class in a review of their prior knowledge regarding Napoleon Bonaparte, which is placed on a descriptive web. As the students silently read the selection, they take notes and jot down questions or inferences for discussion. When students have completed their reading of the memoir, the teacher places them in groups of four to begin their postreading discussion. The groups collaboratively define unknown vocabulary words and tackle questions posted by their members. The teacher leads the students in discussing Napoleon's motives for invading Egypt and how his actions were viewed by the opposing British forces led by Admiral Nelson. In the next class session, groups gather to decide the form of recreation they will use to present Napoleon Bonaparte's memoir. One group of students decides to present a radio broadcast of the invasion from both the French and British perspectives. Members are selected to work on the radio scripts from the two perspectives using a reporter's stance. The group's two radio broadcasts are performed for the class. Immediately after the performance, the teacher leads the class in discerning factual information used in the scripts and in critiquing the two perspectives of the battle.

REFERENCES

Boyd, F., & Thompson, M. (2008). Multimodality and literacy learning: Using multiple texts to enhance content-area learning. In K. Hinchman & H. Sheridan-Thomas (Eds.), *Best practices in adolescent literacy instruction* (pp. 151–164). New York: Guilford Press.

International Reading Association and National Council of Teachers of English. (1996). *Standards for the English language arts.* Newark, DE: International Reading Association & Urbana, IL: National Council of Teachers of English.

Keene, E., & Zimmermann, S. (2007). *Mosaic of thought* (2nd ed.). Portsmouth, NH: Heinemann.

Kress, G., & Van Leeuwen, T. (2001). *Multimodal discourse: The modes and media of contemporary communication.* New York: Oxford University Press.

Love, M. (2005). Multimodality of learning through anchored instruction. *Journal of Adolescent & Adult Literacy, 48,* 300–311.

Conflict Dissection

Strategy 14

Analyzing Relationships in Text

For many years researchers in literacy argued that explicit instruction in narrative text structure was unnecessary. However, recent studies have shown that instruction on comprehending text structure and applying that knowledge is one of the seven most effective educational practices for at-risk students (Flood & Lapp, 2000). Proficient readers automatically identify the structure of a story and are able to use that information to improve their predictions and inferences (Keene & Zimmermann, 2007). However, students from nonmainstream backgrounds may struggle with text structure and may have difficulties recognizing patterns in text (Dickinson, Simmons, & Kameenui, 1995).

Taylor (1992) defined text structure as the underlying building blocks that organize text in predictable and understandable ways. When students understand text structure, their comprehension of deep structure increases and their retention of demanding content improves (Pearson & Camperell, 1994). The *Conflict Dissection* strategy is an explicit instructional sequence to aid adolescent readers' identification of conflict and to deepen their understanding of narrative text structure.

IRA/NCTE Standards for the English Language Arts

1. Students read a wide range of print and nonprint texts to build an understanding of texts, of themselves, and of the cultures of the United States and the world; to acquire new information; to respond to the needs and demands of society and the workplace; and for personal fulfillment. Among these texts are fiction and nonfiction, classic, and contemporary works.
6. Students apply knowledge of language structure, language conventions (e.g., spelling and punctuation), media techniques, figurative language, and genre to create, critique, and discuss print and nonprint texts.

Source: International Reading Association and National Council of Teachers of English (1996).

STEP-BY-STEP PROCEDURE

The purpose of the Conflict Dissection strategy is to help adolescent readers identify plot elements of conflict and resolution. The strategy originated with Macon, Bewell, and Vogt (1990) and can also be adapted for use with expository text structure. As with all comprehension strategies, it is critical for the teacher to engage in scaffolded instruction to guide students to independent use of the strategy.

BEFORE READING

The teacher begins the session by first asking students to define *conflict* and *resolution* on descriptive webs. After summarizing the students' responses, the class defines each term.

1. Before reading the text, the teacher models the strategy with an excerpt from a short story. The teacher defines each of the categories on the graphic organizer:

   - *Somebody/someone:* main character or main group of characters
   - *Wanted/because:* motivation of main character or main group of characters
   - *But:* conflict or problem
   - *So:* resolution of conflict/problem

DURING READING

As students engage in reading, they record their notes and comments on the conflict and resolution of the story.

1. Students are assigned a story or chapter in a novel to be read silently. After reading the selection, they are put into groups to begin the graphic organizer illustrated in Figure 14.1, Conflict Dissection Strategy Chart.

2. Students work in their assigned groups on using the information from the text to complete the chart. The teacher's model used before reading should be visible as a reference during this component.

Figure 14.1	Conflict Dissection Strategy Chart		
Someone	*Wanted/Because*	*But*	*So*
(Main Character)	**(Motivation)**	**(Conflict/Problem)**	**(Solution)**

After Reading

When the groups have completed the graphic organizers, the teacher leads a debriefing session where each group defends their input with references to the text.

1. To complete the activity, students are asked to write a summary based on the information they presented in the graphic organizer.

2. Students practice using the graphic organizer independently for homework or in the next class session.

The Conflict Dissection strategy can become even more challenging as students are asked to complete it again but with another character in the main frame. This exercise enables them to view the conflict or problem from multiple perspectives, which deepens their understanding.

DIFFERENTIATING INSTRUCTION FOR STRIVING READERS

Striving adolescent readers may lack knowledge of text structure to successfully complete the Conflict Dissection graphic organizer (Dickinson et al., 1995). To scaffold their engagement with text, the teacher can work directly with striving readers to discuss conflicts they have experienced in their own lives. When text is related to adolescent students' own lives, it increases their motivation to engage in text and to comprehend (Rothenberg & Watts, 2000). After discussing conflicts in their own lives, the teacher can begin to lead a discussion on how the main character in the text is undergoing a similar situation. This scaffolded reading of the text aids striving readers as they attempt to recognize conflict/resolution patterns in text.

CONSIDERING THE LANGUAGE NEEDS OF ELL STUDENTS

IRA/NCTE Standards for the English Language Arts

10. Students whose first language is not English make use of their first language to develop competency in the English language arts and to develop understanding of content across the curriculum.

Source: International Reading Association and National Council of Teachers of English (1996).

Comprehending text structure is especially difficult for English language learners as they may lack prior knowledge regarding patterns of story structures. However, English language learners can benefit from small group, explicit strategy instruction that engages in "dialogue in context" (Palmer, Shackelford, Miller, & Leclere, 2006/2007). For example, as the teacher meets to work directly with a small group of English language learners, they can engage in discussion regarding the conflict experienced by the main character in the text. English language learners also respond to visual imagery integrated with text, so the teacher may want to guide them in a plot graph that outlines the building tension of the conflict and then its resolution. The visual imagery might aid the group's understanding of how the conflict ebbs and flows throughout the narrative.

AN APPLICATION FOR INSTRUCTION AND LEARNING IN THE ENGLISH LITERATURE CLASSROOM

Ninth graders in English literature class are reading *Ask Me No Questions* by Marina Budhos (2006) about 14-year-old Nadira and her Bangladesh family living in New York City. Nadira's father becomes an illegal immigrant when his residency expires, and in a post-9/11 world they face deportation. The teacher begins the session by asking students to define the term *conflict* and then to make predictions regarding the book based on the title and the blurb on the back of the text. As students read the text, they complete the graphic organizer illustrated in Figure 14.2, Sample of Conflict Dissection Strategy Chart. Students take several homework sessions to complete the text and on the fifth day, the teacher leads a discussion of their responses. As students discuss how Muslims were viewed immediately after the terrorist attacks in 2001, they add to their graphic organizer. At the completion of the session, students provide a summary of the conflict and resolution in *Ask Me No Questions*.

Figure 14.2 Sample of Conflict Dissection Strategy Chart

Someone	Wanted/Because	But	So
(Main Character)	**(Motivation)**	**(Conflict/Problem)**	**(Solution)**
Nadira	Nadira and her family want to stay in the United States.	Nadira's family becomes illegal immigrants when her father's residency expires.	Nadira uses her intelligence to intervene during the trial and to stop the deportation.

REFERENCES

Budhos, M. (2006). *Ask me no questions*. New York: Simon Pulse.

Dickinson, S., Simmons, D., & Kameenui, E. (1995). *Text organization and its relation to reading comprehension: A synthesis of the research. Technical report number 17.* Eugene: University of Oregon. Retrieved November 17, 2009, from http://idea.uoregon.edu/~ncite/documents/techrep/tech17.html

Flood, J., & Lapp, D. (2000). Reading comprehension instruction for at-risk students: Research based practices that can make a difference. In D. Moore, D. Alvermann, & K. Hinchman (Eds.), *Struggling adolescent readers: A collection of teaching strategies* (pp. 138–148). Newark, DE: International Reading Association.

International Reading Association and National Council of Teachers of English. (1996). *Standards for the English language arts.* Newark, DE: International

Reading Association & Urbana, IL: National Council of Teachers of English.

Keene, E., & Zimmermann, S. (2007). *Mosaic of thought* (2nd ed.). Portsmouth, NH: Heinemann.

Macon, J., Bewell, D., & Vogt, M. (1990). *Responses to literature K–8*. Newark, DE: International Reading Association.

Palmer, B., Shackelford, V., Miller, S., & Leclere, J. (2006/2007). Bridging two worlds: Reading comprehension, figurative language instruction, and the English language learner. *Journal of Adolescent & Adult Literacy, 50,* 258–268.

Pearson, D., & Camperell, K. (1994). Comprehension of text structures. In R. B. Ruddell, M. Ruddell, & H. Singer (Eds.), *Theoretical modes and processes of reading* (pp. 448–465). Newark, DE: International Reading Association.

Rothenberg, S., & Watts, S. (2000). Students with learning difficulties meet Shakespeare: Using a scaffolded reading experience. In D. Moore, D. Alvermann, & K. Hinchman (Eds.), *Struggling adolescent readers: A collection of strategies* (pp. 148–157). Newark, DE: International Reading Association.

Taylor, B. (1992). Text structure, comprehension, and recall. In S. Samuels & A. Farstrup (Eds.), *What research has to say about reading instruction* (pp. 220–235). Newark, DE: International Reading Association.

Strategy 15

Jots and Doodles

Visualizing Text to Aid Comprehension

"The sensory and emotional images that surface as we read are a kind of Impressionism of the mind" (Keene & Zimmermann, 2007, p. 174). Visualization is a powerful tool for facilitating reading comprehension (Duke & Pearson, 2002). Proficient readers create visual images in great detail and then use these images to deepen their understanding of text (Keene & Zimmermann, 2007; Snow, 2002). Today's millennial learners use multiple modes of text such as visual imagery to interpret and construct their own meaning (Boyd & Thompson, 2008). Unfortunately the struggling adolescent reader may not evoke imagery while they read and often require explicit strategy instruction in visualization.

According to Meltzer, Smith, and Clark (2001), comprehension strategies that should be taught explicitly are rehearsing, elaborating, and comprehension monitoring. Rehearsing requires students to underline and take notes while they read. Elaborating asks students to create mental images and to summarize. When students monitor for comprehension, they self-question and check for understanding. The Jots and Doodles strategy (Tankersley, 2005) is an effective method for engaging adolescent readers in rehearsing, elaborating, and comprehension monitoring of narrative text.

Source: International Reading Association and National Council of Teachers of English (1996).

IRA/NCTE Standards for the English Language Arts

6. Students apply knowledge of language structure, language conventions (e.g., spelling and punctuation), media techniques, figurative language, and genre to create, critique, and discuss print and nonprint texts.

12. Students use spoken, written, and visual language to accomplish their own purposes (e.g., for learning, enjoyment, persuasion, and the exchange of information).

STEP-BY-STEP PROCEDURE

The purpose of the Jots and Doodles strategy is to help adolescent readers evoke visual images while they read and to monitor their comprehension. As students engage in this strategy, they jot down questions and misunderstandings, note vocabulary words, and illustrate themes.

BEFORE READING

For this session to be successful, the teacher carefully selects narrative text that will evoke mental imagery for the students.

1. The teacher begins the session by presenting a transparency with a section of the text. The teacher reads the text aloud and models how to jot down questions, illustrate images, note unfamiliar words, or take notes while reading.

2. After modeling the strategy, the teacher provides students with a new text passage to read silently.

DURING READING

Students create visual images while they read and record their observations.

1. Students silently read the text, creating doodles of images or themes, noting vocabulary words, taking notes, and writing questions.

2. Students are also encouraged to note when their background knowledge or mental image seems incongruous with the text.

AFTER READING

After students have finished reading the text, they share their jots and doodles with a reading partner. As they compare images, notes, and questions, reading partners collaborate to clarify any misunderstandings or instances when prior knowledge or mental images were incongruous with the text.

1. At the conclusion of the session, the teacher leads the debriefing by asking students to share examples of their doodles and how the images aided comprehension. Any questions that remain unanswered are presented to the whole group and answered by referring to the text.

2. New vocabulary words that partners discussed are gathered and put on the word wall for future reference. The teacher also asks students to share their reflection on the use of the strategy and any problems they encountered with it.

The Jots and Doodles strategy enables adolescent readers to use simple techniques to self-monitor their comprehension while they read. A variation of the strategy is to use poetry or photographs to facilitate visualization of text.

Differentiating Instruction for Striving Readers

Research has shown that aural processing of text is extremely helpful for striving readers (Tankersley, 2005). As striving readers listen to stories or books on tape, they are able to attend to the characters, setting, and the underlying themes. One way to adapt this strategy for striving readers is to provide listening centers with stories on tape. As striving readers listen to the stories, they can engage in the strategy by jotting down their doodles or notes as the story unfolds. This enables them to practice the strategy with narrative text without being hampered by their lack of fluency.

Considering the Language Needs of ELL Students

Source: International Reading Association and National Council of Teachers of English (1996).

IRA/NCTE Standards for the English Language Arts

10. Students whose first language is not English make use of their first language to develop competency in the English language arts and to develop understanding of content across the curriculum.

As teachers, we often assume that students understand a task when given a direction such as "create a mental image." However for many second language learners, this directive may be confusing due to their lack of familiarity with the terms. To provide them with a conceptual understanding of visualization, a preparatory activity may be needed. For example, the teacher may present second language learners with an object and ask them to then close their eyes and try to see it mentally. After creating a mental image, they are asked to describe what they saw and then to illustrate it. This simple exercise will aid ELL students' understanding of the strategy and facilitate their use of it.

An Application for Instruction and Learning in the English Literature Classroom

It is early spring in ninth grade as students ponder the poem "Chicago" by Carl Sandburg. The teacher used his "Sphinx" poem to model the Jots and Doodles strategy, and now students are silently reading the poem, taking notes, jotting down vocabulary words, and creating doodles. When students complete their work, the teacher asks them to work with their reading partner to share any questions, miscomprehensions, as well as their notes. At the conclusion of the session, the teacher leads the debriefing asking for vocabulary words that need clarification. Several groups respond that *husky, brawling,* and *sneer* were troublesome to them. The class brainstorms definitions for each word, and they are placed on the word wall. The teacher asks the students to share their notes and doodles. One responds that the phrase, "tall, bold, slugger set vivid against the little soft cities" prompted his doodle of a huge baseball player with bat at the ready against the New York skyline. The teacher prods the student to explain his inference in the doodle, and he responds, "I think Sandburg was saying Chicago is better than other cities, and he probably meant New York." After students share their jots and doodles, the teacher asks students to summarize their interpretation of the poem, which is written on a reference chart for further discussion.

REFERENCES

Boyd, F., & Thompson, M. (2008). Multimodality and literacy learning: Using multiple texts to enhance content-area learning. In K. Hinchman & H. Sheridan-Thomas (Eds.), *Best practices in adolescent literacy instruction* (pp. 151–164). New York: Guilford Press.

Duke, N., & Pearson, P. D. (2002). Effective practices for developing reading comprehension. In A. E. Farstrup & S. J. Samuels (Eds.), *What research has to say about reading instruction* (pp. 205–243). Newark, DE: International Reading Association.

International Reading Association and National Council of Teachers of English. (1996). *Standards for the English language arts.* Newark, DE: International Reading Association & Urbana, IL: National Council of Teachers of English.

Keene, E., & Zimmermann, S. (2007). *Mosaic of thought* (2nd ed.). Portsmouth, NH: Heinemann.

Meltzer, J., Smith, N., & Clark, H. (2001). *Adolescent literacy resources: Linking the research and practice.* Providence, RI: Brown University.

Snow, C. (2002). *Reading for understanding.* New York: RAND.

Tankersley, K. (2005). *Literacy strategies for grades 4–12: Reinforcing the threads of reading.* Alexandria, VA: Association for Supervision and Curriculum Development.

SECTION IV

Reading Informational Text

Developing Comprehension for Informational Text

There is more treasure in books than in all the pirate's loot on Treasure Island.

—Walt Disney

As teachers we have a high regard for books. We experience a sense of joy at opening a new book, whether it is a novel we read for enjoyment or the required textbook we use with our students. Those first pages reveal the hidden treasures that will be ours. Quickly we claim ownership! When new editions replace some of our old friends, we become reluctant to part with them even though room on our bookshelves is a valued commodity.

Do our students approach their books with similar dispositions as they search for the treasures in their texts? Proficient readers who experience success do appreciate the wealth that books possess. However, those students who struggle to understand and learn from their texts find it difficult to realize the value of the book. The purpose of this section is to provide content area teachers with research-based instructional strategies to use with students for developing skills in comprehending informational texts. As students experience a maturing accomplishment with reading and learning from text, their positive attitudes toward books develop. To further students' comprehension of varied text, Section III provides specific strategies for use with narrative text or fiction, and Section IV offers instructional strategies appropriate for understanding informational text.

WHAT RESEARCH HAS TO SAY ABOUT THE COMPREHENSION OF INFORMATIONAL TEXT

Students comprehend fiction and nonfiction text differently. The National Reading Panel's Report (NICHD, 2000) indicates a significant decline in standardized test scores at the fourth-grade level across the nation. They attribute the fourth-grade slump in reading achievement to the sudden demands for nonfiction or informational reading placed on students who in the primary grades were immersed in reading stories. As students progress through middle and secondary grades, the demands for reading and learning from informational text increase.

Research demonstrates that comprehending narrative and informational text are quite different. Therefore, students require specific strategies for understanding these two different text types. When successful students read, they use different strategies for comprehending narrative and informational texts, and they are flexible in their strategy use while reading. Therefore, effective teachers at all grade levels, primary through secondary, are diligent in teaching appropriate instructional strategies that help students understand and learn from their content area textbooks.

Many terms are used for the two different types of texts. One broad category that is familiar to most is *fiction* and *nonfiction*. Fiction is also referred to as *narrative text* because of the writing style as well as the story structure. The term *nonfiction* is frequently referred to as *expository* as well as *informational* texts. Examples include content area texts, nonfiction literature, and trade books such as biographies, travel, and history. Within this section, we refer to nonfiction and expository texts as informational texts.

NARRATIVE TEXT

Stories that we read for pleasure are quite different than the textbook that has become the tool for learning in content area classrooms. Such differences are due to the internal structure of the texts. A text's internal structure refers to the written organization of the text or the text's framework. Narrative text follows a typical story pattern, discussed at length in Section III. Some shorter stories contain simple story patterns, whereas longer stories are more complex. What makes narrative text easier for students to comprehend than informational text is their familiarity with stories. They know the structure of the narrative because stories are familiar to them. They hear stories throughout the day, listen to stories, gossip using stories, and even their dreams are in the format of stories. Their repeated use of stories provides them with knowledge of the internal structure of story or narrative text. As readers, they use their knowledge of story structure in understanding and predicting story events. Another factor that contributes to the reader's ease in comprehending stories is their ability to connect with story experiences. Many of the stories that students read are constructed on life experiences familiar to their own.

INFORMATIONAL TEXT

Reading and learning from informational text is more challenging to readers. For many striving readers, textbooks that they use daily in content area classrooms become a stumbling block to their learning, limiting their academic progress in the disciplines. Once teachers face the challenges of the textbook, the potentials and possibilities are made visible and achievable. Therefore, let us first explore research to understand why reading a textbook is so difficult for students in content area classrooms. We will then try to answer the question, "How can teachers help students who struggle to understand and learn from the wide range of informational texts that they are required to read?"

Three characteristics of informational text that may become potential sources of difficulty in comprehension are the following: (1) the role of the reader's prior knowledge in understanding the text, (2) the internal structures in informational text, and (3) the features of an informational text.

Prior Knowledge and Informational Text

As discussed in the introduction, comprehension is a constructive process. Skilled readers construct meaning from text as they read by relating what they already know to the concepts within the text. They use their prior knowledge to make connections to new ideas that are introduced in the text, to make inferences and predictions, and to question the author's purposes for writing. This type of reading leads to deep comprehension, and results in students' learning from the text. Readers who do not have the prerequisite knowledge to comprehend text cannot use strategies that lead to their transformation of knowledge. Consider the number of new ideas introduced in content area textbooks that students are expected to read daily. Without background information, little or no understanding of the text takes place. To build meaning around text, students need to know about the key ideas and relate what they know to construct meaning from the text. Preparing students for comprehending challenging texts requires teachers to build text-specific knowledge prior to having students read the text (Watts & Graves, 1997). Thus, effective content area teachers facilitate students' reading by activating and building their prior knowledge.

Informational Text Structures

Readers' knowledge of text structure is another important factor that contributes to their comprehension and learning from informational text. Just as students' prior knowledge serves as an aid in text comprehension, knowing about the internal structure of text will assist them in understanding and remembering information from the text. The internal structure of text refers to how authors organize and present ideas to communicate meanings most effectively. The author selects the specific structure or organizational pattern that is an appropriate fit for the information that is presented. For example, when a sequence of events is presented, the author will use a time order organizational pattern. Researchers (Meyer & Freedle, 1984) have identified the following five most common organizational patterns used by writers in presenting information: (1) description, (2) sequence, (3) comparison, (4) cause–effect, and (5) problem–solution. For most of the patterns, authors use signal words that serve as explicit cues to readers helping them follow the pattern for understanding and remembering the information that is presented. Examples of signal words are *first, second,* and *next.*

As students become familiar with different organizational patterns used in their textbooks, they will use their knowledge of text structure for reading and writing informational text. Skilled readers have knowledge of text structures and use it in comprehending informational text. There are many students who are not aware of the organizational patterns of informational text and could benefit from direct instruction on using the structure for comprehending text (Pressley, 2002; Vacca, 1998). In understanding and learning from complex texts, students need explicit and systematic instruction in using the text's structure (Sweet & Snow, 2003).

Features in Content Area Texts

The textbook has been central to students for acquiring knowledge in a range of disciplines. Teachers' reliance on the textbook varies, ranging from the central tool for learning the discipline to one of the tools used as a source of content. In any case, as middle and secondary students face their texts, these books are often unappealing and formidable. Whether it is reading from a textbook or a nonfiction trade book, there are external features that skilled readers use in comprehending and learning from text. Teachers who help students to identify and use the features of the text will increase their understanding and learning as they read and search for information more efficiently. The following 12 features are commonly found in most textbooks and nonfiction trade books: (1) titles; (2) table of contents; (3) chapter titles; (4) headings and subheadings; (5) margin notes; (6) visuals such as photographs, cartoons, maps, diagrams, and graphs; (7) figures, tables, and lists; (8) bolded, italicized, or highlighted words; (9) beginning-of-the-chapter overviews and objectives; (10) end-of-the-chapter reviews: questions and outlines; (11) index; and (12) glossary.

A Framework for Teaching Comprehension of Informational Text to Adolescent Students

Learning in the 21st century is quite different than it was 20 years ago. In this information age, we bear witness to volumes of new ideas found not only in print but flashing on the screen, appearing in media, compressed into the e-book, and the list goes on. No longer can effective teachers pass along a list of facts to be memorized by the students for weekly and year-end exams. Rather, to be successful in today's world means that students need to learn to be active readers of different text types including informational and that they use appropriate strategies in flexible ways that result in their profound understanding of texts. Duke and Pearson (2002) summarized research to describe the multiple strategies used by skilled readers. Their characteristics are depicted in Figure IV.1, What Skilled Readers Do Before, During, and After Reading. When teachers know the strategies that accomplished readers use while reading, they can then design a framework for effective instruction in reading comprehension.

All students need instruction in reading expository texts that will help them to construct meaning and recall information from text. Students benefit from (a) direct and explicit strategy instruction, (b) knowing how to select the most appropriate strategies that will foster proficient reading, (c) many opportunities that will foster engaged reading that leads to comprehending text, and (d) an understanding of monitoring their own reading. Effective teachers know that learning a strategy takes time. Therefore, they work with students until their strategy application is secure in reading a wide variety of informational text.

Figure IV.1 What Skilled Readers Do Before, During, and After Reading

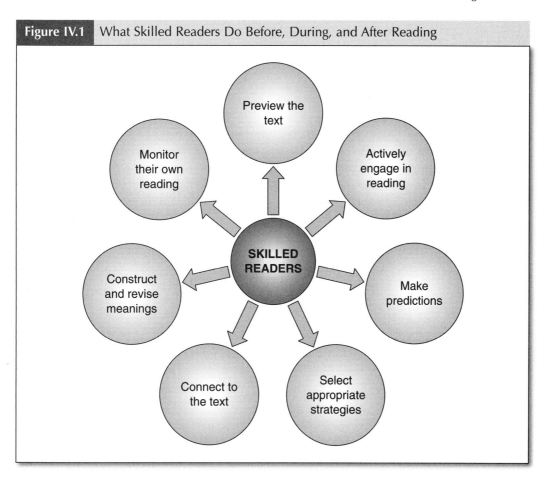

Tips on Teaching Comprehension of Informational Text

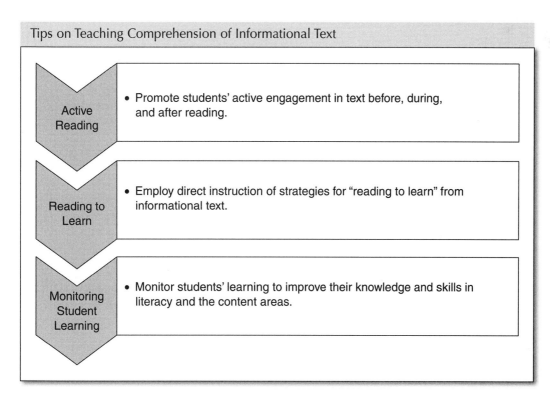

Active Reading	• Promote students' active engagement in text before, during, and after reading.
Reading to Learn	• Employ direct instruction of strategies for "reading to learn" from informational text.
Monitoring Student Learning	• Monitor students' learning to improve their knowledge and skills in literacy and the content areas.

A Strategy for Assessing the Development of Comprehending Informational Text

Assessing student performance is determined by the learning outcomes. For adolescents in content area classrooms, we want students to progress to advanced levels of proficiency in all forms of language arts. In reading from their classroom textbooks as well as from other forms of related texts, students are expected to understand what they have read and to communicate their ideas with others about the content they are learning. Figure IV.2, Rubric for Assessing Student's Reading Comprehension of Informational Text, provides a generic rubric for assessing reading comprehension of informational text. Because it is generic, it may be used to evaluate students' reading comprehension using each of the strategies presented in this section. The rubric is developed to assess four levels of proficiency—from beginning to advanced—and each of the levels is assigned a score. The student's reading proficiency level for comprehending informational text is determined by the total score achieved on the assessment tool.

Figure IV.2	Rubric for Assessing Student's Reading Comprehension of Informational Text			
Criteria	*Beginning* Points = 1	*Developing* Points = 2	*Proficient* Points = 3	*Advanced* Points = 4
Constructs meaning from text	The student experiences difficulty in constructing meaning from the required informational texts.	The student is able to construct meaning from a limited number of required informational texts.	The student is able to construct meaning from most of the informational text that is required reading.	The student is able to construct meaning from wide variety of informational text.
Communicates ideas in writing	With little or no accuracy, the student is able to communicate content area ideas in writing.	With a low degree of accuracy, the student is able to communicate content area ideas in writing.	With a moderate degree of accuracy, the student is able to communicate content area ideas in writing.	With a high degree of accuracy, the student is able to communicate content area ideas in writing.
Effectively engages in discussion	The student rarely participates in discussion, conveying inaccurate information most of the time.	The student participates in discussion to some degree, conveying some information with accuracy.	The student participates in discussions to a moderate degree and conveys most information with accuracy.	The student engages actively in discussion, accurately conveying content information.
Recalls ideas from text	The student recalls little or no information he/she has read and rarely with any degree of accuracy.	The student recalls some information he/she has read with a low degree of accuracy.	The student recalls most information he/she has read with a moderate degree of accuracy.	The student recalls all information he/she has read with a high degree of accuracy.
Score results and levels of reading comprehension	**Advanced level of reading comprehension: 16–13 points** **Proficient level of reading comprehension: 12–9 points** **Developing level of reading comprehension: 8–5 points** **Beginning level of reading comprehension: Below 5 points**			

REFLECTIVE PRACTICE OF TEACHING COMPREHENSION OF INFORMATIONAL TEXT

The litmus test for effective teaching is student learning. Does the teacher have a positive impact on student learning? Therefore, teachers' reflections on their instruction are integrally tied to how well the students have met the learning outcomes. Thinking about the quality of our teaching begins by assessing student learning and leads to using assessment results to make modifications in our teaching. The following questions provide the beginnings of reflective practice that is specifically related to teaching comprehension of informational text:

- Were all students actively engaged in reading? Were the assigned texts motivating and at their reading levels?

- Were all students actively engaged in discussion? If not, what approach can I use to enliven discussions?

- Did students use effective communication skills in talking about the content? Have they begun to appropriate the language of the discipline? How can I change my teaching to foster effective communication skills?

- What types of recall were made by the students? How can I help students to remember the important ideas from their readings, to synthesize, and to summarize information they read?

PROFESSIONAL RESOURCES

Allen, J. (2008). *More tools for teaching content literacy*. Portland, ME: Stenhouse.

Beck, I. L., & McKeown, M. G. (2006). *Improving comprehension with questioning the author: A fresh and expanded view of a powerful approach*. New York: Scholastic.

Godinho, S., & Wilson, J. (2007). *Out of the question: Guiding students to a deeper understanding of what they see, read, hear, and do*. Portland, ME: Stenhouse.

Wood, K. D., & Blanton, W. E. (2009). *Literacy instruction for adolescents: Research-based practice*. New York: Guilford.

Wormeli, R. (2007). *Differentiation: From planning to practice, grades 6–12*. Portland, ME: Stenhouse.

REFERENCES

Duke, N. K., & Pearson, P. D. (2002). Effective practices for developing reading comprehension. In A. E. Farstrup & S. J. Samuels (Eds.), *What research has to say about reading instruction* (pp. 205–242). Newark, DE: International Reading Association.

Meyer, B. J. F., & Freedle, R. D. (1984). Effects of discourse type on recall. *American Educational Research Journal, 21*, 121–143.

National Institute of Child Health and Human Development. (2000). *Report of the National Reading Panel. Teaching children to read: An evidence-based assessment of the scientific research literature on reading and its implications for reading instruction* (NIH Publication No. 00–4769). Washington, DC: Government Printing Office.

Pressley, M. (2002). *Reading instruction that works: The case for balanced teaching* (2nd ed.). New York: Guilford Press.

Sweet, A. P., & Snow, C. E. (Eds.). (2003). *Rethinking reading comprehension*. New York: Guildford Press.

Vacca, R. (1998). Let's not marginalize adolescent literacy. *Journal of Adolescent & Adult Literacy, 41*, 604–609.

Watts, S., & Graves, M. F. (1997). Fostering students' understanding challenging texts. *Middle School Journal, 29*(1), 45–51.

Strategy 16

Questioning the Author (QtA)

Constructing Meaning From the Text

STRATEGY OVERVIEW

Current research supports Questioning the Author (QtA) strategy as a powerful approach to teaching students to read and learn from their content area texts. In their analysis of research on adolescent reading, Torgesen et al. (2007, pp. 17–39) provided recommendations for teaching comprehension. The following two of their recommendations are the basis for the QtA strategy: (1) Provide explicit instruction and supportive practice in the use of effective comprehension strategies throughout the school day. (2) Increase the amount and quality of open sustained discussion of reading content. Using the QtA offers a beneficial strategy that will help students to construct meaning from text through focused discussions on the text that are facilitated by the teacher.

When most students do not understand what they are reading, they believe they lack the appropriate reading skills. However, research cited by Beck, McKeown, Hamilton, and Kucan (1997) reveals that for a number of reasons, textbooks are difficult to comprehend. The failure to understand textbooks is often inherent in the authors' lack of clarity in explaining concepts and issues or their failure to present enough background knowledge for the reader to make appropriate text connections required for understanding. Rather than placing the burden on the reader, students are taught to point to problems within the text itself. The primary purpose of the QtA is to construct meaning from the text. In addition, the strategy develops a disposition within the reader to view authors' writing as imperfect, thus requiring the reader to probe and question the author to clarify the meaning of the text (Beck et al., 1997; Beck & McKeown, 2006). Thus, the QtA offers a process for facilitating students' understanding of the text by teaching them to question the author to clarify the meaning of the text. The major components of the strategy are depicted in Figure 16.1, Components of Questioning the Author (QtA) Strategy.

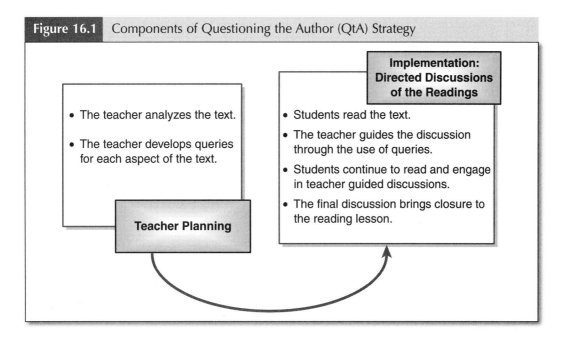

Figure 16.1 Components of Questioning the Author (QtA) Strategy

- The teacher analyzes the text.
- The teacher develops queries for each aspect of the text.

Teacher Planning

Implementation: Directed Discussions of the Readings

- Students read the text.
- The teacher guides the discussion through the use of queries.
- Students continue to read and engage in teacher guided discussions.
- The final discussion brings closure to the reading lesson.

IRA/NCTE Standards for the English Language Arts

1. Students read a wide range of print and nonprint texts to build an understanding of texts, of themselves, and of the cultures of the United States and the world; to acquire new information; to respond to the needs and demands of society and the workplace; and for personal fulfillment. Among these texts are fiction and nonfiction, classic, and contemporary works.

3. Students apply a wide range of strategies to comprehend, interpret, evaluate, and appreciate texts. They draw on their prior experience, their interactions with other readers and writers, their knowledge of word meaning and of other texts, their word identification strategies, and their understanding of textual features (e.g., sound-letter correspondence, sentence structure, context, graphics).

11. Students participate as knowledgeable, reflective, creative, and critical members of a variety of literacy communities.

Source: International Reading Association and National Council of Teachers of English (1996).

STEP-BY-STEP PROCEDURE

The procedure for using the QtA strategy may be understood and implemented through examining its two major components: (1) teacher planning and (2) teacher-led guided discussions.

TEACHER PLANNING

During the planning phase, the teacher prepares instruction by reading the selection from the text, segmenting the text for reading, and developing queries for the discussion.

Step 1: Analyzing the Text

The teacher reads the text from the students' perspectives to anticipate the problems that it will pose to the readers. The teacher asks the following questions when analyzing the text:

- What information does the student need to know to understand the passage?

- What information did the author leave out?

- What terms are introduced by the author that will make the reading difficult to understand?

- What specific aspects of the text need clarification?

After reading and analyzing the text, the teacher segments it into chunks that she believes need clarification for the readers to understand to move on to the next segment of the text. The teacher then prepares for the discussion phase by developing queries that will be posed to the author during students' reading of text.

Step 2: Developing Queries

Queries are a major aspect of the strategy that students will use to construct meaning. They are unlike traditional questions that most teachers use to evaluate students' comprehension after they have read the assigned text. Queries are different. They are used by students during reading to help them construct meaning from the text by asking the author to clarify an ambiguous part of the text. The student knows that oftentimes texts are not written clearly; therefore, they must make sense from what the author has written. The teacher prepares two types of queries for informational text: initiating and follow-up queries. Figure 16.2, Examples of Initiating and Follow-Up Queries, presents two types of queries (Beck et al., 1997, p. 45) that may be applied to a number of texts.

Figure 16.2	Examples of Initiating and Follow-Up Queries
Initiating Queries	*Follow-Up Queries*
• What is the author trying to say here? • What is the author's message? • What is the author talking about?	• What does the author mean here? • Does the author explain it clearly? • Does this make sense with what the author said before? • How does this connect with what the author has told us here? • Does the author tell us why? • Why do you think the author is telling us now?

Implementation

This is the second major component of the QtA strategy. During this phase of the strategy, the teacher directs the students to read a segment of the text and engages them in a discussion where queries are raised about the text for the purpose of helping students to comprehend the text. The teacher models the QtA process by posing queries to get at the author's meaning. Continuing the discussion, the teacher asks students to respond to the queries. When the students' responses to the query show that they have constructed meaning from the text, the teacher will continue the process with another segment of the text. When the students show that the author is not conveying the intended meaning, the teacher poses a follow-up query or provides information for the students to understand the meaning of the text.

To provide structure to the discussion, Beck et al. (1997) have categorized responses, calling them *discussion movers*, made by the teacher as she facilitates the discussion. For example, the teacher may begin by modeling a response to the text using a query to the author. This is called *modeling*. Another example that is offered occurs when the student is having difficulty in stating a response. The teacher restates the student's response for clarity. This is called *revoicing*. The teacher continues to engage students in the discussion about the text through the use of QtA. Discussion movers are further explained in Figure 16.3, QtA Discussion Movers.

Figure 16.3	QtA Discussion Movers

- **Marking:** Teacher's response to student's comments that will highlight an important idea that was made.
- **Turning back:** Teacher's response to student's comment that will require further development of thought and figuring out ideas, or it may turn the student's attention back to the text for further clarification of ideas.
- **Revoicing:** When the student is having difficulty expressing a response, the teacher will restate the comment to help clarify the comment.
- **Modeling:** The teacher models a response to the text or the process of using queries and responses to build meaning from the text.
- **Annotating:** The teacher offers information to fill the gaps that the author left.
- **Recapping:** The teacher summarizes the information that has been constructed by the students as they interacted with the text.

The teacher brings closure to the discussion of the readings by recapping or summarizing the information that students have learned from their readings.

DIFFERENTIATING INSTRUCTION FOR STRIVING READERS

As emphasized in the introduction, the textbook is difficult to understand for most readers. For many striving readers, textbooks are overwhelming. Therefore, when first using the QtA strategy with students reading below grade level, select content rich materials that are written at an appropriate reading level. To further support striving readers, provide more demonstrations of how to pose queries and facilitate their responses. Follow-up queries may be adjusted to the students' responses with the teacher showing students how to go back to the text to get more information or figure out what the author is telling us.

CONSIDERING THE LANGUAGE NEEDS OF ELL STUDENTS

IRA/NCTE Standards for the English Language Arts

10. Students whose first language is not English make use of their first language to develop competency in the English language arts and to develop understanding of content across the curriculum.

Source: International Reading Association and National Council of Teachers of English (1996).

The QtA strategy will help ELL students construct meaning from the texts when they understand the purpose of the strategy. Therefore, the teacher should clearly articulate the process and the purpose for using QtA through modeling, demonstrations, and guidance. Further, begin with text materials that are at the students' readability level, provide the necessary background information to understand the ideas, and whenever possible, use picture story books for young adults that focus on the topic of study.

AN APPLICATION FOR INSTRUCTION AND LEARNING IN THE SOCIAL STUDIES CLASSROOM

Students are reading about World War II from their textbooks. To further develop content in that area, the teacher provides additional readings from literature. To understand the reign of terror that the Nazi regime imposed on the people from the perspective of the young adult, the students read a book *Resistance: Teen Partisans and Resisters Who Fought Nazi Tyranny* by Charles Anflick (1999). The teacher engaged students in reading and discussing this book using the QtA strategy.

The preparation phase began with the teacher's reading the book from the students' perspective and taking into account the students' reading skills as well as their prior knowledge needed for comprehension. The book contains six very short chapters that include photographs. The teacher decided to use the book for one week and integrate the readings into daily lessons to align the supplementary readings with the textbook to further develop the topic of study. Chapter 1 provides the background information for the book and helps the readers understand the terms *Nazis, holocaust, kristallnacht,* and *resistance.*

The teacher began the lesson on World War II with a brief discussion on the assigned textbook readings that was followed by the additional classroom readings from *Resistance: Teen Partisans and Resisters Who Fought Nazi Tyranny.* The teacher segmented Chapter 1 into three parts. For each of the segments, the teacher developed queries that were used to move the discussion and help students to think deeply about the readings for the purpose of constructing meaning. The students read the chapter about Hitler's rise to power and the National Socialist Party, the effects of the passage of the Nuremberg Laws on the lives of the Jewish people, Kristallnacht, and teenagers as resisters to Hitler and the Nazis. After students read each segment, the teacher facilitated the discussion by demonstrating how to construct meaning by questioning the author. For example, after students read the first segment, the teacher began the discussion, "Some of the statements that we have read may not be clear. Let's ask the author what he meant by certain statements and words." The teacher continues, "We need to go back to the book. What did the author mean by the statement 'Nazis deliberately confused them into thinking that perhaps everything would be fine'?" One student responded, "The author describes it later on in the last sentence. He said, 'By hiding this information, the Nazis and their collaborators destroyed millions of people.'" The teacher drew attention to the student's insightful response and continued until the discussion of the first reading segment was complete. She then directed students to continue to read the second segment, reading and discussing the text until they have completed Chapter 1. The teacher emphasized that the text may not be clear, but we can go back to the text and figure out what the author meant. When the student responded, the teacher urged him to confirm his meaning from the text.

Once students learn how to pose queries to the author, they will assume greater responsibility for questioning the author. A more effective approach that the teacher employed was to first use the QtA strategy with large group discussions, modeling and demonstrating how to figure out what the author meant and to use the text to confirm the meaning. When the students are familiar and secure with using the strategy, the teacher moves them to small-group discussions.

REFERENCES

Anflick, C. (1999). *Teen witnesses to the holocaust. Resistance: Teen partisans and resisters who fought Nazi tyranny.* New York: Rosen.

Beck, I. L., & McKeown, M. G. (2006). *Improving comprehension with questioning the author: A fresh and expanded view of a powerful approach.* New York: Scholastic.

Beck, I. L., McKeown, M. G., Hamilton, R. L., & Kucan, L. (1997). *Questioning the author: An approach for enhancing student engagement with text.* Newark, DE: International Reading Association.

International Reading Association and National Council of Teachers of English. (1996). *Standards for the English language arts.* Newark, DE: International Reading Association & Urbana, IL: National Council of Teachers of English.

Torgesen, J. K., Houston, D. D., Roberts, G., Vaught, S., Wexler, J., Francis, D. J., et al. (2007). *Academic literacy instruction for adolescents: A guidance document from the center on instruction.* Portsmouth, NH: RMC Research Corporation, Center on Instruction.

Strategy 17

Text Structure Strategy

Using Graphic Organizers to Learn From Informational Text

STRATEGY OVERVIEW

The purpose of the Text Structure strategy is to provide students with an understanding of the variety of text structures or writing patterns that authors use to convey their ideas. Students' knowledge of text structures may be used for improving their reading, writing, and learning from textbooks as well as other forms of informational text.

Authors use different types of text structures or writing patterns that will best communicate the ideas and concepts they are writing about. In our previous sections, we examined the differences between narrative or fictional text with expository or informational text. One major difference noted is the text structures or writing patterns that are used in each of these text types. When students make a transition from reading fiction to informational texts, the writing patterns or text structures used by authors may affect how they comprehend from text and the information they recall. Therefore, it would benefit readers to know the structures used in their textbooks and other informational books. Teaching students to identify text structures through the use of graphic organizers would further promote their comprehension of text (Vacca et al., 2006) and would allow them to skillfully use text structures in their reading and writing (Harvey & Goudvis, 2000; Stead, 2001).

The five most frequently used writing patterns or text structures in writing informational text are the following: (1) descriptive, (2) sequential, (3) cause/effect, (4) compare/contrast, and (5) problem/solution. To recognize specific types of text structures, skilled readers often use related signal words or phrases. For example, *as a result of, the effects are, because of* are signal words that are typically used with the cause/effect text structure. When skilled readers identify these signal words within the text, they are cued to search for a cause and effect within the text. The definition and list of signal words/phases for each of the five text structures are provided in Figure 17.1, Text Structures, Descriptions, and Signal Words and Phrases.

Research related to teaching students text structure to promote literacy indicates that instruction should include the following: (a) text structure awareness and its importance, (b) how to use text structure while reading, (c) guided and independent practice in the use of text structure, and (d) the application of the strategy to different texts (Dickson, Simmons, & Kameenui, 1998). Further research by Armbruster, Anderson, and Ostertag (1989) emphasizes the importance of the use of graphic organizers or visual representations of the organizational writing patterns or text structure in teaching this strategy.

Figure 17.1 Text Structures, Descriptions, and Signal Words and Phrases

Descriptive	Sequential	Cause/Effect	Compare/Contrast	Problem/Solution
Descriptive text structures provide a full account of people, places, ideas, and events through explanations and descriptions.	Sequential text structures provide a description of events in the order in which they occur.	Cause/effect structures offer an explanation of the cause(s) and the effect(s) of phenomena.	Compare/contrast discusses the similarities and differences between two people, places, events, or issues.	The problem is identified and described along with the description of how it was solved.
Signal Words and Phrases				
the following, for example, such as, to illustrate, furthermore, additionally	first, second, third, next initially . . . finally before . . . after then, to begin with	as a result of, the effects of, because of, consequently, if this . . . then that, therefore	different than, unlike the . . . similar in that, as compared to, opposite from, as opposed to	a solution to the problem, evidence shows that the stated problem, the results are, it was solved by, leading to the solution described below

Figures 17.2 through 17.7 provide frames for each of the five writing patterns used by authors of informational text. For the *cause/effect* text structure, there are two frames, one showing one cause with multiple effects and a second showing multiple causes having a single effect. As students use the graphics, they will become sensitive to the writing patterns within informational text. Using this strategy will help students learn about the text structures, which they can use for reading and writing.

GRAPHIC ORGANIZERS FOR TEXT STRUCTURES FOR INFORMATIONAL TEXT

Figure 17.2 Descriptive Text Structure

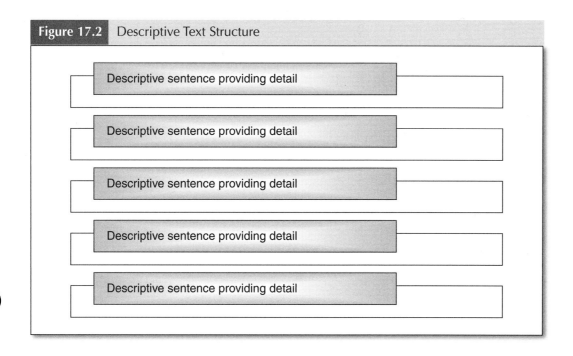

Descriptive sentence providing detail

Descriptive sentence providing detail

Descriptive sentence providing detail

Descriptive sentence providing detail

Descriptive sentence providing detail

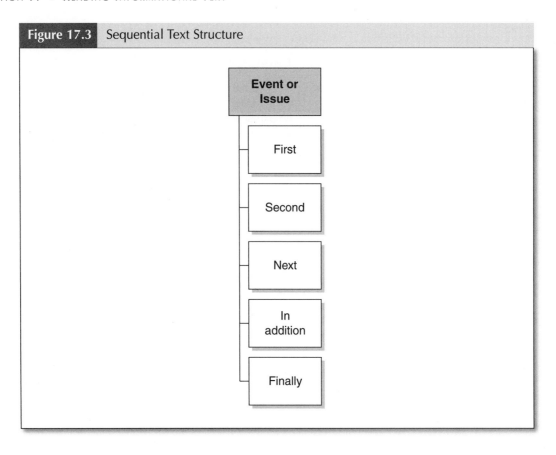

Figure 17.3 Sequential Text Structure

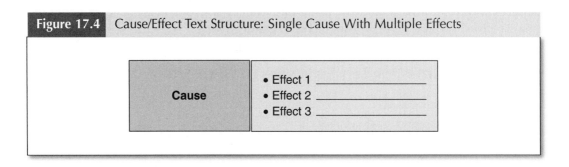

Figure 17.4 Cause/Effect Text Structure: Single Cause With Multiple Effects

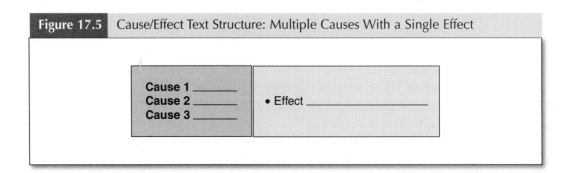

Figure 17.5 Cause/Effect Text Structure: Multiple Causes With a Single Effect

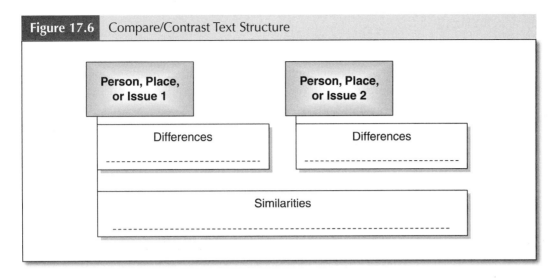

Figure 17.6   Compare/Contrast Text Structure

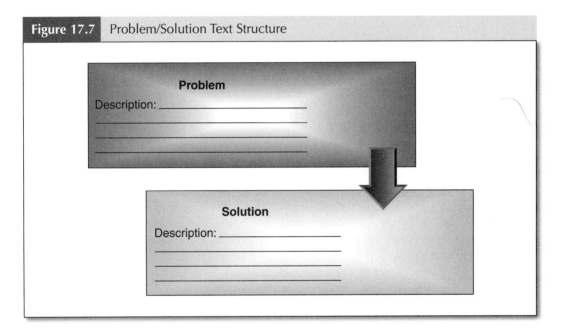

Figure 17.7   Problem/Solution Text Structure

IRA/NCTE Standards for the English Language Arts

3. Students apply a wide range of strategies to comprehend, interpret, evaluate, and appreciate texts. They draw on their prior experience, their interactions with other readers and writers, their knowledge of word meaning and of other texts, their word identification strategies, and their understanding of textual features (e.g., sound-letter correspondence, sentence structure, context, graphics).

5. Students employ a wide range of strategies as they write and use different writing process elements appropriately to communicate with different audiences for a variety of purposes.

Source: International Reading Association and National Council of Teachers of English (1996).

STEP-BY-STEP PROCEDURE

Strategy instruction begins by helping students learn that authors use certain writing patterns to convey specific information. They will learn how to identify and use text structures to understand text, take notes, or organize information for their own writing. During strategy instruction, students are monitored during reading as they take notes from text as well as after reading when they use their notes to summarize information within the text. The teacher provides practice using a wide range of materials to ensure that students have acquired independence in strategy use. Prior to the lesson, the teacher prepares by examining the readings to determine the text structures that are used. When more than one structure is presented in the readings, the teacher decides if teaching the major organizational pattern would be more beneficial to the students. This is especially important in teaching students in middle grades. Teaching two or three structures and comparing them would be an effective approach for those who have stronger literacy skills.

BEFORE READING

The teacher begins this phase of the instruction by using demonstrations and direct instruction on the specific text structure(s) in the readings.

- First provide an explanation of how informational text is written and then offer a brief description of the major types of text structures. For each of the five text structures, present students with the list of signal words, showing how they serve as cues or signals to the reader in understanding and finding certain types of information. Within this introduction, the emphasis is on the importance of knowing about text structures for a better understanding of what one reads.
- Next focus the instruction on the text structure that will be found in the readings. Show the graphic organizer, the description of the text structure, and its accompanying signal words, and provide a thorough explanation of that text structure.
- Using a system such as an electronic whiteboard or Elmo, display an example of the text with the text structure that is being taught.
- Read the text aloud to demonstrate how a reader uses the information about text structure to understand the information within the text. Begin by showing students how the reader previews the text, finds the signal words, identifies the type of text structure or writing pattern, and uses it to understand and classify the information within the text.
- After an examination of the text, demonstrate how the information is organized by writing it in the appropriate area on the graphic organizer.
- Using the completed graphic organizer, model to students how it may be used to write a summary statement of the passage. Modeling this relationship will help students use text structures in writing summaries and organizing their own ideas for informational writing.

DURING READING

This phase of instruction offers students the opportunities for strategy use under the direction of the teacher.

- Assign students the appropriate readings from the text.
- Prior to their reading, direct students to survey the text to determine the text structure. Assist students in determining the text structure by helping them to identify the signal words and preview the text to determine the author's purpose.
- Direct students to read the text and use the appropriate graphic organizer to take notes.

AFTER READING

During this phase of instruction, students receive feedback on working with text structure while reading, note taking, and writing brief summaries of what they read.

- Engage students in a discussion to help clarify meanings from their readings. During the discussion, show students the relationship between the content and the author's organization of the information.

- Offer feedback to students with respect to their use of the graphic organizer for note taking.

- Direct students to use their graphic organizers and their understanding of text structure to write simple summaries that include a main idea and supporting details.

DIFFERENTIATING INSTRUCTION FOR STRIVING READERS

Striving readers may not remember the various types of text structures and their accompanying signal words; they may not know how to identify and use text structure while reading, completing the graphic organizer, and using the completed graphic organizer to write a brief summary. To facilitate striving readers in their use of text structure, employ the checklist presented in Figure 17.8, Checks When Using Text Structure as a reminder of each step in the strategy. Display it as a reminder for all students. Finally, but most importantly, provide ongoing monitoring and guidance of students' strategy use and their application to other texts.

Figure 17.8	Checks When Using Text Structure

☑ Did I preview the text to look for the AUTHOR'S PURPOSE?

☑ Did I preview the text to identify the SIGNAL WORDS?

☑ Did I determine the type of TEXT STRUCTURE from the signal words and information?

☑ Did I select the appropriate GRAPHIC ORGANIZER?

☑ Did I complete the graphic organizer for NOTE TAKING during reading?

☑ Did I use the completed graphic organizer to WRITE A BRIEF SUMMARY?

☑ Did I ASK A FRIEND OR THE TEACHER for assistance when I was confused?

CONSIDERING THE LANGUAGE NEEDS OF ELL STUDENTS

IRA/NCTE Standards for the English Language Arts

10. Students whose first language is not English make use of their first language to develop competency in the English language arts and to develop understanding of content across the curriculum.

Source: International Reading Association and National Council of Teachers of English (1996).

Signal words help students to understand the text structure and aid in overall comprehension and recall of information. Many signal words and phrases are more abstract in nature. English learners find abstract words difficult to comprehend and remember. Words like *additionally, moreover,* and *furthermore,* and phrases like *as a result of* are abstract; for English language learners to use such signals, they need a clear understanding of the meaning and usage of such words.

AN APPLICATION FOR INSTRUCTION AND LEARNING IN THE MUSIC CLASSROOM

Students in 11th-grade music class have learned about the elements of writing songs. Their textbook readings were on the topic "melody form" in which the author first describes the approach many songwriters use: Find the melody and the lyric comes later. The author used a number of descriptive text structures throughout his explanations of the melody form. The teacher introduced the lesson by telling the students they would be reading about the importance of the melody in the composition of the song as well as aspects of the melody.

The teacher prepared the students with a lesson on how authors use various writing patterns to convey ideas, provided graphics for each of the five text structures, defined the text structures and identified their accompanying signal words, and finally, showed how each writing pattern was used in their textbooks by the author. The teacher then focused on the descriptive text structure and presented its graphic organizer along with the signal words. After introducing the students to the readings, the teacher asked them to survey the text for signal words that indicated descriptive writing patterns. When students identified one or two signal words and phrases, the teacher pointed to additional signal words in the text that cued the reader on how the author organized the information. The teacher directed the students to read the assigned passages. After reading, the students used their graphic organizers to take notes from the text. At the conclusion of their reading and note taking, the students used their notes to write a summary of their reading.

REFERENCES

Armbruster, B. B., Anderson, T. H., & Ostertag, J. (1989). Teaching text structure to improve reading and writing. *The Reading Teacher, 43,* 130–137.

Dickson, S. V., Simmons, D. C., & Kameenui, E. J. (1998). Text organization: Research bases. In D. C. Simmons & E. J. Kameenui (Eds.), *What reading research tells us about children with diverse learning needs: Bases and basics* (pp. 239–277). Mahwah, NJ: Lawrence Erlbaum.

Harvey, S., & Goudvis, A. (2000). *Strategies that work: Teaching comprehension to enhance understanding.* York, ME: Stenhouse.

International Reading Association and National Council of Teachers of English. (1996). *Standards for the English language arts.* Newark, DE: International Reading Association & Urbana, IL: National Council of Teachers of English.

Stead, T. (2001). *Is that a fact? Teaching nonfiction writing.* Portland, ME: Stenhouse.

Vacca, J. L., Vacca, R. T., Gove, M. K., Burkey, L. C. Lenhart, L. A., & McKeon, C. A. (2006). *Reading and learning* (6th ed.). Boston: Allyn & Bacon.

Connect to It

Strategy 18

Making Personal, Text, and
World Connections to Text

The purpose of Connect to It strategy is to provide students with an understanding of what they are reading as they work to relate the text to their own lives, to other texts that they have read or heard about, as well as to the world that they know. Thus, students are taught to make connections from the text to themselves, to other texts, and to the world. Proficient readers and writers take advantage of this powerful strategy before, during, and after reading for deepening their understanding of the text. Harvey and Goudvis (2000) have identified the following three types of connections that students make with the text: (1) text-to-self, (2) text-to-text, and (3) text-to-world that are depicted in Figure 18.1, Making Text Connections for Deepening Comprehension.

| Figure 18.1 | Making Text Connections for Deepening Comprehension |

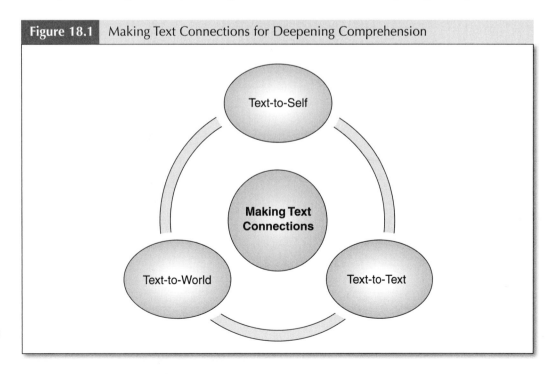

Consider the benefits for students when they learn to connect to the text they are reading. Students become engaged with their readings, as they draw on their personal experiences and use their prior knowledge to connect with the text. For many students, the consequences are rewarding: They learn new information that results in the transformation of their knowledge. According to Cambourne (2002, p. 36), such learning occurs when students take the information, knowledge, or skills and make it their own. Without transformation, learning is shallow and not usable. Thus, the goal of the Connect-to-It strategy leads to transformation of knowledge.

DEFINING TEXT CONNECTIONS

Proficient readers connect to the text without exerting energy; they are mindless of the strategy that they are using in making such connections. To understand the nature of connecting to text, think of your own reading habits and how you reflect on text. You may put yourself into the role of the hero or heroine; you may think about another book that is similar to the one you are reading; or you may compare the event in the text to similar events in the world around you. In doing so, you are making connections to what you are reading. Figure 18.2, Defining Text Connections provides definitions of three types of text connections and examples that skilled readers make.

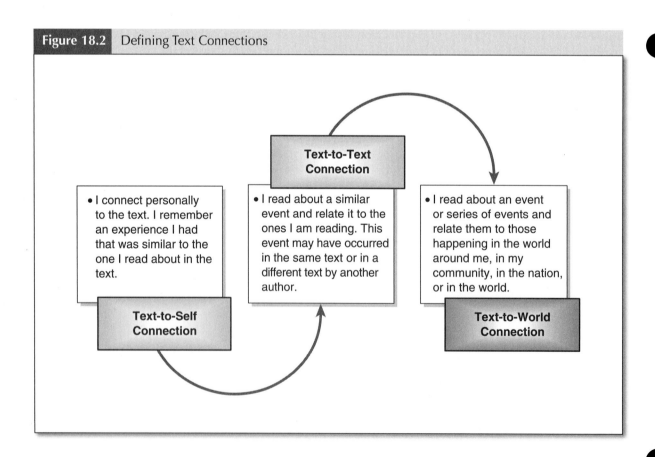

| Figure 18.2 | Defining Text Connections |

Text-to-Text Connection

- I connect personally to the text. I remember an experience I had that was similar to the one I read about in the text.

Text-to-Self Connection

- I read about a similar event and relate it to the ones I am reading. This event may have occurred in the same text or in a different text by another author.

- I read about an event or series of events and relate them to those happening in the world around me, in my community, in the nation, or in the world.

Text-to-World Connection

Source: International Reading Association and National Council of Teachers of English (1996).

> ## IRA/NCTE Standards for the English Language Arts
>
> 1. Students read a wide range of print and nonprint texts to build an understanding of texts, of themselves, and of the cultures of the United States and the world; to acquire new information; to respond to the needs and demands of society and the workplace; and for personal fulfillment. Among these texts are fiction and nonfiction, classic, and contemporary works.
>
> 3. Students apply a wide range of strategies to comprehend, interpret, evaluate, and appreciate texts. They draw on their prior experience, their interactions with other readers and writers, their knowledge of word meaning and of other texts, their word identification strategies, and their understanding of textual features (e.g., sound-letter correspondence, sentence structure, context, graphics).
>
> 12. Students use spoken, written, and visual language to accomplish their own purposes (e.g., for learning, enjoyment, persuasion, and the exchange of information).

STEP-BY-STEP PROCEDURE

In helping students to make connections to the text, the teacher structures the lesson around three phases: before reading, during reading, and after reading, which will provide an opportunity for the students to learn the strategy and think deeper about the text. As the students read, the teacher monitors their strategy use, and they share the range of connections that they made during reading. Each piece of reading differs; therefore, the type of connections that may be made is dependent on the reader and the text. The teacher prepares for the lesson by reading the text and thinking through the connections that may be evoked before, during, and after reading.

BEFORE READING

Within this phase of the reading, the teacher models the important types of connections that they may make while they are reading.

1. Prepare the students for reading by providing them with an introduction to the topic.

2. Engage students in a discussion that focuses on an overview of the chapter, providing students with an understanding of the content that they will read about.

3. Describe the three different ways that readers connect to the information they are reading and emphasize the importance of understanding and remembering what they read.

4. Demonstrate how to connect to the text through similar personal experiences, text events, as well as world events. For example, model a text-to-self connection by reading a paragraph aloud and asking the students to describe the event that was

just read. After focusing on the textual information, ask the students if they remember any such event in their own lives that was similar. Highlight the similarities between the event in the text and the personal experiences.

5. Continue to model each type of connection, text-to-text and text-to-world events. Throughout the discussion, encourage students to make personal, text, and world connections.

DURING READING

The students are ready to read the assigned text independently, during which they will be required to connect with the text.

1. Support students' strategy use by displaying Figure 18.3, Text-to-Self, Text-to-Text, and Text-to-World Connections, as a reminder to connect to the text.

2. Provide students with copies of the graphic to post in their journals and direct them to read a portion of the text, stop at intervals, make a connection, and record it in their journals.

3. As the students read and write in their journals, monitor their strategy use, offering assistance to those readers who may be experiencing difficulty in making connections.

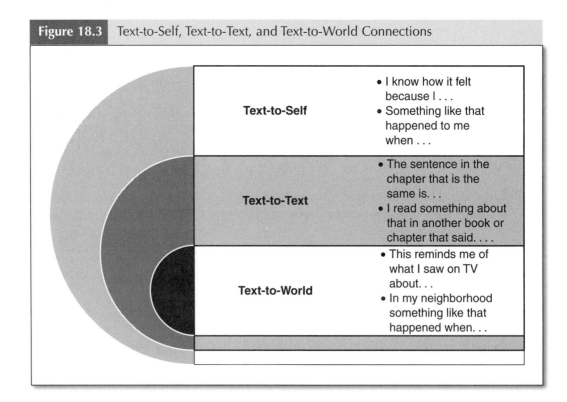

Figure 18.3 Text-to-Self, Text-to-Text, and Text-to-World Connections

Text-to-Self	• I know how it felt because I . . . • Something like that happened to me when . . .
Text-to-Text	• The sentence in the chapter that is the same is. . . • I read something about that in another book or chapter that said. . . .
Text-to-World	• This reminds me of what I saw on TV about. . . • In my neighborhood something like that happened when. . .

AFTER READING

After students have read the assigned readings, they reflect on their journal entries and recall the connections they have made to the text. Students are given time to engage in small-group discussions about the connections they have made. This is an important aspect of instruction that helps students to integrate the information they have read with their own set of related concepts and personal experiences that helped them to connect to the text.

1. Provide time for small-group discussion, encouraging students to compare the connections they have made.

2. Avoid confusion when first introducing this strategy by focusing on one type of connection at a time.

3. Encourage each small group to select two or three connections to share with the class.

DIFFERENTIATING INSTRUCTION FOR STRIVING READERS

Students who have difficulty in comprehending text also experience problems in understanding directions and applying a new strategy. Therefore, make the following modifications for students who have reading problems: (a) Begin with one connection at a time. Because text-to-self is the easiest to understand, use this type of connection to demonstrate how readers connect to the text. (b) In addition to describing and modeling the strategy, use a think-aloud, writing one or two examples of text connections on the chalkboard. (c) Select appropriate reading material, readings that are at students' skill and interest levels. (d) Finally, monitor students' work until they feel secure in using the strategy.

CONSIDERING THE LANGUAGE NEEDS OF ELL STUDENTS

IRA/NCTE Standards for the English Language Arts

10. Students whose first language is not English make use of their first language to develop competency in the English language arts and to develop understanding of content across the curriculum.

Source: International Reading Association and National Council of Teachers of English (1996).

Learning how to make a wide range of connections to the text will deepen students' understanding. This is especially true for ELL students. As teachers, we may not be aware that ELL students may not interpret "connecting to the text" the same way native language learners do. For ELL students to learn and implement the strategy, it is critical for them to understand the concept of *connecting to text*. Therefore, to teach the underlying meaning of the concept, have the students first learn the concept and application in their native language and then use it on their English texts may be very helpful.

An Application for Instruction and Learning in the Mathematics, Science, and Technology Classroom

Students in the 11th-grade math, science, and technology classrooms are learning more advanced concepts in statistics. The purpose of their understanding and using statistics is to be able to apply it to science research projects. The teacher began with a review of the simple concepts of mean, median, mode, range, standard deviation, and regression to the mean. After students read the chapter, the teacher returned to the mathematical concepts so that students could make text connections. Making text connections of the statistical concepts to self, text, and world was especially helpful to students as they applied them to their science research. The teacher began with the concepts of mean, median, and mode and asked the students to make a connection to their personal experiences. Students used the graphic organizer to jot down a few text-to-self connections that included their mean weekly allowance, the average number of hours they watch TV, play video games, talk on the phone, text, and hang out with friends. Students proceeded to search their texts to determine connections within their math textbook as well as in their science books to make a text-to-text connection. The teacher then distributed an article taken from a science magazine that uses statistics within a study on the effects of smoking among teens, adults at work, and the elderly who have smoked or continue to smoke. Students were requested to make world connections to those in the study.

References

Cambourne, B. (2002). Holistic, integrated approaches to reading and the language arts instruction: The constructivist framework of an instructional theory. In A. E. Farstrup & S. J. Samuels (Eds.), *What research has to say about reading comprehension* (p. 36). Newark, DE: International Reading Association.

Harvey, S., & Goudvis, A. (2000). *Strategies that work: Teaching comprehension to enhance understanding.* York, ME: Stenhouse.

International Reading Association and National Council of Teachers of English. (1996). *Standards for the English language arts.* Newark, DE: International Reading Association & Urbana, IL: National Council of Teachers of English.

Quick Writes

Strategy 19

Integrating Language for
Understanding Text

The overall goal of the Quick Write strategy is to facilitate students' understanding of informational text through the use of a set of integrated language activities. Before students read, they briefly write all they know about the topic. Readance, Moore, and Rickelman (2000) suggested that quick writes are effective ways for teachers to assess students' prior knowledge before reading new material. Moore, Moore, Cunningham, and Cunningham (2006) emphasized the importance of writing in the content areas as a way of expanding students' thinking and communication skills about concepts within the discipline. They suggested that the Quick Write strategy is an effective way for teachers to promote thinking and writing about the subject areas. Variations of the strategy have demonstrated the effectiveness when used throughout each phase of reading, especially when discussions of the readings are emphasized as a strategic component of Quick Write strategy.

After the teacher introduces the topic of study, students briefly discuss the central ideas. To activate prior knowledge of the topic before reading, they engage in a 3-minute quick write; they use their quick writes during reading to deepen their knowledge of the topic and correct misconceptions; after reading, students return to their pre-reading quick writes for the purpose of revising them by including the new information on the topic they learned from their readings.

IRA/NCTE Standards for the English Language Arts

3. Students apply a wide range of strategies to comprehend, interpret, evaluate, and appreciate texts. They draw on their prior experience, their interactions with other readers and writers, their knowledge of word meaning and of other texts, their word identification strategies, and their understanding of textual features (e.g., sound-letter correspondence, sentence structure, context, graphics).

11. Students participate as knowledgeable, reflective, creative, and critical members of a variety of literacy communities. Students use spoken, written, and visual language to accomplish their own purposes (e.g., for learning, enjoyment, persuasion, and the exchange of information).

Source: International Reading Association and National Council of Teachers of English (1996).

STEP-BY-STEP PROCEDURE

The teacher prepares for the lesson by designing an introduction to the topic of study and developing probing questions that will be used by students to activate their prior knowledge on the topic. To facilitate the process, the teacher uses the graphic organizer shown in Figure 19.1, Prereading and Postreading Quick Write, by projecting it on the electronic white board or distributing copies to the students.

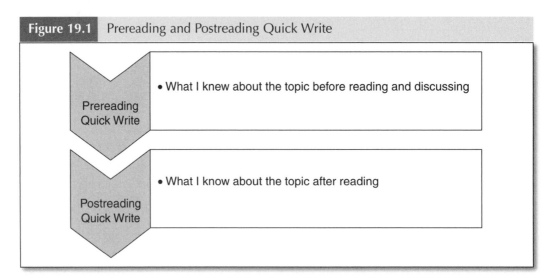

Figure 19.1 Prereading and Postreading Quick Write

Prereading Quick Write
• What I knew about the topic before reading and discussing

Postreading Quick Write
• What I know about the topic after reading

BEFORE READING

The purpose of using the Quick Write strategy prior to reading the text is to help students activate their prior knowledge that is necessary for their comprehension of the readings. Students' quick writes will allow the teacher to assess what students already know and what they need to learn about the topic of study.

1. Provide an overview of the content that will be studied.

2. Help students to activate their prior knowledge through the following:

    a. Ask a probing question related to the readings.

    b. Have students respond to the question through a brief whole-class or small-group discussion.

    c. Direct students to take 3 minutes to write all they know about the topic. The teacher provides a follow-up question that is intended to further jog their minds about knowledge related to their readings.

3. Ask students to share their completed quick writes with the class and use their responses to assess their prior knowledge to help them establish goals for reading the text.

DURING READING

1. After assigning students their readings, direct them to read their quick writes.

2. Encourage students to ask themselves questions as they read to expand their knowledge of the topic.

3. Direct students to use their learning journals to jot down notes and questions as they read.

AFTER READING

1. Provide a few minutes of discussion after reading.

2. Ask students to share with the class the additional information that they learned from their readings about the topic.

3. Direct students to write a summary of the important information on the topic.

4. Have students compare their prereading and postreading quick writes to understand the value of the quick writes.

DIFFERENTIATING INSTRUCTION FOR STRIVING READERS

Striving readers need additional help to understand and use quick writes. Teachers may facilitate their understanding and use of this strategy by doing the following: (1) modeling quick writes and using group quick writes as a way to scaffold the process, (2) working with students to help them identify new information while they are reading, (3) modeling how to develop postreading quick writes that help them to integrate the new information from their notes, and (4) using the group's postreading quick writes to create a group summary.

CONSIDERING THE LANGUAGE NEEDS OF ELL STUDENTS

IRA/NCTE Standards for the English Language Arts

10. Students whose first language is not English make use of their first language to develop competency in the English language arts and to develop understanding of content across the curriculum.

Source: International Reading Association and National Council of Teachers of English (1996).

Many ELL students have content knowledge of the topic but cannot communicate their ideas in oral or written language. Small-group discussion of prior knowledge is crucial as well as the use of the key words in students' native languages and the English language to stimulate the discussion. A teacher-facilitated discussion where background knowledge is built is helpful. Oftentimes, content area texts, such as social studies, science, and art have pictures and graphics with labels to help in the discussion and development of concepts. Once students had the opportunity to participate in a guided discussion, they may engage in a quick write of what they have talked about.

AN APPLICATION FOR INSTRUCTION AND LEARNING IN THE PHYSICAL EDUCATION CLASSROOM

In the 11th-grade physical education class, the students were learning about cardiovascular fitness. The teacher introduced the topic with a brief discussion on the role of physical fitness for people at all ages and physical fitness levels. The emphasis in the discussion was on the wide range of effects of physical activity on a person's well-being. Before reading from the text that focused on establishing a personal wellness profile, defining one's fitness and wellness goals, students participated in a brief discussion on the positive effects of having a personal wellness program. After the small group discussions, students were directed to write for 5 minutes on everything they know related to this topic. As students read about personal wellness programs, they used their learning journals to expand their knowledge and raise questions about areas of interests or a confusing fact or concept. Within the postreading discussion, students shared what they learned in designing a personal wellness profile and setting personal fitness and wellness goals. After their discussion, they returned to their prereading quick writes and their learning logs to help them write a postreading quick write summarizing what they learned from their readings and discussions.

REFERENCES

International Reading Association and National Council of Teachers of English. (1996). *Standards for the English language arts.* Newark, DE: International Reading Association & Urbana, IL: National Council of Teachers of English.

Moore, D. W., Moore, S. A., Cunningham, P. M., & Cunningham, J. W. (2006). *Developing readers and writers in the content areas K–12* (5th ed.). Boston: Allyn & Bacon.

Readance, J. E., Moore, D. W., & Rickelman, R. J. (2000). *Prereading activities for content area reading and learning* (3rd ed.). Newark, DE: International Reading Association.

Inquiry Charts (I-Charts)

Organizing Information for Learning From Texts

Strategy 20

Technology has caused dramatic effects on the world in which we live including how we teach and how students learn. Each day access to information becomes easier. Students are directed to multiple sources of information that may be acquired from one screen. With such a wide range of information from print and electronic texts, there is an emergent potential for knowledge acquisition by all our students; however, organizing the information for learning may be a challenge for most students. The Inquiry Chart (I-Chart) strategy provides a systematic approach to facilitate students in classifying and categorizing abundant amounts of information for learning.

With students having access to multiple sources of data, consider the number of factors that will help them to use the available information wisely. First, a wide range of reading materials will present various viewpoints on a topic to students. Such a variety of perspectives allows for rich conversations among students and results in reading and thinking critically about issues (Blachowicz & Ogle, 2001). The second concern has to do with organizing large amounts of information for learning. Presenting students with an abundance of information on one topic may be overwhelming and confusing. Their use of the I-Chart will prove helpful in organizing information and identifying the most relevant facts they need for learning from their reading.

The I-Chart strategy (Hoffman, 1992) is a data table that assists students in organizing information they retrieved from a wide range of materials. This strategy works well in classrooms where teachers require students to engage in group research using multiple sources of information. Students use a chart that guides them in keeping a record of texts, making reference to their research questions, categorizing information, and synthesizing numerous facts and ideas for report writing. As students begin to think about their topic of study, they also evaluate their own knowledge, develop questions on what kinds of information they need, and identify sources for information gathering. Thus, the main purpose for using the I-Chart strategy is to assist students in developing questions, accessing and organizing information for understanding, and reporting and presenting research findings. The I-Chart strategy works well with informational text but may be adapted for studies of literature as well.

When students are not familiar with the I-Chart strategy, when they are reluctant to engage in research, or when students are in middle school, the teacher may introduce the strategy for conducting a class research project by modeling many of the aspects for using I–Charts effectively.

Source: International Reading Association and National Council of Teachers of English (1996).

IRA/NCTE Standards for the English Language Arts

1. Students read a wide range of print and nonprint texts to build an understanding of texts, of themselves, and of the cultures of the United States and the world; to acquire new information; to respond to the needs and demands of society and the workplace; and for personal fulfillment. Among these texts are fiction and nonfiction, classic, and contemporary works.

2. Students read a wide range of literature from many periods in many genres to build an understanding of the many dimensions (e.g., philosophical, ethical, aesthetic) of human experience.

8. Students use a variety of technological and informational resources (e.g., libraries, databases, computer networks, video) to gather and synthesize information and to create and communicate knowledge.

11. Students participate as knowledgeable, reflective, creative, and critical members of a variety of literacy communities.

STEP-BY-STEP PROCEDURE

There are three stages for the implementation of the I-Chart strategy. Stage 1 includes planning and organizing for inquiry; Stage 2 includes conducting research and sharing information, and Stage 3 includes writing and reporting inquiry findings.

STAGE I: PLANNING AND ORGANIZING

This stage of the strategy consists of teaching the process of inquiry, topic development, crafting appropriate questions for research, and gathering data sources.

Step 1: Introduction

Within the first step, the teacher will introduce the process of inquiry to the students. When students are not familiar with researching a topic using the method of inquiry, the teacher may decide to use a single topic of study for the class. The teacher proceeds to engage the students in a discussion about the topic to help them activate prior knowledge related to the subject being researched. As students actively participate in the discussion, they listen to others and begin to think about what they know. When students have a clear sense of the topic, the teacher begins to define the process of research by describing the steps in using the I-Chart. The students continue to talk about aspects of the topic as they begin to use the I-Chart shown in Figure 20.1, I-Chart Data Table.

Figure 20.1	I-Chart Data Table

Topic for Research:_____

Information Sources	Questions for Research					Interesting Facts
	#1	**#2**	**#3**	**#4**	**New**	
What we know						
Textbook						
Encyclopedia						
Newspaper articles						
Magazine article						
Internet sites & media						
Summary statements						

Step 2: Asking Questions

After the students have shared and recorded what they know about the topic, the teacher elicits questions for research. Well-crafted questions are essential for research, and as teachers know, oftentimes it is the question that is more important than the answer. "Asking engaging and researchable questions leads to effective inquiries. Engaging questions elicit a sense of connectedness" (Moore, Moore, Cunningham, & Cunningham, 2006, p. 246). Therefore, the teacher discusses the question's importance in researching a topic and models writing one or two effective questions. As this phase proceeds, students record their questions at the top of the I-Chart. The teacher may highlight a question demonstrating how it will lead the students on the perfect search for information. After students have completed developing their questions, the teacher discusses how inquiry on a topic will lead to new questions. She then encourages students to continue to ask questions throughout their research project.

Step 3: Identifying Data Sources

Like any research project, identifying the sources of information is critical. The teacher and students work together to find reading materials that address the questions. Sometimes teachers begin with the textbooks because they offer a snapshot of the topic of study. Important materials will include trade books, newspapers, magazine articles, primary sources, Internet sites, media that includes films and music, comics, and people, both experts and those with related information on the topic.

STAGE II: CONDUCTING RESEARCH

During this aspect of the inquiry, students begin to examine the wide variety of sources by looking for information to answer their questions. They read, take notes, and share information with others.

Step 1: Reading and Recording

The teacher begins by reviewing what students already know and helping them to examine their own perspectives on a topic. Students then refocus their efforts on the questions for the purpose of deepening their understanding of the topic and examining their viewpoints. Students are given a time to select and read relevant materials. As they read, students take notes related to the questions and record interesting facts they believe are pertinent to the topic.

Step 2: Sharing

After each reading period, students are given the opportunity to share their findings for their question. Their peers are encouraged to respond by confirming their findings, making connections, or offering a different perspective based on information they have gathered. When students are learning the process of inquiry and how to use the I-Chart for the first time, the teacher may record their findings on a class chart as a model for conducting research and offer feedback to the students to develop and strengthen their skills.

STAGE III: INTEGRATING AND EVALUATING

Stage III is the final stage of the I-Chart strategy. Students conclude their research by (a) summarizing the information gleaned from the variety of data sources, (b) comparing the information that they already knew with the new information from different sources, (c) continuing to research new questions, and (d) reporting information to the group.

Step 1: Summarizing the Information

Students are now faced with notes from sizeable amounts of information. To answer their research questions, they need to synthesize all of their facts and data. The teacher directs students to think about each question, extract the information from their notes that relates to the question being addressed, and write a coherent summary statement that addresses the question. Students are required to think critically in teasing out the appropriate information, and in some cases, evaluating conflicting facts. The final aspect of this step is to have students write their summary statements on the I-Chart. Summarizing information into one or two sentences may be a challenge for middle school students. For younger students, the teacher may need to spend time demonstrating to them how to select relevant information and the main ideas that are needed in writing a summary statement.

Step 2: Comparing

Students examine information from various data sources and compare it to their beliefs or to their preexisting knowledge for the purpose of determining misconceptions they may have had about the topic of study. This aspect of research is very important because it leads to their transformation of knowledge and their understanding of different perspectives on the topic.

Step 3: Continuing Research

As a result of evaluating and analyzing information garnered from research, students develop new questions that will require further research. Students continue the inquiry process to answer these new questions.

Step 4: Reporting Information

This final step of the strategy requires students to report on the information they found. Depending on how the I-Chart strategy is used—with the whole group, small cooperative groups, or with individual students—determines the nature of reporting. For example, the teacher may require that students use I-Charts for an individual research project and develop their own formal written report. In another context, when working as a whole group, individual students may report to the class on a single question using an oral presentation.

DIFFERENTIATING INSTRUCTION FOR STRIVING READERS

Striving readers often have difficulty doing research using multiple texts. Their difficulty may be confounded by addressing more than one question at one time. To help striving readers begin to understand the process of research, differentiate instruction in one or more of the following ways: (a) use a limited number of texts that are rich in content and target students' readability and interest levels, (b) limit the number of questions to one or two, (c) design the I-chart to show the changes in the number of questions and data sources so as to avoid any confusion, and (d) offer ongoing assistance and monitoring during the research process.

Considering the Language Needs of ELL Students

Source: International Reading Association and National Council of Teachers of English (1996).

IRA/NCTE Standards for the English Language Arts

10. Students whose first language is not English make use of their first language to develop competency in the English language arts and to develop understanding of content across the curriculum.

Help students to craft research questions that they will fully understand and will guide them in their research. Work with students in finding the appropriate resources and encourage them to use a range of trade books that are content rich and to use texts that employ contextual language and offer illustrations and diagrams of concepts. Selective Internet sites, media, and picture books may be very beneficial in providing information to students. ELL students need ongoing assistance and guidance in selecting and using materials for researching information. When students demonstrate their lack of understanding of a certain text, try another.

An Application for Instruction and Learning in the Environmental Science Classroom

Students in the sixth grade were beginning a research project in science. Because this was their first time engaging in research, the teacher decided to model the process of conducting research with the class and worked in small groups to answer questions. Beginning with the first stage of the I-Chart strategy, the teacher prepared the students through a discussion of the topic on the "changing environment." She decided to introduce the students to controversies related to environmental issues. She read a newspaper article about the high prices of gasoline that appeared in the local news. Both the students and teacher decided on the topic of "global warming" for their research project. Because of controversies around the topic and the multiple perspectives voiced by scientists, politicians, talk show hosts, and business owners, the teacher believed that the topic would be engaging and helpful to students in viewing issues from different perspectives.

The teacher then introduced the students to the I-Chart as part of the process of organizing research. She began the first steps of the process: (a) establishing the topic, (b) assisting students to craft research questions related to "global warming" that would help them derive enough information on the topic, (c) engaging them in a discussion to activate their prior knowledge, (d) dividing them into groups related to the research questions, and (e) providing source materials for research.

In the next phase of the research project, the students worked in small groups to find information that specifically related to their question. The teacher guided the groups as they were conducting research, reading, recording, and sharing their information. Each student used their I–Chart to help them organize the information they found related to their question. As students read information from various sources, they took notes and wrote them on the I-Chart shown in Figure 20.2, I-Chart for Global Warming: In Progress. When students from each small group felt that they completed their research,

Figure 20.2	I-Chart for Global Warming: In Progress					
	Questions for Research					
Information Sources	#1 How does global warming occur?	#2 Is the threat of global warming real?	#3 How do humans cause global warming?	#4 What are the current and future effects?	New If global warming is real, can it be reversed?	Interesting Facts
What we know	Pollution of the atmosphere.	Some scientists and politicians do not believe it is real, and others do.	Pollution is a main cause of global warming.	Glaciers are shrinking.	We can prevent it by reducing the pollution caused by changing the energy sources we use.	Arctic Sea ice lost its thickness over the recent decades.
Textbook	Releasing so much carbon dioxide into the air is causing global warming.	Global warming has begun because the earth is getting warmer.	Many different types of scientists do not believe that global warming exists.	Certain animals will become extinct because of global warming.	All countries must work together.	SUVs send out 43% more global warming pollution than cars.
Newspaper articles			More forests are being replaced by homes. Few trees mean less CO_2 is removed by photosynthesis.	Ice Ages are bound to happen.	Some scientists and reporters feel that global warming is not real and nature takes care of the earth.	Humans have changed what is in the atmosphere and how the land is used, which is a major cause.
Trade books	Radiation from the earth's core causes global warming.	There are some meteorologists and climatologists who believe in global warming.	Human activity has caused more CO_2 to be released in the atmosphere than can be removed naturally.	Bird populations around the North Sea decreased in 2004 because the sand eels left these warmer waters.	Most scientists agree that people must act immediately to limit the warming effect by a few degrees.	In 300 years the levels of CO_2 have increased, which caused the temperatures to increase as well.

(Continued)

Figure 20.2	(Continued)					
	Questions for Research					
Information Sources	**#1 How does global warming occur?**	**#2 Is the threat of global warming real?**	**#3 How do humans cause global warming?**	**#4 What are the current and future effects?**	**New If global warming is real, can it be reversed?**	*Interesting Facts*
Internet sites & media		Many scientists have conducted experiments and studies to show that there is a threat to the environment from CO_2.	Factories and burning fossil fuels place 65% of the extra CO_2 to be released in the atmosphere.	Shrinking glaciers cause the oceans to get higher.	Some supporters of Kyoto Protocol think that it may help, but it will not solve the problem.	There are many different viewpoints related to whether the Kyoto Protocol can help global warming.
Summary statements		Most people, especially scientists, believe global warming is here and is a threat to the environment.				

they compared the information they had. They were encouraged to present more than one point of view and document ideas with data sources. The information was then integrated in a brief report that answered the group's question. Each small group reported their information to the class.

REFERENCES

Blachowicz, C., & Ogle, D. (2001). *Reading comprehension: Strategies for independent learners*. New York: Guilford Press.

Hoffman, J. V. (1992). Critical reading/thinking across the curriculum: Using I-charts to support learning. *Language Arts, 69*, 121–127.

International Reading Association and National Council of Teachers of English. (1996). *Standards for the English language arts*. Newark, DE: International Reading Association & Urbana, IL: National Council of Teachers of English.

Moore, D. W., Moore, S. A., Cunningham, P. M., & Cunningham, J. W. (2006). *Developing readers and writers in the content areas K–12* (5th ed.). Boston: Allyn & Bacon.

Media and Digital Literacies

Developing Comprehension for Media and Digital Literacies

*In times of change, learners inherit the Earth, while the learned find themselves
beautifully equipped to deal with a world that no longer exists.*

—Eric Hoffer

Today's adolescents use their cell phones to capture as favorite songs on the radio and then browses the Internet to download the song. They surf the Web for information, create their own blog or Web sites, and share videos or other digital imagery with peers. Text messaging is their primary form of communication with their friends, replacing the telephone culture of their parents' generation. Yet when the majority of adolescents enter school, they leave this digital world behind them. Today's adolescent needs 21st-century skills to perform in the workplace and technology provides the context and medium to develop them.

WHAT RESEARCH HAS TO SAY ABOUT THE COMPREHENSION OF MEDIA AND DIGITAL LITERACIES

How does online reading comprehension differ from processing the printed page? Recent research is beginning to shed more light on a process that is not easily visible.

Reading online text is much more complex than processing the printed page and therefore more demanding of the reader. This section provides the research framework for effective comprehension of digital literacies.

21ST-CENTURY LEARNERS

In today's digital world, technology is infused into every aspect of our life whether it be banking, cell phones, games, even grocery shopping. To compete in the global marketplace, it is increasingly apparent that students need to master the skills necessary for this brave new world (Biancarosa & Snow, 2004). Across organizations and nations, today's workplace demands highly skilled workers capable of collaboratively analyzing and synthesizing information on the Web and across modalities to answer complex problems (Leu, Kinzer, Coiro, & Cammack, 2004). To remain employed and lead productive lives in the global marketplace, adolescent learners need to become proficient in 21st-century skills.

So what are the 21st-century skills? Today's learner must become proficient in core subject areas such as language arts, world languages, mathematics, economics, science, geography, history, government, civics, and the arts (International Society for Technology in Education [ISTE], 2008). Technology is the medium for applying knowledge of these core subjects as students tackle complex problems or questions on the Internet or through digital media (Henry, 2006). The core difference between schools preparing students for the digital age as opposed to the industrial age is their approach to knowledge. Schools ready for the digital age recognize that students have to be equipped to deal with the reams of information available on the Web, rather than memorizing facts from a single printed textbook (Collier, 2007; Yancey, 2009).

To successfully search for information on the Web, the adolescent learner needs 21st-century skills to process the myriad information on the Internet and to analyze it critically (International Reading Association, 2009). Skills in such areas as creativity and innovation, critical thinking and problem solving, as well as communication and collaboration are key to unlocking the complex nature of the digital age ISTE, 2007). Yet very few students are equipped to even evaluate the links that appear on a search engine (Barone & Wright, 2008).

Literacy in information and communications technology is the ability to search and evaluate Internet sites, communicate through e-mail or instant messaging, and to use word processing or digital imagery to create meaning (ISTE, 2007). As with printed text, struggling readers are especially challenged by the reams of information they must peruse and the analysis of complex information, which all appear legitimate to them (Henry, 2006). Even more troubling is the continuing digital divide between affluent and poor districts in regard to the integration of technology (Leu et al., 2004). In less affluent districts, the curriculum remains driven by state assessments and therefore adolescent learners have limited instruction in the new literacies. Yet students in affluent districts are acquiring the skills that will enable them to become competitive in the 21st-century marketplace (Barone & Wright, 2008). It is increasingly apparent that comprehension of digital media is now a basic skill such as phonemic awareness that must be addressed across all age groups and reading levels.

NEW LITERACIES

What are the new literacies and how do they differ from traditional views of reading and writing? Across the centuries, literacy has been transformed by society and the tools of the age such as the book or the printing press (O'Brien & Scharber, 2008; Warschauer, 2006). The critical difference today is that change is occurring at such a rapid pace due to new technology (Leu et al., 2004). As our tools such as iPods, digital cameras, or hand-held computers change, how we read and write in multiple media formats is transformed (National Council of Teachers of English, 2008).

At the core of this transformation is the Internet and information communication technology (Leu, 2002). To be proficient in this arena, the learner must have the skills, strategies, and dispositions to adapt to rapidly changing formats, tools, and contexts (Leu et al., 2004). Skills such as identifying questions, locating information, critically analyzing and synthesizing the information to present the answers to others are essential for proficiency in this new domain (Wyatt-Smith & Elkins, 2008). Foundational skills of literacy such as phonemic awareness, vocabulary, and comprehension are the building blocks of fluency in the digital age (Leu et al., 2004). New literacies do not replace these foundational skills, but they are essential to develop the rate and level of reading needed to meet the processing demands of the Internet (O'Brien & Scharber, 2008).

ONLINE READING COMPREHENSION SKILLS

The processing of reading online digital text is radically different from comprehending printed matter (Barone & Wright, 2008; Coiro & Dobler, 2007). To comprehend online text, adolescent learners must engage in an inquiry-based process (Coiro, 2005). They need to be able to pose the right questions, choose a viable search engine, evaluate the results of the search, synthesize and evaluate the findings, and then interpret their results (Mokhitari, Kymes, & Edwards, 2008). If you are a struggling reader with a poor reading rate, the reams of information that you need to skim and interpret become overwhelming (Henry, 2006).

To gain fluency with digital texts, adolescent learners must also be able to decode symbols unique to surfing the Web such as the strategic use of color, icons that are hyperlinked, or interactive maps and graphs (Leu et al., 2004). Another challenge facing learners when they engage in the processing of digital text is deciding which link to follow and evaluating whether information on that site is valid (Coiro & Dobler, 2007). One of the drawbacks of the Internet is that anyone can publish false information. If adolescent readers are unaware of this danger or unable to evaluate sources of information, they will not be able to adequately address complex problems (National Council of Teachers of English, 2008).

As students gauge the value of Web sites or determine an author's stance on the Web, they are developing strategic knowledge, which is critical to reach proficiency in the processing of digital text (Leu et al., 2004). Taking a critical stance when surfing the Web is an essential comprehension skill in determining the value of available information (Coiro, 2005). Yet for many struggling readers, the ability to view text from multiple perspectives or to infer the author's bias is severely hampered by their inability to read accurately and speedily (O'Brien & Scharber, 2008); therefore, the role of the teacher in modeling, guiding, and providing independent practice of these online comprehension skills is as critical as with printed text.

A FRAMEWORK FOR TEACHING COMPREHENSION OF MEDIA AND DIGITAL LITERACIES TO ADOLESCENT LEARNERS

To comprehend digital texts, adolescent learners must be fluent and engage in inquiry-based learning. Struggling readers and writers need explicit models of how to search for information and to evaluate appropriate links. The following suggestions provide the foundation for comprehension of new literacies:

1. Effective comprehension instruction of digital text must use the Internet as a foundational text for guided practice in processing online information (Coiro & Dobler, 2007).

2. Comprehension of digital text is different from processing printed information and demands higher levels of critical thinking and reading speed (O'Brien & Scharber, 2008).

3. To process digital text, adolescent learners need to be able to pose the right questions, choose a viable search engine, evaluate the results of the search, synthesize and evaluate the findings, and then interpret their results (Mokhitari et al., 2008).

4. Explicit instruction in how to pose questions, choose a search engine, summarize and evaluate information is needed to become fluent in the new literacies (Coiro & Dobler, 2007).

5. Adolescent learners need foundational skills such as vocabulary and comprehension as well as the building blocks of the new literacies such as decoding of symbols, strategic use of icons, and comprehension of digital images (Leu et al., 2004).

In this section, "Developing Comprehension of Media and Digital Literacies," five instructional strategies are presented for use in content area classrooms. The strategies are presented as guides for teachers of adolescent learners to adapt and use for their specific discipline and student profile.

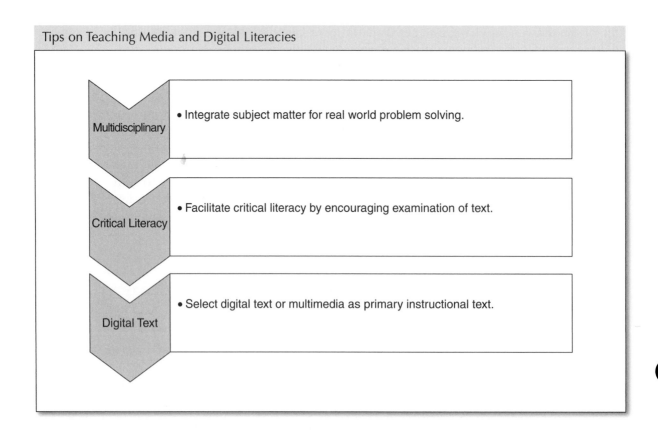

Tips on Teaching Media and Digital Literacies

Multidisciplinary
- Integrate subject matter for real world problem solving.

Critical Literacy
- Facilitate critical literacy by encouraging examination of text.

Digital Text
- Select digital text or multimedia as primary instructional text.

A Strategy for Assessing Comprehension of Digital Text

Educators continue to grapple with definitive ways to assess proficiency in information communication technology. The National Educational Technology Standards (ISTE, 2007) provide teachers across the grades with performance benchmarks that can be modified to fit the technology or instructional context. However, the global educational community has outlined the following essential elements as an assessment framework (UNESCO, 2008):

- Recognize and identify information needed
- Locate and evaluate the quality of information
- Store and retrieve information
- Make effective and ethical use of information
- Apply information to create and communicate knowledge

The performance-based assessment illustrated in Figure V.1, Rubric for Assessment of Comprehension of Media and Digital Texts, is designed to be a portfolio rubric for

Figure V.1	Rubric for Assessment of Comprehension of Media and Digital Texts			
	Advanced	*Target*	*Developing*	*Below Standard*
Content	Content is relevant to purpose. Students have included multiple sources of information. Research is accurate and sources of information are valid. (4 points)	Content is relevant to purpose. Students have included varied sources of information. Research is accurate and sources of information are valid. (3 points)	Content is relevant to purpose. Students have included some sources of information. Research is accurate and sources of information are valid. (2 points)	Content is not relevant to purpose. Students have not included sources of information. Research is inaccurate and sources of information are invalid. (1–0 points)
Technology	Project includes graphics, animation, audio tracks, and at least 5 distinct features (4 points)	Project includes graphics, animation, audio tracks, and at least 3 distinct features (3 points)	Project includes some graphics, animation, audio tracks, and at least 2 distinct features (2 points)	Project does not include graphics, animation, audio tracks, and has no distinct features (1–0 points)
Production	Project is expertly edited for video, audio features and has no errors. (4 points)	Project is edited for video, audio features and has no errors. (3 points)	Project is partially edited for video, audio features and has a few errors. (2 points)	Project is not edited for video, audio features and has multiple errors. (1–0)
Collaboration	Students work expertly to discuss problems and to identify solutions (4 points)	Students work to discuss problems and to identify solutions (3 points)	Students work to discuss some problems and to identify solutions (2 points)	Students do not work to discuss problems nor to identify solutions (1–0 points)
Advanced: (20–14) Target: (13–9) Developing: (8–5) Below Standard: (4–0)				

various projects such as Wikis, podcasts, or multimedia presentations. Teachers can select various elements in the rubric to focus on one type of performance or use it holistically to assess a semester's worth of performances in one particular content area.

REFLECTIVE PRACTICE ON TEACHING DIGITAL AND MEDIA LITERACIES

The new literacies are dialectic in nature and therefore are constantly changing due to technology (Leu, 2002). To shift toward the new paradigm of 21st-century learning, a reflective stance that examines practice and implements changes is vitally necessary. After examining the data from the rubric in V.1, Rubric for Assessment of Comprehension of Media and Digital Texts, the reflective practitioner can analyze which areas adolescent learners need to improve. For example, if they are not using critical thinking, then focused sessions on examining Web sites for factual errors or biases might be needed. To keep current, teachers also need to keep informed about the technology their students are using at home and reflect on ways to bring it into the classroom.

PROFESSIONAL RESOURCES

Brooks-Young, S. (2007). *Digital age literacy for teachers: Applying technology standards to everyday practice.* Washington, DC: International Society for Technology in Education.

Hendron, J. (2008). *RSS feeds for educators: Blogs, newsfeeds, podcasts & wikis in the classroom.* Washington, DC: International Society for Technology in Education.

Richardson, W. (2008). *Blogs, wikis, podcasts, and other powerful web tools for the classroom.* Thousand Oaks, CA: Corwin Press.

Williams, B. (2007). *Educators podcast guide.* Washington, DC: International Society for Technology in Education.

REFERENCES

Barone, D., & Wright, T. (2008). Literacy instruction with digital and media technology. *The Reading Teacher, 62,* 292–302.

Biancarosa, G., & Snow, C. (2004). *Reading next: A vision for action and research in middle and high school literacy.* A report to the Carnegie Corporation of New York. Washington, DC: Alliance for Excellent Education.

Coiro, J. & Dobler, E. (2007). Exploring the online reading comprehension strategies used by sixth grade skilled readers to search and locate information on the internet. *Reading Research Quarterly, 42,* pp. 214–259.

Coiro, J. (2005). Making sense of online text. *Educational Leadership, 62,* pp. 30–37.

Collier, L. (2007). The shift to 21st century literacies. *The Council Chronicle,* pp. 4–8.

Henry, L. A. (2006). SEARCHing for an answer: The critical role of new literacies while reading on the internet. *The Reading Teacher, 59,* 614–627.

International Reading Association. (2009). *New literacies and 21st century technologies: A position statement of the International Reading Association.* Newark, DE: International Reading Association. Retrieved November 23, 2009, from http://www.reading.org/Libraries/Position_Statements_and_Resolutions/ps1067_NewLiteracies21stCentury.sflb.ashx

International Society for Technology in Education. (2007). *National educational technology standards for students* (2nd ed.). Eugene, OR: Author.

International Society for Technology in Education. (2008). *Maximizing the impact: The pivotal role of technology in a 21st century education system.* Retrieved November 21, 2009, from www.iste.org

Leu, D. (2002). The new literacies: Research on reading instruction with the internet. In A. E. Farstrup & S. J. Samuels (Eds.), *What research has to say about reading instruction* (3rd ed., pp. 310–336). Newark, DE: International Reading Association.

Leu, D., Kinzer, C., Coiro, J., & Cammack, D. (2004). Toward a theory of new literacies emerging from the internet and other information and communication technologies. In R. Ruddell & N. Unrau (Eds.), *Theoretical models and processes of reading* (5th ed., pp. 1570–1613). Newark, DE: International Reading Association.

Mokhtari, K., Kymes, A., & Edwards, P. (2008). Assessing the new literacies of online reading comprehension. *The Reading Teacher, 62,* 354–357.

National Council of Teachers of English. (2008). *Definition of 21st century literacies.* Retrieved November 23, 2009, from http://www.ncte.org/library/NCTEFiles/Resources/PolicyResearch/21stCenturyResearchBrief.pdf

O'Brien, D., & Scharber, C. (2008). Digital literacies. *Journal of Adult & Adolescent Literacy, 52,* 66–68.

United Nations Educational, Scientific and Cultural Organization. (2008). *Towards literacy information indicators.* Retrieved November 21, 2009, from http://www.ictliteracy.info/rf.pdf/InfmtnLiteracyIndic.pdf

Warschauer, M. (2006). *Laptops and literacy: Learning in the wireless classroom.* New York: Teacher's College Press.

Wyatt-Smith, C., & Elkins, J. (2008). Multimodal reading comprehension in online environments. In J. Coiro, M. Knobel, C. Lankshear, & D. Leu (Eds.), *Handbook of research on new literacies* (pp. 899–941). New York: Routledge.

Yancey, K. (2009). *Writing in the 21st century.* Retrieved November 21, 2009, from http://www.ncte.org/library/NCTEFiles/Press/Yancey_final.pdf

Strategy
21

Think and Check

Contextualizing and Corroborating Online Information

STRATEGY OVERVIEW

Which site is credible? How do I know that the author is using facts not opinions? Such questions are rarely asked by adolescent learners as they busily cut and paste responses from the Web, lacking the strategies necessary to process digital text (Henry, 2006). Reading on the Internet can be a daunting task for any adolescent learner due to its vast stores of information and hyperlinks (Schmar-Dobler, 2003). Struggling readers especially have difficulties skimming information and analyzing it. Compounding the problem is the accessibility of "malinformation," information that can be harmful, as well as "misinformation," which is false or incomplete information (Kuiper & Volman, 2008).

The *Think and Check* strategy is a collaborative instructional activity where adolescent learners are given guided instruction in how to examine critically and use information on the Internet (Damico & Baildon, 2007). In this activity, students work in pairs to answer research questions, critique sources on the Web, examine evidence, summarize, and interpret it for presentation. The role of the teacher is to model how to corroborate and use information for research across the curriculum. The following step-by-step procedures describe how to implement the Think and Check strategy with adolescent readers.

Source: International Reading Association and National Council of Teachers of English (1996).

IRA/NCTE Standards for the English Language Arts

1. Students read a wide range of print and nonprint texts to build an understanding of texts, of themselves, and of the cultures of the United States and the world; to acquire new information; to respond to the needs and demands of society and the workplace; and for personal fulfillment. Among these texts are fiction and nonfiction, classic, and contemporary works.

2. Students read a wide range of literature from many periods in many genres to build an understanding of the many dimensions (e.g., philosophical, ethical, aesthetic) of human experience.

8. Students use a variety of technological and informational resources (e.g., libraries, databases, computer networks, video) to gather and synthesize information and to create and communicate knowledge.

11. Students participate as knowledgeable, reflective, creative, and critical members of a variety of literacy communities.

STEP-BY-STEP PROCEDURE

BEFORE READING

For students to be skillful investigators on the Web, they must have background knowledge of the topic they are researching. Therefore, this strategy should be done at the mid-point or end of a unit of study. Before students begin this strategy, the teacher should have selected credible sites to begin research on the Web.

1. The teacher leads the class in a brainstorming session on the topic. As students respond with categories and details of information, a concept web is created on the SMART Board or chart paper.

2. Students are put in pairs and asked to formulate a research question related to the topic. For example, were the claims raised by the American colonies valid in the Declaration of Independence?

3. The teacher provides students with a list of starter search engines for the topic and introduces the Think and Check graphic illustrated in Figure 21.1. The teacher uses a think-aloud to model how she knows each site is credible and addresses the points raised on the Think and Check graphic.

Figure 21.1	Think and Check Strategy

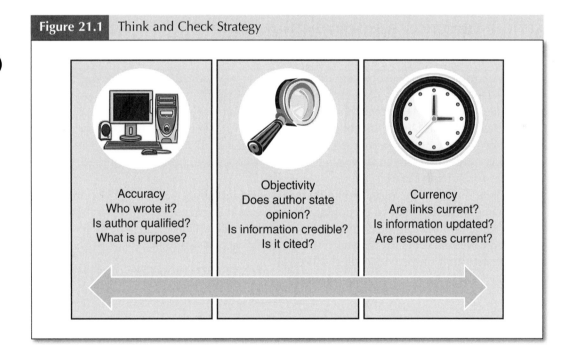

Accuracy
Who wrote it?
Is author qualified?
What is purpose?

Objectivity
Does author state opinion?
Is information credible?
Is it cited?

Currency
Are links current?
Is information updated?
Are resources current?

DURING READING

The following components may take several sessions for the students to complete.

1. Students use the starter search sites provided by the teacher. As one partner surfs the Web, the other records their responses to the prompts on the Think and Check graphic organizer.

2. As they skim information on each site, they bookmark those recorded as credible to provide a list of bookmarked sites with their report. Partners discuss the evidence

on each site and use the hyperlinks to gather more background knowledge on the topic or to address new research questions that may arise as a result of their search.

3. When students discern that they have compiled enough evidence to answer their research question, they use the Think and Check graphic to summarize the information.

AFTER READING

After students have completed their search on the Web, they analyze the information provided in the summary and prepare to present it to their peers.

1. Students decide the format for presenting their response to the research question. They may use audio, media, or digital text to report on their findings. During the presentation, one partner provides the findings of their search while the other student cites the evidence for their work and the credibility of their sources.

2. At the conclusion of the session, the teacher leads a debriefing session, which records strategies students used to discern which sites were credible and to confirm evidence. After everyone has shared their strategies, the teacher compiles the information onto a reference chart entitled "How to Select Web Sites for Research."

DIFFERENTIATING INSTRUCTION FOR STRIVING READERS

Quickly skimming and processing digital text is very difficult for striving readers (Schmar-Dobler, 2003). As with their reading of the printed page, striving readers lack the strategies to surf the Internet and to cope with unknown vocabulary or passages they do not comprehend. Due to its collaborative nature, the Think and Check instructional activity provides a built-in support in that the striving reader is paired with a more fluent reader. However, to improve and become independent, the striving reader needs strategies for surfing the Net.

Teachers may intervene by providing an explicit modeling session for striving readers by using a think-aloud to demonstrate strategies for when they do not know words or lack adequate background knowledge to process digital text. Striving readers may also need bookmarked sites that use videos and imagery to supplement text to comprehend the information provided on the Web site.

CONSIDERING THE LANGUAGE NEEDS OF ELL STUDENTS

Source: International Reading Association and National Council of Teachers of English (1996).

IRA/NCTE Standards for the English Language Arts

10. Students whose first language is not English make use of their first language to develop competency in the English language arts and to develop understanding of content across the curriculum.

Similar to striving readers, English language learners need additional layers of support with the processing of digital text. Several Web sites exist that provide translations of the English language into myriad languages from around the world. These sites should be bookmarked for English language learners so that when they come across unknown vocabulary words, they can translate them into their native language. English language learners will also need bookmarked sites that include e-books or audio books. When English language learners are provided these supplemental tools, they are more willing to participate in the instructional activity and will successfully complete it.

AN APPLICATION FOR INSTRUCTION AND LEARNING IN THE SOCIAL STUDIES CLASSROOM

Ninth graders have just completed a unit on the Great Depression. Their teacher begins the culminating activity of the unit by showing the class the Library of Congress Web site and its available links. Using Figure 21.1, the teacher demonstrates through a think-aloud how she knows the site is credible, examines the information on the site for bias, and discusses new vocabulary words. After the demonstration, the students are paired to develop their own research question regarding the Great Depression. One pair of students chooses to research, "Was it possible to prevent the Great Depression?" The students use their Think and Check sheet (Figure 21.1) to record their work and evidence. After the second class session of research, the students decide to present their information in a news show format with video clips. When students complete the presentation, the teacher facilitates a discussion on which sites were the most used and credible on the Great Depression. Students also comment on problems they encountered while gathering information for the presentation and how they resolved them. The teacher compiles the strategies students used while they were surfing the Internet, and then she posts them on a reference chart for future use.

REFERENCES

Damico, J., & Baildon, M. (2007). Examining ways readers engage with web sites during think-aloud sessions. *Journal of Adolescent and Adult Literacy, 51,* 254–263.

Henry, L. A. (2006). SEARCHing for an answer: The critical role of new literacies while reading on the internet. *The Reading Teacher, 59,* 614–627.

International Reading Association and National Council of Teachers of English. (1996). *Standards for the English language arts.* Newark, DE: International Reading Association & Urbana, IL: National Council of Teachers of English.

Kuiper, E., & Volman, M. (2008). The web as a source of information for students in K–12 education. In J. Coiro, M. Knobel, C. Lankshear, & D. Leu (Eds.), *Handbooks of research on new literacies* (pp. 241–267). New York: Routledge.

Schmar-Dobler, E. (2003). Reading on the internet: The link between literacy and technology. *Journal of Adolescent and Adult Literacy, 47,* 80–86.

Strategy 22

Digital Storytelling

Creating Digital Text

STRATEGY OVERVIEW

Across the centuries one constant has been humankind's desire to tell a story and enthrall an audience. As our tools have changed, the medium for transmitting our stories has varied starting with primarily oral means to staged theatrics, radio/television broadcasts, and now the Internet. The potential audience for today's narratives is global, and adolescent learners can receive feedback on their work from peers in other countries. Adolescents use YouTube and social networking sites to create their multimedia productions, which may be original or based on plots from books, movies, or favorite television shows.

Digital Storytelling uses multimedia to engage the adolescent learner in reading and writing for authentic purposes (Kajder & Swenson, 2004). The visual nature of the instructional strategy enables struggling readers to gain competency in intermediality (Collier, 2007). As they combine visual imagery, audio tracks, digital texts, and graphics, the blending of various media outlets motivates and engages the struggling adolescent reader in ways never before seen with the printed page (Coiro, 2003; McKenna, Reinking, Labbo, & Kieffer, 1999).

Source: International Reading Association and National Council of Teachers of English (1996).

> ### IRA/NCTE Standards for the English Language Arts
>
> 4. Students adjust their use of spoken, written, and visual language (e.g., conventions, style, vocabulary) to communicate effectively with a variety of audiences and for different purposes.
>
> 5. Students employ a wide range of strategies as they write and use different writing process elements appropriately to communicate with different audiences for a variety of purposes.
>
> 6. Students apply knowledge of language structure, language conventions (e.g., spelling and punctuation), media techniques, figurative language, and genre to create, critique, and discuss print and nonprint texts.

STEP-BY-STEP PROCEDURE

This strategy takes place over several class sessions for approximately 2 weeks and can be adapted for schools with very little digital equipment. It is important that students understand that digital stories must be 80% content and only 20% video/sound effects to meet the assignment requirements (Kajder, 2006).

PREPARATION

The session begins with the teacher asking students, "What makes a great story?" The teacher records the characteristics of great stories and then asks students to recall family stories about favorite or quirky relatives.

1. Students are put into pairs and asked to discuss the stories they recalled about a favorite or quirky relative.

2. With their partner, students record their storyline on the graphic shown in Figure 22.1. Partners compare the basic plotline with the characteristics of great stories, which they brainstormed earlier. If necessary, partners supplement the plot with fictional events or characters to make the story more interesting.

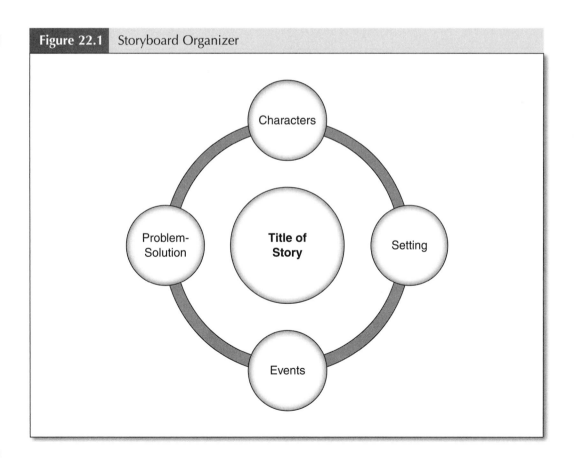

Figure 22.1   Storyboard Organizer

Characters

Problem-Solution

Title of Story

Setting

Events

CREATION

The teacher directs students to search their photo albums at home and bring in key photos to class.

1. Students use a storyboard to map out their story and write the narrative under each box. Partners critique one another's work and offer suggestions to improve the plot.

2. With their partners, they analyze the photos they brought from home and decide where to place them on their storyboard. Before the end of the class session, students must decide what other images are needed to supplement the family photos.

3. Students are given a digital camera if they already do not own one to use for homework. Their assignment is to take the supplemental images for their storyboard with the digital camera.

4. When students have compiled their digital photos, they return to the storyboard and decide if the narrative under each image needs revisions.

PRODUCTION

Partners use iMovie software to create their digital family narrative. If this is not available, students may use whatever is available to them such as PowerPoint or YouTube.

1. After students have scanned their family photos and uploaded digital images, they create an audio track with the story's narration. Students may choose to add a second track of background music.

2. When the digital stories are completed, students upload them to the class homepage for peers to critique and to offer feedback. The teacher may also lead students in a discussion on the different processes involved with digital storytelling as compared with written narratives.

DIFFERENTIATING INSTRUCTION FOR STRIVING READERS

Many striving readers are creating blogs on their home computers, writing alternate plots for their favorite books or movies on fanfiction sites for their peers, or illustrating their own graphic knowledge. Yet they separate these authentic ways of reading and writing from academic literacy and do not perceive themselves as successful readers or writers (Kajder, 2006). Digital storytelling allows them to use these same skills in the classroom. A modification for striving readers may be for them to create a personal narrative about a problem or critical event in their lives. Writing about their own stories is self-motivating and will increase engagement in the task (Kajder, 2006). Striving readers then use digital images to represent the feelings or thoughts evoked by their personal narratives. Due to the personal nature of their work, students may choose whether to upload them on the class Web site.

CONSIDERING THE LANGUAGE NEEDS OF ELL STUDENTS

Source: International Reading Association and National Council of Teachers of English (1996).

IRA/NCTE Standards for the English Language Arts

10. Students whose first language is not English make use of their first language to develop competency in the English language arts and to develop understanding of content across the curriculum.

According to research, the ability to visualize as students read and to use those images to process text is a critical comprehension skill (Keene & Zimmermann, 2007). Imagery enables English language learners to draw on their background knowledge to comprehend new vocabulary words or concepts. Digital storytelling is a unique strategy in that its primary medium is visual. As with striving readers, when English language learners are asked to tell their own personal narratives, they are able to organize content, construct meaning, and process text (Kajder, 2006). Since English language learners in the majority of American middle and high school classrooms have varying levels of fluency in their second language, they will need a partner to help them construct the accompanying narrative to their digital story. Software programs such as *Translate It!* offer translations of common words into English, and English language learners may prefer this option to increase their independence and to protect their privacy.

AN APPLICATION FOR INSTRUCTION AND LEARNING IN THE BIOLOGY CLASSROOM

Monday morning in a 10th-grade Biology classroom, the students are completing a unit on the history of science and have studied famous scientists with a focus on women and minorities. The teacher explains that the culminating project will be to create a digital narrative of one of the scientists they studied. To provide a model, the teacher shows a short 10-minute clip from Ken Burns' Civil War documentary and explains that this is a more elaborate version of what each group will accomplish. The class discusses how Ken Burns used photographs, images of documents, and music from the time to tell the story of the Civil War.

Students are then placed in groups of three and are given the name of the scientist they will research. Bob's group begins to use search engines on the Web to research Marie Curie and to bookmark favorite sites with digital photographs of her life. One of the students in the group finds a site dedicated to Marie Curie, which contains digital images of some of her journals and documents. After several research sessions, group members gather to begin storyboarding their digital narrative about Marie Curie. Students decide to present the narrative in a chronological fashion and begin the story with her birth and family members. To create the storyboard, group members synthesize their information and collaborate on which key images or information should be included. Once the storyboard is complete, group members are asked to use their digital cameras to capture supplementary images, which will tell the story of Marie Curie's life. The group convenes for several more sessions to upload the images, create an audio commentary, and provide background music. Before uploading the digital narrative to the class Web site, the group edits the video and ensures that it has enough content information to satisfy the assignment requirements.

REFERENCES

Coiro, J. (2003). Reading comprehension on the internet: Expanding our understanding of reading to encompass the new literacies. *The Reading Teacher, 56,* 458–465.

Collier, L. (2007). The shift to 21st century literacies. *The Council Chronicle,* pp. 4–8.

International Reading Association and National Council of Teachers of English. (1996). *Standards for the English language arts.* Newark, DE: International Reading Association & Urbana, IL: National Council of Teachers of English.

Kajder, S. (2006). *Bringing the outside in: Visual ways to engage reluctant readers.* Portland, ME: Stenhouse.

Kajder, S., & Swenson, J. (2004). Digital images in the language arts classroom. *Learning and Leading with Technology, 31,* 42–46.

Keene, E., & Zimmermann, S. (2007). *Mosaic of thought* (2nd ed.). Portsmouth, NH: Heinemann.

McKenna, M., Reinking, D., Labbo, L., & Kieffer, R. (1999). The electronic transformation of literacy and its implications for the struggling reader. *Reading and Writing Quarterly, 15,* 111–126.

Strategy

23

Wikibooks

Collaborative Research Projects

The Internet is providing myriad ways for adolescent learners to work collaboratively on projects known as wikis. The basic concept of a Wiki is that any registered user on the site may edit the collaborative text and contribute their point of information as illustrated on Wikipedia, one of the most famous social network sites (Goodwin-Jones, 2003). As individuals or groups share their knowledge on Wiki sites, they are socially constructing a repository of information on a scale never foreseen by Vygotsky, the social constructivist (Ferdig & Trammell, 2004).

Today's millennial learner represents a generation that has been exposed to reams of information presented from multiple perspectives at the touch of a computer mouse (Kajder, 2006). Yet many are struggling to process the vast array of facts at their fingertips and need instruction in summarizing, analyzing, and critiquing digital text. Wikis provide adolescent learners with a collaborative project to research any topic and to create an online community that constructs knowledge together for a global audience (Goodwin-Jones, 2003).

IRA/NCTE Standards for the English Language Arts

1. Students read a wide range of print and nonprint texts to build an understanding of texts, of themselves, and of the cultures of the United States and the world; to acquire new information; to respond to the needs and demands of society and the workplace; and for personal fulfillment. Among these texts are fiction and nonfiction, classic, and contemporary works.

2. Students read a wide range of literature from many periods in many genres to build an understanding of the many dimensions (e.g., philosophical, ethical, aesthetic) of human experience.

8. Students use a variety of technological and informational resources (e.g., libraries, databases, computer networks, video) to gather and synthesize information and to create and communicate knowledge.

11. Students participate as knowledgeable, reflective, creative, and critical members of a variety of literacy communities.

Source: International Reading Association and National Council of Teachers of English (1996).

Step-by-Step Procedure

Wikibooks provide adolescent readers with a collaborative online project that entails critical thinking, creativity, and collaboration. The purpose of the strategy is to facilitate adolescent learner's summarization, analysis, and critique of digital text on a focus topic. The teacher acts as facilitator, providing core bookmarks and points of clarification.

Before Writing

Before the session, the teacher leads a discussion on the novel the class has just finished, such as *Pride and Prejudice*. The teacher shows the students examples of versions of the same plot in movies such as *Bridget Jones' Diary* and explains that they will create a Wikibook on their retelling of the classic.

1. The teacher leads a brainstorming session using the possible variations of the novel:
   - Setting the novel in a different time period
   - Presenting the story in another country or culture
   - Changing the ending or key event in the plot
2. The teacher shows the class a video on YouTube, which describes how Wikis work, and the students also discuss their knowledge of Wikipedia.
3. Students are placed in groups of three to begin to discuss their version of *Pride and Prejudice*.

During Writing

The teacher provides each group with the story map illustrated in Figure 22.1,

1. Students map out their plot and discuss the characters, setting, and key events in their version and how they differ from the classic by Jane Austen.
2. When they are finished drafting their story map, the leader of the group begins the Wikibook by entering the first chapter or section. The teacher decides the length that each student will contribute as it may vary according to ability level.
3. Each group member takes a turn contributing to the Wikibook and elaborates on past posts if necessary.

After Writing

When the group has entered the basic framework of their story, they return to the story map to ascertain if the story on the Wiki adhered to the original plot.

1. Students collaborate to edit their Wikibook and to make revisions to the plot, setting, or characters.
2. Students may choose to include background music, imagery, or audio tracks to supplement their text.

3. Wikibooks can be used across the content areas such as science, social studies, the arts, or mathematics. The teacher may choose a core topic to research or a focus question to explore. Adolescent learners of varying technological skills can quickly grasp the basic procedures for creating a Wikibook or site.

DIFFERENTIATING INSTRUCTION FOR STRIVING READERS

Striving readers are often constricted by their limited prior knowledge on a topic. One of the benefits of using a Wiki to apply a concept or skill is the social construction of knowledge (Ferdig & Trammell, 2004). As striving readers read the comments of their peers on a topic or see their video contribution, they are assimilating this information into their own knowledge base. To increase student learning, striving readers may also be paired with more advanced readers to contribute to the Wiki assignment.

CONSIDERING THE LANGUAGE NEEDS OF ELL STUDENTS

IRA/NCTE Standards for the English Language Arts

10. Students whose first language is not English make use of their first language to develop competency in the English language arts and to develop understanding of content across the curriculum.

Source: International Reading Association and National Council of Teachers of English (1996).

Visualization is a critical skill for English language learners and striving readers (Keene & Zimmermann, 2007). To complete an assignment on the altering of a plot such as *Pride and Prejudice* or to contribute to a discussion on academic content, English language learners may need to see a movie adaptation of the novel or a documentary on the topic. Once English language learners are able to visualize the plot or the academic topic, their comprehension and engagement in the task increases considerably.

AN APPLICATION FOR INSTRUCTION AND LEARNING IN THE GEOMETRY CLASSROOM

Seniors are busy working in pairs at their computers in geometry class. They are all logged onto different Wiki pages that have been uploaded by their teacher onto a Wiki site. The teacher has several pairs working on the same theorem. Brian's group has logged onto the Wiki site and is busily discussing and checking the work posted by another group. All of the groups are working on Theorem 2: *The straight line that bisects the vertex angle of an isosceles triangle is the perpendicular bisector of the base.* After all of the groups have posted their proofs on the Wiki site, the teacher gives them access to look at one another's pages to compare responses. Students discuss discrepancies and comment on each other's proofs.

REFERENCES

Ferdig, R., & Trammell, K. (2004). Content delivery in the blogsphere. *The Journal Online: Technological Horizons in Education.* Retrieved November 23, 2009, from http://defiant.corban.edu/jjohnson/Pages/Teaching/BloggingBlogosphere.pdf

Goodwin-Jones, R. (2003). Blogs and wikis: Environments for online collaboration. *Language, Learning, & Technology, 7,* 12–16.

International Reading Association and National Council of Teachers of English. (1996). *Standards for the English language arts.* Newark, DE: International Reading Association & Urbana, IL: National Council of Teachers of English.

Kajder, S. (2006). *Bringing the outside in: Visual ways to engage reluctant readers.* Portland, ME: Stenhouse.

Keene, E., & Zimmermann, S. (2007). *Mosaic of thought* (2nd ed.). Portsmouth, NH: Heinemann.

Strategy 24

Podcasting

Merging Media for Understanding

Many adolescents today leave disparate literacy lives, often leaving the digital world behind when they enter the classroom (Vasudevan, 2006/2007). Multimodal text allows learners of all ages to create, collaborate, problem solve, and think critically as they engage in 21st-century learning. Podcasting has been gaining momentum since 2005 as an exciting new multimodal medium for adolescent learning as it enables adolescent learners to engage in global discourse (King & Gura, 2007; Richardson, 2009; Rozema, 2007).

A podcast is an audio file that is broadcast on the Internet and distributed via a Really Simple Syndication (RSS; King & Gura, 2007, p. 8). Podcasts can be individual episodes, or they can be a series of a show or regular radio broadcast (King & Gura, 2007; Trier, 2007). Podcast users enjoy its time-shifting aspect as episodes can be enjoyed at any time as the user downloads the file onto their MP3 player (Trier, 2007). In addition, the RSS feed enables a global audience to respond to the content of the podcast and to offer feedback to its authors (King & Gura, 2007). Podcasts also cross disciplinary lines so adolescent learners can create audio files on an array of topics and formats (Thompson, 2008).

IRA/NCTE Standards for the English Language Arts

1. Students read a wide range of print and nonprint texts to build an understanding of texts, of themselves, and of the cultures of the United States and the world; to acquire new information; to respond to the needs and demands of society and the workplace; and for personal fulfillment. Among these texts are fiction and nonfiction, classic, and contemporary works.

2. Students read a wide range of literature from many periods in many genres to build an understanding of the many dimensions (e.g., philosophical, ethical, aesthetic) of human experience.

8. Students use a variety of technological and informational resources (e.g., libraries, databases, computer networks, video) to gather and synthesize information and to create and communicate knowledge.

11. Students participate as knowledgeable, reflective, creative, and critical members of a variety of literacy communities.

Source: International Reading Association and National Council of Teachers of English (1996).

STEP-BY-STEP PROCEDURE

To implement the strategy, the classroom will need a desktop microphone, laptop, and software for making graphic wave audio patterns (King & Gura, 2007). This strategy is designed to be implemented over the course of a week or longer depending on the skill levels of the students.

COLLABORATING

The teacher begins the session by asking students if they have ever downloaded and listened to a podcast. After sharing a few responses, the teacher allows the students to listen to a podcast about the bicentennial of Lincoln's birth. The students will be researching content for a podcast entitled, "The Land of Lincoln Today," which will explore his legacy and impact on America in our time. Each team will be given a different episode of the podcast to create.

Before assembling into teams, the teacher assigns the following roles:

- *Fact checker:* proofs all aspects of the script for accuracy

- *Mediator:* resolves any disputes that may arise

- *Editor:* corrects the script for grammatical/style errors

- *Writer:* prepares the final script for broadcasting

CREATING AND PROBLEM SOLVING

After students have been assigned to teams, they begin to research the content for their podcast. The teacher has provided each team with a list of bookmarks to begin their search on Lincoln's legacy.

1. Students brainstorm subtopics of their episode "The Impact of Emancipation" and are assigned one to research.

2. After completing their search for information on the subtopic, students convene to share notes and to discuss the major points they wish to include using Figure 24.1 to plot their broadcast.

3. When the team has reached consensus regarding the salient points to include, team members prepare scripts for their subtopics, which will be broadcast. The editor and fact checker will examine each script for accuracy and grammatical/style issues. Team members may be asked to research additional information or to revise their script as this is a cyclical process.

4. After the final script has been approved, the team rehearses the podcast and saves it as a draft file for the teacher to approve. When the team is given permission to upload the file, the podcast is sent for distribution on the Internet.

| Figure 24.1 | Preparation Guide for Podcasting |

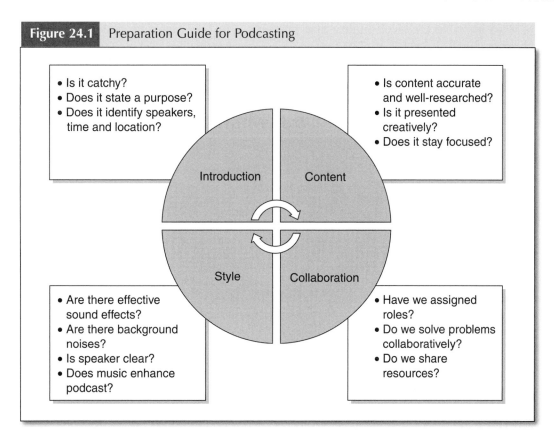

- Is it catchy?
- Does it state a purpose?
- Does it identify speakers, time and location?

Introduction

- Is content accurate and well-researched?
- Is it presented creatively?
- Does it stay focused?

Content

Style

- Are there effective sound effects?
- Are there background noises?
- Is speaker clear?
- Does music enhance podcast?

Collaboration

- Have we assigned roles?
- Do we solve problems collaboratively?
- Do we share resources?

CRITICAL THINKING

Almost immediately after uploading their podcast, the team will begin to receive feedback regarding the content of their broadcast.

1. A week after uploading their podcast, the team selects questions regarding content or critical feedback on the broadcast.

2. Students write a response to their subscribers' feedback and prepare a reflection to share with the class on what they learned regarding the process of creating a podcast.

DIFFERENTIATING INSTRUCTION FOR STRIVING READERS

Podcasting provides striving readers with a wonderful tool to increase their conceptual knowledge base and to engage in classroom discussions (Richardson, 2009). Due to the vast array of free podcasts available on sites such as iTunes, teachers can download broadcasts of discussions on topics across the disciplines. Striving readers are able to listen to the podcasts on topics such as President Lincoln and increase their knowledge base to improve their vocabulary and participate in classroom discussions (Franz & Hopper, 2007).

CONSIDERING THE LANGUAGE NEEDS OF ELL STUDENTS

Source: International Reading Association and National Council of Teachers of English (1996).

IRA/NCTE Standards for the English Language Arts

10. Students whose first language is not English make use of their first language to develop competency in the English language arts and to develop understanding of content across the curriculum.

Teachers of English language learners have been excited for several years about the myriad uses of podcasting for their students. Several Web sites provide podcasts with differing levels of fluency with English for students to download and practice on their own time (Stanley, 2008). In addition, the collaborative nature of creating a podcast enables English language learners to learn from their more fluent peers and to use multiple sources of information such as videos on the Internet to search for information. Adolescent English language learners are often embarrassed to converse with their peers if their fluency is limited. Since team members rehearse their scripts several times before podcasts are finalized, English language learners are given the opportunity to master their speaking skills at home or outside of the class period.

AN APPLICATION FOR INSTRUCTION AND LEARNING IN THE MUSIC CLASSROOM

Tenth graders have completed their study of modern American composers. As a final assignment, they are placed in groups and are asked to create a podcast on a selected composer such as Leonard Bernstein and his impact on modern music. Students brainstorm ideas related to their composer and then assign subtopics for individual research such as biographical information and early influences. After students have completed their research on the American composer, the fact checker and mediator lead the discussion of the group's results. Students are asked to write a script for their component, which is edited and then rehearsed. The group decides on audio tracks to supplement their broadcast and then they record and save it for the teacher's review. After all the podcasts have been uploaded to the class Web site, students critique one another's work and rank them for information, presentation, and professionalism.

REFERENCES

Franz, D., & Hopper, P. (2007). Is there room in math reform for preservice teachers to use reading strategies? National Implications. *National Forum of Teacher Education Journal, 17,* 1–9.

International Reading Association and National Council of Teachers of English. (1996). *Standards for the English language arts.* Newark, DE: International Reading Association & Urbana, IL: National Council of Teachers of English.

King, K., & Gura, M. (2007). *Podcasting for teachers: Using a new technology to revolutionize teaching and learning.* New York: Information Age.

Richardson, W. (2009). *Blogs, Wikis, Podcasts, and other powerful web tools for the classroom* (2nd ed.). Thousand Oaks, CA: Corwin Press.

Rozema, R. (2007). The book report, version 2.0: Podcasting on young adult novels. *English Journal, 97*(1), 31–37.

Stanley, G. (2008). Podcasting: Audio on the internet comes of age. *Teaching English as a Second or Foreign Language Journal: The Electronic Journal for English as a Second Language.* Retrieved November 29, 2009, from http: www.tesl-ej.org/wordpress/past-issues/volume9/ej36/ej36int/

Thompson, M. (2008). Multimodal teaching and learning: Creating spaces for content teaching. *Journal of Adolescent and Adult Literacy, 52,* 144–153.

Trier, J. (2007). "Cool" engagements with YouTube: Part I. *Journal of Adolescent and Adult Literacy, 50,* 408–413.

Vasudevan, L. (2006/2007). Looking for angels: Knowing adolescents by engaging their multimodal literacy practices. *Journal of Adolescent & Adult Literacy, 50,* 252–257.

Strategy
25

Book Trailers

Insights and Discoveries About Texts

STRATEGY OVERVIEW

Reluctant and struggling adolescent readers view the printed text with dread. Yet the same learners are often *mediacentric* and can easily navigate their way around YouTube or the Internet (Gunter & Kenny, 2008). Book trailers are similar to movie trailers in that they give readers a quick summary of the text to entice them to pick up the printed volume and engage in reading in a video format. The winning combination of story, technology, the arts, and entertainment engages reluctant and struggling readers and motivates them to become excited about text (Kenny, 2007).

In addition to increasing motivation, book trailers also provide adolescent readers with an organizational format to visualize the plot of a story, which facilitates comprehension (Gunter & Kenny, 2008; Keene & Zimmerman, 2007). Similar to podcasting, to create the book trailer, students must summarize the plot, collaborate on the salient features of the text, and problem solve during the production process (Rozema, 2007; Trier, 2007). Yet the power of the narrative remains the core element across mediacentric stories as adolescent readers engage in one of the oldest form of knowing: reading (Kenny, 2007).

Source: International Reading Association and National Council of Teachers of English (1996).

IRA/NCTE Standards for the English Language Arts

2. Students read a wide range of literature from many periods in many genres to build an understanding of the many dimensions (e.g., philosophical, ethical, aesthetic) of human experience.

8. Students use a variety of technological and informational resources (e.g., libraries, databases, computer networks, video) to gather and synthesize information and to create and communicate knowledge.

9. Students develop an understanding of and respect for diversity in language use, patterns, and dialects across cultures, ethnic groups, geographic regions, and social roles.

11. Students participate as knowledgeable, reflective, creative, and critical members of a variety of literacy communities.

STEP-BY-STEP PROCEDURE

The purpose of the *Book Trailer* strategy is to motivate adolescent readers to engage with the printed text and become knowledgeable about narrative formats. This strategy is implemented after the class has completed a book study of a well-known novel. Since it involves video production, the strategy may take 4 weeks or more to implement depending on the literacy levels of the students.

BEFORE PRODUCTION

To create a book trailer, students must identify the central theme of the novel and its plot. During the first session, the teacher facilitates a *book talk* about the story elements.

1. The teacher begins the session by asking students to do a quick-write on their response to the novel. After a few students have shared their initial responses to the story, the teacher begins to connect students' comments with story elements.

2. The teacher distributes Figure 25.1, Book Trailer Organizer, and asks students to work with a partner to identify main characters, setting, problem, and resolution. When students have completed the graphic organizer, the teacher records their responses related to the novel's theme.

3. The teacher shows students the Digital Book Talk site http://video.google.com/videosearch?q=+booktalk&hl=en#. Students discuss media features such as music, graphics, and why certain book trailers were more effective than others.

| Figure 25.1 | Book Trailer Organizer |

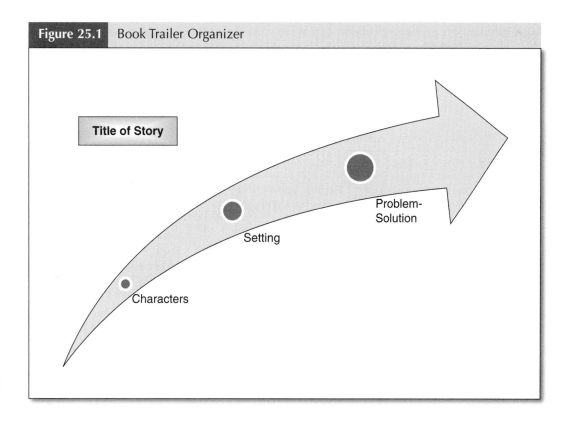

Title of Story

Characters

Setting

Problem-Solution

DURING PRODUCTION

Students will need software such as iMovie or Moviemaker to produce their book trailer. However, if the school does not have this software, YouTube may be used for more simplistic video versions.

1. Students are placed into teams and begin their collaboration by discussing the theme of their book trailer. Each team is given a 2-minute timeframe for their book trailer so the video must be succinct.

2. Each group discusses the key characters and images they want to create in their book trailer and ways to entice their peers to pick up the book.

3. In the next session, the group completes a storyboard, which times each frame and lays out their plans for the book trailer. After each frame is illustrated, the group decides on music, sound effects, and visual images to use.

4. After using iMovie to create their book trailer, they edit their video and create an audio track to narrate their videos.

AFTER PRODUCTION

After the groups have finished the production of their trailers, each one is presented and discussed. The class uses the rubric shown in Figure 25.2 to critique each book trailer.

1. At the conclusion of the presentations, the teacher tallies the scores on the rubrics and announces the top two book trailers. The top two videos are uploaded to the class Web site for comment from a global audience.

2. In the final session, the teacher leads a debriefing session on problems with the production process and how they were solved. Students are also asked to write a brief reflection on how their thinking about the book changed as a result of producing the book trailer.

Figure 25.2	Rubric for Assessing Book Trailers		
Element	Beginning	Developing	Advanced
Story content	Does not identify key story elements and theme (2–0 points)	Partially identifies key story elements and theme (4–3 points)	Succinctly identifies key story elements and theme (5 points)
Engagement	Does not engage the audience immediately with image, graphics, sound (2–0 points)	Somewhat engages the audience immediately with image, graphics, sound (4–3 points)	Engages the audience immediately with image, graphics, sound (5 points)
Direction	Not all of the story parts are present, nor are they well-developed, or produced in a logical sequence (2–0 points)	Majority of story parts are present, are well-developed, and produced in a logical sequence (4–3 points)	All story parts are present, are well-developed, and produced in a logical sequence (5 points)

Element	Beginning	Developing	Advanced
Video production	Book trailer does not have a professional appearance with graphics and sound (2–0 points)	Book trailer has a somewhat professional appearance with graphics and sound (4–3 points)	Book trailer has a professional appearance with graphics and sound (5 points)
TOTAL= /20			

The Book Trailer strategy is particularly suited for mediacentric students as it builds on their strengths to engage them in reading; however, it is also a powerful instructional tool for reluctant and striving readers.

DIFFERENTIATING INSTRUCTION FOR STRIVING READERS

Striving adolescent readers have spent years of their lives in downward spirals of failure and learned helplessness (O'Brien, 2003). Yet while many feel incompetent when processing printed text, their sense of self-efficacy improves when producing digital text or multimedia (O'Brien, 2001). The Book Trailer strategy gives striving readers the opportunity to choose digital images, software tools, graphics, and audio tracks, which increases motivation (O'Brien, 2003; Wilber, 2008). To increase engagement in the activity, striving readers may choose from a selection of novels that are on their reading level yet still deal with the same theme or concept. After reading their novel, the collaborative nature of the Book Trailer strategy provides another scaffold to improve student learning.

CONSIDERING THE LANGUAGE NEEDS OF ELL STUDENTS

IRA/NCTE Standards for the English Language Arts

10. Students whose first language is not English make use of their first language to develop competency in the English language arts and to develop understanding of content across the curriculum.

Source: International Reading Association and National Council of Teachers of English (1996).

To create a book trailer about the novel they have read, English language learners must infer "the big idea" or theme of the story. It is often difficult for second language learners or striving readers to grasp what is meant by the big idea or the theme. To prepare them for the Book Trailer strategy, the teacher may conduct a small guided reading activity using paintings by Norman Rockwell to practice making inferences. Paintings such as

"The Four Freedoms" can be used to discuss the main idea illustrated as well as supporting details that contribute to the concept. When English language learners become more proficient in identifying the big idea from paintings or photographs, they are ready to tackle the same cognitive process with printed and digital text.

An Application for Instruction and Learning in the Art Classroom

Eleventh graders have been studying the Impressionist movement. As a culminating activity, they will create a trailer that engages other students in the study of this artistic movement. The teacher begins the project by asking students to do a quick write of their prior knowledge of the Impressionist movement and central artists in the period such as Claude Monet. Once students have discussed their knowledge of this movement, the teacher shows a clip from the Metropolitan Museum in New York and Musee d'Orsay in Paris about their collection of Impressionist paintings. After viewing the clips, the students critique them and decide which video features they would like to imitate and which ones should be discarded. After several sessions of examining which artists and paintings to include in the video trailer, the students choose one theme expressed in the paintings to explore in their video trailer such as "the study of nature" and begin to storyboard their images. Working collaboratively, the students add music, digital images, graphics, and a narrative track. When all video trailers are completed, the students use the rubric illustrated in Figure 25.2 to critique one another's work and to select the highest-rated video.

References

Gunter, G., & Kenny, R. (2008). Digital booktalk: Digital media for reluctant readers. *Contemporary Issues in Technology and Teacher Education, 8*(1). Retrieved November 23, 2009, from http://www.citejournal.org/vol8/iss1/currentpractice/article1.cfm

International Reading Association and National Council of Teachers of English. (1996). *Standards for the English language arts*. Newark, DE: International Reading Association & Urbana, IL: National Council of Teachers of English.

Keene, E., & Zimmermann, S. (2007). *Mosaic of thought* (2nd ed.). Portsmouth, NH: Heinemann.

Kenny, R. (2007). Digital narrative as a change agent to teach reading to media-centric students. *International Journal of Social Sciences, 2*(3). Retrieved November 23, 2009 from http://www.waset.org/journals/ijss/v2/v2-3-29.pdf

O'Brien, D. (2001). *"At-risk" adolescents: Redefining competence through the multiliteracies of intermediality,* visual arts, and representation. Retrieved November 23, 2009, from http://www.readingonline.org/newliteracies/obrien/index.html

O'Brien, D. (2003). Juxtaposing traditional and intermedial literacies to redefine the competence of struggling adolescents. *Reading Online.* Retrieved November 21, 2009, from http://www.readingonline.org/newliteracies/obrien2/

Rozema, R. (2007). The book report, version 2.0: Podcasting on young adult novels. *The English Journal, 97*(1), 31–37.

Trier, J. (2007). "Cool" engagements with YouTube: Part I. *Journal of Adolescent and Adult Literacy, 50,* 408–413.

Wilber, D. (2008). iLife: Understanding and connecting to the digital literacies of adolescents. In K. Hinchman & H. Sheridan-Thomas (Eds.), *Best practices in adolescent literacy instruction* (pp. 57–77). New York: Guilford Press.

SECTION VI

Critical Thinking

Developing Students' Critical Thinking Skills

The principle goal of education in the schools should be creating men and women who are capable of doing new things, not simply repeating what other generations have done; men and women who are creative, inventive and discoverers, who can be critical and verify, and not accept everything they are offered.

—Jean Piaget

Matthew Robson, a teen in Great Britain, recently surprised mainstream media with the results of a teen survey of the daily literacy and technological diaries of today's adolescent (Pavia & Kishtwari, 2009). The 15-year-old British student polled his fellow teens and discovered that the majority were using social networking sites, texting, surfing the Web, or playing video games. Responses noted gender and age differences in that primarily boys were playing video games, while girls communicated through Facebook. No one twittered; in fact, twittering was considered only for the "elderly." Matt also commented that adolescents never read newspapers because they can get a summary of the news on television or on the Internet. This glimpse into the multiple literacies of today's adolescent is notable for the absence of printed text. Yet despite the Google generation's skilled ability to access information, they are in need of strategies to process and critically evaluate it (University College London, CIBER Group, 2008). The multimodal nature of the average teen's digital diary also alerts educators of the need to develop critical thinking across both print and nonprint texts.

What Research Has to Say About the Development of Critical Thinking

How do we teach adolescent readers to critically process and evaluate text? Researchers and theorists concur that today's teen requires explicit strategy instruction for deeper comprehension of multimodal texts and content area reading. This section provides the research framework for the development of critical thinking across modalities and content areas.

Universal Literacy

As the world adapts to the information age brought about by the Internet, universal literacy has become a global expectation. Universal literacy is the expectation that all individuals will be able to critically process text and to interpret it (Considine, Horton, & Moorman, 2009). As our concept of text is transformed to include digital and other nonprint sources, this raising of the literacy bar across the globe is coming at a critical period in our history. Seventy percent of American high school graduates lack the critical thinking skills necessary to process and analyze the reams of information of the digital age and are therefore limited in terms of career prospects (Deshler, Palinscar, Biancarosa, & Nair, 2007). It can be inferred that these graduates did not receive explicit instruction on processing and evaluating multimodal texts.

Critical thinking for the digital age encompasses the strategies and skills necessary to "unpack" the layers of meaning in multimodal text (Xu, 2008). Multimodal texts represent the range of modes in which we communicate and inform such as photographs, magazines, Web sites, video clips, music, paintings, blogs, digital stories, and gestures (Boyd & Thompson, 2008). To access and analyze such texts, today's adolescent needs explicit instruction in critical thinking strategies that can be differentiated for multimodal texts and different content areas (Duke & Pearson, 2002; Keene, 2008).

The National Assessment of Educational Progress (NAEP) has modified its core cognitive skills to frame this conversation regarding critical thinking for the digital age. The 2009 National Assessment of Educational Progress framework (National Assessment Governing Board, 2005) has selected three cognitive skills as critical for developing higher-level thinking:

- *Locate and recall:* This cognitive skill represents the literal level of comprehension such as identification of the main idea or locating supporting details. To process text at higher levels, students must be able to summarize and recall key concepts.

- *Integrate and interpret:* This slightly higher level of processing text demands that the learner connects the new concept to existing schema and elaborates on it. When the reader is able to draw on background knowledge while reading, predictions, inferences, and conclusions can be drawn.

- *Critique and evaluate:* The highest level of processing asks readers to critique text based on their knowledge regarding text structure, content knowledge, and understanding of the discourse community. Readers are able to view multiple perspectives and to critique text for objectivity or accuracy.

The ability to critique and evaluate text is especially difficult for striving readers. Striving readers often lack foundational skills such as word identification and fluency (Deshler et al., 2007). They also need explicit instruction in literal comprehension skills such as finding the main idea, summarizing, and questioning before, during, and after reading (McDonald, Thorley, Stanley, & Moore, 2009). However, research has shown that when striving readers are engaged and motivated, they will focus their attention on processing difficult text and on obtaining the strategies necessary to do so (Hanson, 2009). As effective teachers soon realize, all learners but especially adolescent ones need to feel an emotional connection to the text or content area to be engaged in the process (Keene, 2008).

MULTIPLE LITERACIES

One method for generating an emotional connection between the adolescent learner and the text is to create a bridge between their "inside" and "outside" school literacies (Xu, 2008). As today's adolescent learner text messages or surfs the Net, they are engaging in locating and recalling of informational text across modalities (Considine et al., 2009). Yet teens often enter the classroom to find a disconnect between their digital world and the walls of their classroom (Brown, 2008). Effective teachers draw on adolescent learners' multiple literacies and use them to develop critical thinking skills (Deshler et al., 2007).

To critically evaluate and interpret text, adolescent learners need breadth and depth of conceptual understanding across disciplines (Duke & Pearson, 2002). Multimodal texts such as photographs, music, video clips, digital stories, gestures, or paintings provide engaging and motivational ways to construct conceptual understanding and to make personal connections to their outside school literacies (Hanson, 2009). As students unpack the meaning in photographs, gestures, or movie clips, they are evaluating and analyzing the message (Boyd & Thompson, 2008). These critical thinking skills require the learner to consider the purpose of the message, the intended audience, and to discern bias (Considine et al., 2009). Effective teachers model, demonstrate, and provide feedback as adolescent learners use these critical thinking skills to process content area text. Responsive teachers use assessment data to individualize instruction and to build bridges for learning.

RESPONSIVE PEDAGOGY

Responsive pedagogy assesses students' skills, gauges their literacy practices and identity, and forms an instructional plan (Brown, 2008). Responsive teachers construct bridges between students' out-of-school literacies and the content area (Brown, 2008; Xu, 2008). How do they accomplish this feat? Effective and responsive teachers use multimodal texts to create that emotional connection to the academic discipline that will engage the adolescent learner (Hanson, 2009; Keene, 2008). As adolescent learners compare their textbook reading with related content material in movies, photographs, music, or paintings, they are using multiple sources of information from their world to process complex concepts (Boyd & Thompson, 2008). As they process and analyze multimodal texts, responsive teachers use accountable talk and writing to engage adolescent learners in the discourse community (Allington, Johnston, & Day, 2002).

A discourse community is the language and literacy specific to a community or discipline (Jetton & Dole, 2004). The complex nature of content area literacy requires a set of skills and strategies that are specific to a discipline (Vacca, 2002). Each discipline has its own vocabulary and discourse that must be mastered to critically interpret and evaluate its texts (Jetton & Dole, 2004). To become fluent in a content area, learners must master the tasks of the discipline such as character analysis in the field of English. Students' mastery of discipline tasks is largely due to subject matter knowledge. Responsive and effective teachers scaffold this process by engaging adolescent learners in accountable talk.

Accountable talk occurs when learners use the vocabulary of the discipline to summarize, explain, clarify, challenge, interpret, and critique (Gunning, 2008). When adolescent learners apply and practice the discourse of the discipline, they internalize its concepts and generate inferences and elaborations (Vacca, 2002). Similarly, writing across the curriculum scaffolds adolescent learners' acquisition of academic vocabulary and their knowledge of text structures within a specific domain (Jetton & Dole, 2004). When students use their understanding of expository text structure to construct their own writing samples, they demonstrate mastery of academic discourse (Gunning, 2008; Keene, 2008). As adolescent learners acquire fluency in accountable talk, their ability to engage in critical thinking improves demonstrating the relationship between cognition and oral language.

A FRAMEWORK FOR TEACHING CRITICAL THINKING SKILLS TO ADOLESCENT STUDENTS

To develop critical thinking, adolescent learners need explicit instruction in evaluating and interpreting multimodal texts. The following suggestions provide the foundation for development of critical thinking:

1. Critical thinking for the digital age encompasses print as well as nonprint materials across multiple modalities (Considine et al., 2009).

2. To critically process and evaluate multimodal texts, adolescent learners need the foundational skills such as word identification and fluency (Deshler et al., 2007).

3. When adolescent learners feel a personal or emotional connection to the subject matter, their level of engagement and motivation is improved (Hanson, 2009).

4. Explicit instruction in the vocabulary and discourse of the content area discipline is necessary to master specific tasks (Vacca, 2002).

5. Responsive teachers connect adolescent learners' outside sources of knowledge with academic content to construct conceptual understanding, engagement, and critical thinking (Brown, 2008; Xu, 2008).

This section, "Developing Students' Critical Thinking Skills," presents five instructional strategies, which are guides for teachers of adolescent learners to adapt and use for their specific discipline.

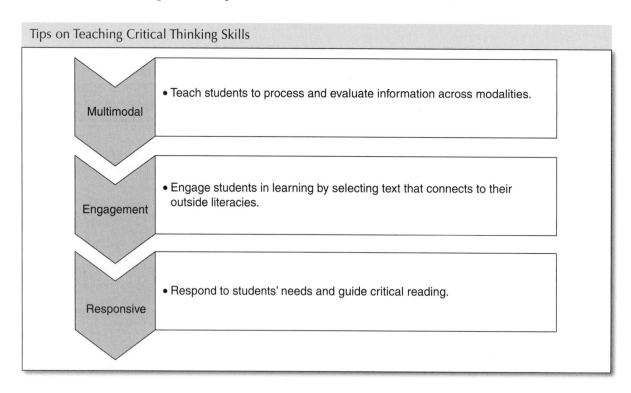

Tips on Teaching Critical Thinking Skills

Multimodal
• Teach students to process and evaluate information across modalities.

Engagement
• Engage students in learning by selecting text that connects to their outside literacies.

Responsive
• Respond to students' needs and guide critical reading.

A Strategy for Assessing the Development of Critical Thinking Skills

The digital revolution has reiterated the need for improved critical thinking across the curriculum. To process and analyze massive amounts of online information, adolescent students need to be able to clarify ideas, analyze evidence, synthesize arguments, and identify biases (Jago, 2009). It is essential for students to reflect on their abilities to process information in critical ways. The holistic rubric illustrated in Figure VI.1 may be used by students to reflect on their critical thinking or by the

Figure VI.1	Assessment of Critical Thinking			
Critical Thinking Component	*Advanced*	*Target*	*Developing*	*Needs Improvement*
Problem solving	Student uses multiple sources to critically identify and analyze problem (4 points)	Student uses several sources to critically identify and analyze problem (3 points)	Student begins to critically identify and analyze problem (2 points)	Student is not able to critically identify and analyze problem (1 point)
Research	Student uses multiple sources to research problem and synthesizes evidence (4 points)	Student uses several sources to research problem and synthesizes evidence (3 points)	Student partially uses multiple sources to research problem and synthesizes evidence (2 points)	Student does not use sources to research problem and synthesizes evidence (1 point)
Application	Student critically applies research and new information to construct new ideas (4 points)	Student applies research and new information to construct new ideas (3 points)	Student partially applies research and new information to construct new ideas (2 points)	Student does not apply research and new information to construct new ideas (1 point)
Consider	Student critically considers biases, context, and other perspectives in problem-solving process (4 points)	Student considers biases, context, and other perspectives in problem-solving process (3 points)	Student partially considers biases, context, and other perspectives in problem-solving process (2 points)	Student *does not* consider biases, context, and other perspectives in problem-solving process (1 point)
Synthesis	Student critically synthesizes information to construct new ideas or solutions (4 points)	Student synthesizes information to construct new ideas or solutions (3 points)	Student partially synthesizes information to construct new ideas or solutions (2 points)	Student does not synthesize information to construct new ideas or solutions (1 point)
Advanced: 20–16 points Target: 15–11 points Developing: 10–6 points Beginning: 5–1 points				

teacher as a performance assessment. Key components of critical thinking are the following:

- Identification and analysis of the problem or question
- Research and synthesis of supporting data or evidence
- Application of ideas or information
- Consideration of context, other perspectives, or biases
- Synthesis of ideas for solutions or answers

Teachers can meet with students to discuss their ratings on the rubric to improve their critical thinking. As adolescent learners record their own progress over the course of the term, they begin to note gaps in their critical thinking skills. This reflection provides the teacher with an opportunity to facilitate further guided practice in the areas in need of improvement and to teach responsively.

REFLECTIVE PRACTICE ON TEACHING CRITICAL THINKING SKILLS

The ability to analyze, evaluate, and synthesize information is a critical skill for the 21st century. To critically evaluate and interpret text, adolescent learners need breadth and depth of conceptual understanding across disciplines (Duke & Pearson, 2002). Visit an effective teacher in your discipline and record your observations of the following:

- How does the teacher use multimodal texts to motivate and engage students?
- What strategies does the teacher employ to integrate students' cognitive, cultural, and linguistic backgrounds with the content area?
- How does the teacher engage students in academic discourse?

After you have recorded your observations, share them with a colleague and discuss how you can implement these best practices in your own lessons.

PROFESSIONAL RESOURCES

Atwell, N. (2007). *The reading zone: How to help kids become skilled, passionate, habitual, critical readers.* New York: Scholastic.

Gallagher, K. (2009). *Article of the week.* Portland, ME: Stenhouse.

Harvey, S. (2007). *Strategies that work: Teaching comprehension for understanding and engagement.* Portland, ME: Stenhouse.

Tovani, C. (2000). *I read it, but I don't get it: Comprehension strategies for adolescent learners.* Portland, ME: Stenhouse.

References

Allington, R., Johnston, P., & Day, J. (2002). Exemplary fourth-grade teachers. *Language Arts, 79,* 462–466.

Boyd, F. B., & Thompson, M. K. (2008). Multimodality and literacy learning: Using multiple texts to enhance content area learning. In K. Hinchman & H. Sheridan-Thomas (Eds.), *Best practices in adolescent literacy instruction* (pp. 151–163). New York: Guilford Press.

Brown, R. (2008). Strategy matters: Comprehension instruction for older youth. In K. Hinchman & H. Sheridan-Thomas (Eds.), *Best practices in adolescent literacy instruction* (pp. 114–131). New York: Guilford Press.

Considine, D., Horton, J., & Moorman, G. (2009). Teaching and reading the millennial generation through media literacy. *Journal of Adolescent and Adult Literacy, 52,* 471–481.

Deshler, D., Palinscar, A. S., Biancarosa, G., & Nair, M. (2007). *Informed choices for struggling adolescent readers.* Newark, DE: International Reading Association and Carnegie Corporation.

Duke, N., & Pearson, P. D. (2002). Effective practices for developing reading comprehension. In A. E. Farstrup & S. J. Samuels (Eds.), *What research has to say about reading instruction* (3rd ed., pp. 205–242). Newark, DE: International Reading Association.

Gunning, T. (2008). *Developing higher-level literacy in all students.* Boston: Allyn & Bacon.

Hanson, J. (2009). Multiple literacies in the content classroom: High school students' connections to U.S. history. *Journal of Adolescent and Adult Literacy, 52,* 597–606.

Jago, C. (2009). *Writing in the 21st century: Crash! The currency crisis in American culture.* Report retrieved from www.nwp.org/cs/public/download/nwp_file/12468/Crash!_The_Currency_Crisis_in_American_Culture.pdf?x-r=pcfile_d

Jetton, T., & Dole, J. A. (2004). *Adolescent literacy: Research and practice.* New York: Guilford Press.

Keene, E. (2008). *To understand: New horizons in reading comprehension.* Portsmouth, NH: Heinemann.

McDonald, T., Thorley, C., Stanley, R., & Moore, D. (2009). The San Diego striving readers project: Building academic success for adolescent readers. *Journal of Adolescent and Adult Literacy, 52,* 720–722.

National Assessment Governing Board. (2005). *Reading framework for the 2009 National Assessment of Educational Progress.* Washington, DC: American Institutes for Research.

Pavia, W., & Kishtwari, S. (2009). Twitter is for old people, work experience wiz kid tells bankers. *Times Online.* Retrieved December 4, 2009, from http://www.timesonline.co.uk/tol/news/uk/article6703399.ece

University College London CIBER Group. (2008). *Information behavior of the researcher of the future (CIBER Briefing Paper 9).* London: Author. Retrieved December 4, 2009, from http://www.jisc.ac.uk/media/documents/programmes/reppres/gg_final_keynote_11012008.pdf

Vacca, R. (2002). Making a difference in adolescents' school lives: Visible and invisible aspects of content area reading. In A. E. Farstrup & S. J. Samuels (Eds.), *What research has to say about reading instruction* (3rd ed., 184–205). Newark, DE: International Reading Association.

Xu, S. H. (2008). Rethinking literacy learning and teaching: Intersections of adolescents' in school and out of school literacy practices. In K. Hinchman & H. Sheridan-Thomas (Eds.), *Best practices in adolescent literacy instruction* (pp. 39–57). New York: Guilford Press.

Strategy
26

SCAMPER

Collaborative Analysis of Text

STRATEGY OVERVIEW

By the time adolescent learners enter middle school, they have encountered thousands of texts and participated in multiple strategies to analyze them. Their familiarity with academic learning may lead to ennui and lack of engagement with text. One way to motivate and engage adolescent learners is the SCAMPER strategy. The SCAMPER (**S**ubstitute, **C**ombine, **A**dapt, **M**odify, **P**ut, **E**liminate, **R**everse/rearrange) instructional strategy stimulates creative thinking and "out of the box" processing of text (Eberle, 1997). This strategy can be adapted across content areas and is typically implemented when students have acquired background knowledge on a concept or unit of study.

The SCAMPER strategy enables adolescent learners to access, analyze, and evaluate text to construct new ideas or solutions (Hobbs, 2005). The complex nature of multimodal texts in the information age requires learners to interpret and evaluate text across time, space, and context (Alvermann, 2009). In this activity, students work in groups to creatively construct alternative solutions or elaborations on a unit of study. The following step-by-step procedures describe how to implement the SCAMPER strategy with adolescent readers.

Source: International Reading Association and National Council of Teachers of English (1996).

IRA/NCTE Standards for the English Language Arts

1. Students read a wide range of print and nonprint texts to build an understanding of texts, of themselves, and of the cultures of the United States and the world; to acquire new information; to respond to the needs and demands of society and the workplace; and for personal fulfillment. Among these texts are fiction and nonfiction, classic, and contemporary works.
6. Students apply knowledge of language structure, language conventions (e.g., spelling and punctuation), media techniques, figurative language, and genre to create, critique, and discuss print and nonprint texts.
9. Students develop an understanding of and respect for diversity in language use, patterns, and dialects across cultures, ethnic groups, geographic regions, and social roles.
11. Students participate as knowledgeable, reflective, creative, and critical members of a variety of literacy communities.

Before beginning the instructional sequence, teachers introduce the SCAMPER strategy by describing each component and its purpose. The components are:

- Substitute a person, place, time, or situation
- Combine or synthesize ideas, situations, contexts
- Adapt or adjust a problem or concept to suit a new purpose
- Modify, magnify, or minify the size, traits, or dimensions of the concept or problem
- Put to other uses or contexts
- Eliminate a feature of the concept, story, or problem
- Rearrange or reverse the sequence of the story, concept, or context

Adolescent learners need adequate background knowledge to successfully master the SCAMPER strategy; therefore, it should be implemented toward the midpoint or end of a unit of study.

BEFORE READING

In order for students to be skillful investigators on the Web, they must have background knowledge of the topic they are researching. Before students begin this strategy, the teacher should have researched credible sites on the Web.

1. The teacher demonstrates how to implement the strategy by using the legend of Robin Hood as an example. Students are asked to summarize the legend before beginning the demonstration.

2. During the demonstration of the SCAMPER strategy, the teacher asks specific prompts for each component:
   a. Substitute: How would the Robin Hood legend change if it took place in Los Angeles in 2009?
   b. Combine: How would the plot change if I added characters from other legends?
   c. Adapt: How would Robin Hood adapt if evil Sir Guy of Gisborne were secretly helping the poor?
   d. Modify: How would the plot change if Robin Hood acted alone?
   e. Put to other uses: How would the plot change if the purpose of my story were to promote anticapitalism among the people?
   f. Eliminate: How would the story change if there weren't a Friar Tuck?
   g. Rearrange or reverse sequence: How would the audience react if we began the legend with King Richard and his participation in the Crusades?

3. After demonstrating the strategy, the teacher leads the class in a discussion of how the SCAMPER strategy helped them to "revisualize" the Robin Hood legend and how it will be applied to the content area. Students receive the SCAMPER graphic illustrated in Figure 26.1 to begin their task.

DURING READING

The following components may take several sessions for the students to complete.

1. Working in groups of three, students discuss the main concept or problem and use the prompts provided in SCAMPER Topic Strategy Guide (Figure 26.1) to generate ideas.

2. Students are encouraged to use multimodal texts such as Web sites, digital resources, or textbooks to generate alternative concepts and solutions for each prompt. One student assigned as the group recorder notes any roadblocks the group encounters and how they are resolved.

3. When students have completed their SCAMPER Topic Strategy Guide (Figure 26.1), they rehearse their presentation to the class and prepare to address questions raised by their peers.

Figure 26.1	SCAMPER Topic Strategy Guide

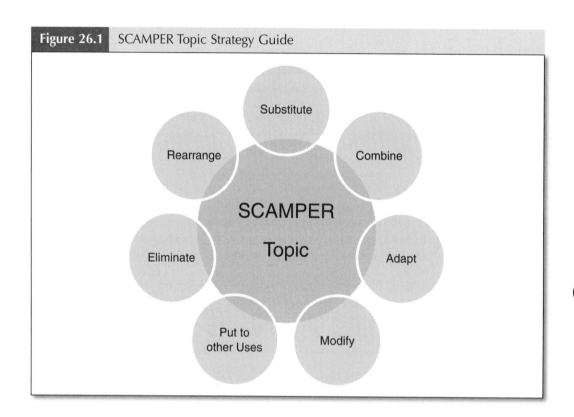

AFTER READING

After students have completed the SCAMPER strategy, they share their creative thinking with classmates.

1. Students present their SCAMPER Topic Strategy Guide on a SMART board or overhead transparency. As they share their findings, students discuss their synthesis and analysis of information, which led to the group's responses at each prompt.

2. After groups have presented, the teacher leads a discussion that summarizes the myriad creative annotations or solutions that were generated through the SCAMPER strategy.

3. At the conclusion of the session, the teacher leads a debriefing session for students to note any roadblocks they encountered with the SCAMPER strategy. The discussion also focuses on how the strategy can be applied to creative problem solving when dealing with personal issues in their private lives.

DIFFERENTIATING INSTRUCTION FOR STRIVING READERS

The majority of striving readers want to participate with their peers in tackling more difficult text; however, they often lack the skills or confidence to do so (Ivey, 2000). The SCAMPER strategy can be modified to accommodate the various reading levels of striving readers in content area classes. For example, in social studies classes striving readers may choose newspapers or magazines to implement the creative thinking activity.

Research has shown that when adolescent learners are provided a choice in reading materials, their level of engagement and motivation increases (Hanson, 2009). Newspapers in print or online offer adolescent readers a menu of topics to peak their interest in current events, the arts, or sports and usually are on a middle school reading level. Teachers may use a current events article to demonstrate the strategy or to provide striving readers with guided practice before it is used independently with academic content.

CONSIDERING THE LANGUAGE NEEDS OF ELL STUDENTS

IRA/NCTE Standards for the English Language Arts

10. Students whose first language is not English make use of their first language to develop competency in the English language arts and to develop understanding of content across the curriculum.

Source: International Reading Association and National Council of Teachers of English (1996).

The concept of creating alternative solutions or elaborations might be confusing for ELL students to grasp. Picture books provide great resources for teachers to illustrate creative thinking, especially *The True Story of the Three Little Pigs* (Scieszka & Smith, 1996). Using the book, teachers can use the SCAMPER Topic Strategy Guide (see Figure 26.1) to demonstrate how the authors of the book made several creative substitutions and adaptations to construct their story. ELL students can work in pairs to practice the strategy with other picture books featuring creative adaptations such as *The Frog Prince Continued* (Scieszka, 1994).

AN APPLICATION FOR INSTRUCTION AND LEARNING IN THE PSYCHOLOGY CLASSROOM

Twelfth graders in an advanced placement psychology class are studying human development from prenatal through the toddler years. Students have completed the first two course topics on the syllabus, which focus on prenatal care and the development of the fetus in the uterus. As a review and extension activity, the teacher assigns the students to groups of three to complete the following SCAMPER prompts (see Figure 26.1):

- **S**ubstitute: How would the fetus develop if it were another type of mammal?

- **C**ombine: How would maternal or paternal drug abuse impact the development of the fetus?

- **A**dapt: How would the fetus adapt if an in utero operation were needed to repair a defective gene or organ?

- **M**odify: How would twins or triplets develop in utero?

- **P**ut to other uses: How can our understanding of prenatal nutrition prevent birth defects?

- **E**liminate: How would the fetus evolve if it were reproduced through cloning?

- **R**earrange or reverse sequence: In what ways does the aging process mirror the infancy/toddler years of development?

When student groups have completed their strategy sheet, they share their thinking with the class. The teacher prompts students to give examples of how their peers' responses sparked their own creative thinking and generated alternative solutions or elaborations.

References

Alvermann, D. (2009). Sociocultural connections of adolescence and young people's literacies. In L. Christenbury, R. Bomer, & P. Smagorinsky (Eds.), *Handbook of adolescent literacy* (pp. 80–98). New York: Guilford Press.

Eberle, B. (1997). *SCAMPER: Games for imaginative development.* Waco, TX: Prufrock Press.

Hanson, J. (2009). Multiple literacies in the content classroom: High school students' connections to U.S. history. *Journal of Adolescent and Adult Literacy, 52,* 597–606.

Hobbs, R. (2005). Literacy for the information age. In J. Flood, S. B. Heath, & D. Lapp (Eds.), *Handbook of research on teaching literacy through the communicative and visual arts* (pp. 7–14). Newark, DE: International Reading Association.

International Reading Association and National Council of Teachers of English. (1996). *Standards for the English language arts.* Newark, DE: International Reading Association & Urbana, IL: National Council of Teachers of English.

Ivey, G. (2000). Reflections on teaching struggling middle school readers. In D. Moore, D. Alvermann, & K. Hinchman (Eds.), *Struggling adolescent readers: A collection of teaching strategies* (pp. 27–39). Newark, DE: International Reading Association.

Scieszka, J. (1994). *The frog prince continued.* New York: Puffin.

Scieszka, J., & Smith, L. (1996). *True story of the 3 little pigs.* New York: Puffin.

Six Thinking Hats

Facilitating Different Modes of Thinking

Strategy 27

Today's adolescent will read and write on more advanced levels as adults than at any time in history (Moje, Young, Readance,& Moore, 2000). Due to the wealth of multimodal text available to them at the click of a button, they will need to be critical consumers of information. Critical literacy requires higher-order thinking skills such as inferring, reasoning, and problem solving (McDonald, Thorley, Stanley, & Moore, 2009). Evaluating multimodal text for biases or inaccuracies is a critical skill for the Google generation. In addition, the ability to use that information to create or innovate is forecasted to be essential to a thriving economy (Paris & Strom, 2009).

As we near completion of the first decade of the millennium, many theorists and policy makers are asking schools to focus on creative or divergent thinking (Jackson, 2009). As technology levels the playing field in regard to access to information, thriving economies will be rooted in innovation and creative problem solving. Creative problem solving, especially when rooted in a project-based activity, allows adolescent learners to view a problem or situation from myriad perspectives and to generate divergent thinking (Jackson, 2009). The Six Thinking Hats strategy by Edward de Bono (1999) is particularly suited to fostering divergent thinking.

In this strategy, adolescent learners view a topic or problem by wearing a range of different "hats." The purpose of the instructional strategy is to facilitate divergent thinking and awareness that as situations or contexts change, how we view a topic or problem must also be transformed.

Source: International Reading Association and National Council of Teachers of English (1996).

IRA/NCTE Standards for the English Language Arts

7. Students conduct research on issues and interests by generating ideas and questions, and by posing problems. They gather, evaluate, and synthesize data from a variety of sources (e.g., print and nonprint texts, artifacts, people) to communicate their discoveries in ways that suit their purpose and audience.

8. Students use a variety of technological and informational resources (e.g., libraries, databases, computer networks, video) to gather and synthesize information and to create and communicate knowledge.

9. Students develop an understanding of and respect for diversity in language use, patterns, and dialects across cultures, ethnic groups, geographic regions, and social roles.

11. Students participate as knowledgeable, reflective, creative, and critical members of a variety of literacy communities.

STEP-BY-STEP PROCEDURE

The Six Thinking Hats strategy focuses on viewing a problem or topic from six different perspectives. The best way to implement this strategy is during a project-based unit. This strategy will require several sessions to research the topic and complete the problem-solving process. The six different thinking hats are as follows:

- *White hat:* Focuses on information already available

- *Black hat:* Examines the problems or difficulties associated with the topic

- *Yellow hat:* Centers on the benefits and values

- *Red hat:* Studies the emotions or feelings that are generated by the topic or problem

- *Green hat:* Requires imaginative or creative thinking about the problem or topic

- *Blue hat:* Focuses on metacognitive or reflective thinking about the problem-solving process

PREPARATION

The session begins with the teacher asking students, "When did you have to solve a difficult problem? What did you do?" The teacher notes their responses on chart paper and discusses the steps or strategies they used to solve the problem. To implement the Six Thinking Hats strategy, students should have prior knowledge about the topic or problem area. In this example, the teacher has focused on the problem of global warming since it is an extension activity in their biology textbook and the students are completing the chapter.

1. Students are put into pairs and asked to discuss the prompt, "What is global warming?"

2. With their partner, students record their definitions, and the teacher constructs a class statement regarding global warming based on their responses. Afterwards, the teacher distributes a graphic organizer for the Six Thinking Hats strategy and explains each of the six areas.

Figure 27.1	Six Thinking Hats

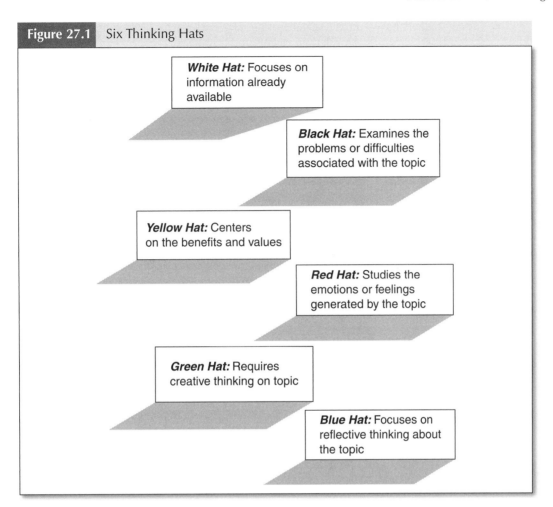

CREATIVE THINKING

The teacher instructs students to use print, digital, and multimodal texts to generate ideas for each of the six thinking hats. The teacher focuses their efforts by providing a prompt for each thinking hat (see Figure 27.1):

- *White hat:* What facts/research are available on global warming?

- *Black hat:* How will global warming impact our planet/country/state?

- *Yellow hat:* How are countries adapting and creating jobs based on the "green" industry?

- *Red hat:* How do people respond to the problem of global warming?

- *Green hat:* What are some creative solutions or innovations to deal with the problem?

- *Blue hat:* How did your group work together to generate ideas for each area? Were there any problems?

1. Students use the graphic organizer to record their responses to each prompt. One member of the group is assigned to journal their creative process to respond to the blue hat or other reflective prompt.

2. Students jot down their sources of information for each thinking hat so that they can defend their creative solutions based on available research or theories.

3. When students have completed generating responses for each thinking hat, they prepare an oral presentation for their peers on the process. Each member of the group reports on a thinking hat and provides their peers with the rationale for each response.

4. As each group reports out, the teacher constructs an overall profile of students' responses to each prompt on the SMART Board or overhead projector. After discussing the generated solutions or responses to each prompt, students discern patterns for each thinking hat.

REFLECTION

The blue hat is a critical component of this instructional strategy as it requires students to reflect on their creative problem solving and collaboration.

1. After students reported out their responses to each prompt, the teacher leads a discussion on their thinking processes. Problems encountered during the implementation of the strategy are discussed and students are encouraged to share their solutions to any difficulties.

2. At the closure of the session, the teacher revisits the chart from the first class that listed problems students faced in their own lives. The teacher leads a discussion on how the Six Thinking Hats strategy can be applied to dealing with problems in their everyday lives.

DIFFERENTIATING INSTRUCTION FOR STRIVING READERS

According to research, striving readers need "preloading" of information to critically comprehend text (Johannessen & McCann, 2009). Preloading of information entails providing striving readers with the background information they will need to construct new concepts or to process text. This is especially critical for striving readers' successful engagement in the Six Thinking Hats instructional strategy. To preload striving readers with background knowledge, the teacher provides them with a list of Web sites and online text regarding the selected topic before the other students are introduced to the strategy. Striving readers work in pairs to generate a descriptive web on the topic and to discuss it with one another. This preloading session enables striving readers to participate in the Six Thinking Hats instructional strategy with confidence and enthusiasm.

CONSIDERING THE LANGUAGE NEEDS OF ELL STUDENTS

Source: International Reading Association and National Council of Teachers of English (1996).

IRA/NCTE Standards for the English Language Arts

10. Students whose first language is not English make use of their first language to develop competency in the English language arts and to develop understanding of content across the curriculum.

English language learners, similar to striving readers, need content preparation to participate fully in critical thinking activities. One way to prepare second language learners for participating in the Six Thinking Hats instructional strategy is to provide key vocabulary words for the content area topic that is explored (Blake & Majors, 2000). Teachers can create a word list of key vocabulary words with an accompanying podcast. A podcast will provide sentences with the words in context, which will provide second language learners with the pronunciation for each word. Providing key vocabulary words in context on the podcast enables second language learners to develop background knowledge on the topic so that they can participate in the instructional strategy.

AN APPLICATION FOR INSTRUCTION AND LEARNING IN THE SCIENCE CLASSROOM

Tenth-grade students have just completed a unit on infectious diseases. The teacher has assigned each group a different infectious disease to research and explore through the Six Thinking Hats instructional strategy. One group has been assigned the H1N1 flu pandemic, which will take several sessions to complete.

Their first action is to respond to the white hat prompt that entails information on the topic. Students surf the Net for figures on the spread of the flu across the globe as well as the number of deaths it has caused. For the black hat prompt, student record the huge amounts of money governments are allotting to fighting the disease as well as the problems with containing the disease in the age of air travel. Students encounter problems in generating benefits and values regarding H1N1 flu and need further support from the teacher. The teacher provides the group with pre-selected bookmark sites that focus on new drugs being developed collaboratively by several nations to fight the pandemic. However for the red hat prompt, the group has no difficulty in finding news broadcasts on the Internet that express the emotional response of loved ones who lost family members to the H1N1 flu. The group discusses possible creative solutions to respond to the green hat prompt. After conducting further research on medical innovations, the group decides to record possible genetic experiments to fight the pandemic on the molecular level. When the graphic organizer is completed, the group reflects on their progress for the blue hat prompt. They discuss how they could have solved their problem generating a response to the yellow hat prompt by investigating the topic further before they sought intervention.

REFERENCES

Blake, M., & Majors, P. (2000). Recycled words: Holistic instruction for LEP students. In D. Moore, D. Alvermann, & K. Hinchman (Eds.), *Struggling adolescent readers: A collection of teaching strategies* (pp. 116–122). Newark, DE: International Reading Association.

DeBono, E. (1999). *Six thinking hats.* Boston: Back Bay Books.

International Reading Association and National Council of Teachers of English. (1996). *Standards for the English language arts.* Newark, DE: International Reading Association & Urbana, IL: National Council of Teachers of English.

Jackson, A. (2009). New middle schools for new futures. *Middle School Journal, 40*(5), 6–11.

Johannessen, L., & McCann, T. (2009). Adolescents who struggle with literacy. In L . Christenbury, R. Bomer, & P. Smagorinsky (Eds.), *Handbook of adolescent literacy* (pp. 65–80). New York: Guilford Press.

McDonald, T., Thorley, C., Stanley, R., & Moore, D. (2009). The San Diego striving readers project: Building academic success for adolescent readers. *Journal of Adolescent and Adult Literacy, 52,* 720–722.

Moje, E., Young, J., Readance, J., & Moore, D. (2000). Reinventing adolescent literacy for new times: Perennial and millennial issues. *Journal of Adolescent and Adult Literacy, 43,* 400–411.

Paris, S., & Strom, R. (2009). *Adolescents in the internet age.* Charlotte, NC: Information Age Publishers.

Academic Controversy

Strategy
28

Taking Sides on the Issue

Academic language proficiency is the ability to analyze complex ideas, critique evidence or opinions, and to use language to communicate (Zwiers, 2008). Academic Controversy (Johnson & Johnson, 1995) is an instructional strategy that facilitates academic language and thinking as students problem solve, reason, and analyze a topic from multiple points of view. Adolescent students tend to cling to their own perspectives on issues, rooted in their culture or belief system (Lenski & Lewis, 2008). Academic Controversy provides a collaborative framework for adolescent learners to explore other points of view on a controversial topic or pertinent issue and to attain academic language proficiency.

As students engage in accountable talk and academic writing, they are required to listen more carefully, examine points of view, provide and critique evidence (Probst, 2007). When adolescent learners work with their peers to research a topic, construct a brief on it, provide a persuasive argument, and then present opposing sides on the issue, they internalize the process of critical thinking (Costa & Marzano, 2001). The Academic Controversy instructional strategy provides adolescent learners with guided practice in using academic language and thinking to support opinions with evidence to reach consensus on an issue.

IRA/NCTE Standards for the English Language Arts

4. Students adjust their use of spoken, written, and visual language (e.g., conventions, style, vocabulary) to communicate effectively with a variety of audiences and for different purposes.

5. Students employ a wide range of strategies as they write and use different writing process elements appropriately to communicate with different audiences for a variety of purposes.

8. Students use a variety of technological and informational resources (e.g., libraries, databases, computer networks, video) to gather and synthesize information and to create and communicate knowledge.

9. Students develop an understanding of and respect for diversity in language use, patterns, and dialects across cultures, ethnic groups, geographic regions, and social roles.

Source: International Reading Association and National Council of Teachers of English (1996).

Step-by-Step Procedure

Academic Controversy is best implemented as a group activity; however, it can be adapted for individual students. Before beginning the session, it is critical that the teacher discusses several ground rules regarding academic discussion. Rules can be posted on chart paper for display during the activity or written on a SMART Board for reference. The rules are as follows:

- Respect and listen to one another even though we may disagree.
- Critique ideas, opinions, and not persons.
- State evidence and research to support position.
- Work together to reach a rational consensus.
- Change perspectives or opinions based on evidence rather than emotions.
- Keep an open mind throughout the discussion.

Before discussion

Before the academic discussion, the teacher presents the topic that will be explored, *Genetic engineering: Beneficial or harmful?* After presenting the topic, the teacher asks students to define genetic engineering and to provide their description of it.

The teacher assigns students to quads with each group comprised of student pairs representing pro and con sides of the issue. To prepare for the discussion, students work with their partner to research factual information on the topic from around the globe. The teacher provides focus questions to guide their research:

- What are some of the benefits of genetic engineering?
- How can it be harmful to individuals and society?
- How is genetic engineering unfolding around the globe?

1. Students are given the graphic organizer presented in Figure 28.1, Academic Controversy: Pros and Cons, to prepare for their discussion.

2. After researching the pros and cons of the topic, students work with their partner to outline their argument as assigned by the teacher. Students also choose the mode of their argument, which may be a video, a PowerPoint presentation, or an oral persuasive argument.

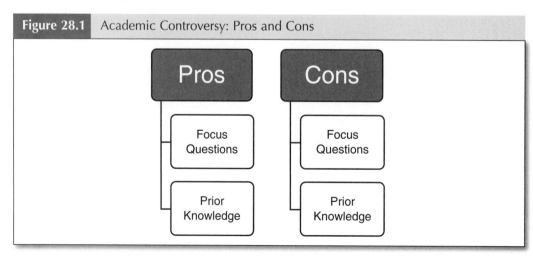

Figure 28.1 Academic Controversy: Pros and Cons

During Discussion

The teacher provides each group with a note-taking sheet as illustrated in Figure 28.2 to organize their thoughts during the discussion.

1. Students meet with their quad and present the position that supports genetic engineering. The remaining pair uses the note-taking sheet to jot down pertinent facts and questions regarding the presentation. The pair of students who are listening to the position are not allowed to interrupt with questions during the presentation.

2. After the presentation, the opposing pair is given 1 minute to challenge with questions and concerns regarding the pair's argument. Students responding to each challenge must support their answers with facts and research rather than opinion or emotion.

3. Next, the process is repeated with the pair presenting the position against genetic engineering. After their persuasive argument against genetic engineering, they are challenged for 1 minute by students representing the opposing perspective.

4. For the last component of the discussion, students flip positions, and now they argue the opposing point of view as persuasively as they did previously for the other perspective. Again, students representing the opposing point of view challenge their arguments and evidence.

| Figure 28.2 | Academic Controversy: Note-Taking Sheet |

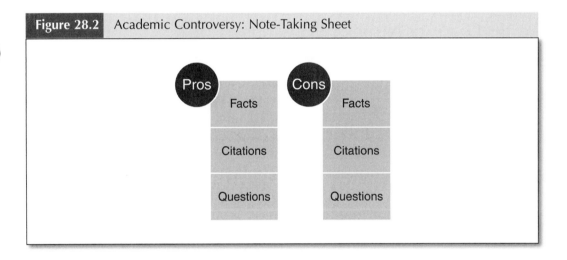

After discussion

Immediately after each quad finishes their presentations, students reflect on their note-taking sheet on new concepts or opinions that were developed during the discussion. They also record how their thinking on the issues may have changed as a result of viewing it from opposing points of view.

1. Students report out their reflections with one member of the group recording how perspectives were changed as a result of the discussion.

2. With one student working as the facilitator, the group collaborates to reach consensus on the issue. However, all members of the group are required to base their decision on the evidence. Students use their note-taking sheet to corroborate their thinking on the issue of genetic engineering.

3. After each quad has completed their deliberations, the teacher asks the facilitators to report out their position on the topic. Responses are recorded on a chart with the evidence to support each quad's point of view. The teacher also leads a debriefing on how groups reached consensus and notes any communication difficulties or behavioral issues.

DIFFERENTIATING INSTRUCTION FOR STRIVING READERS

Engaging in academic language enables striving readers to learn from their more knowledgeable peers on various topics presented for discussion (Fisher & Frey, 2007). To participate fully in the instructional strategy, striving readers can listen to podcasts on the topic. After listening to various sources, striving readers use their note-taking sheet as illustrated in Figure 28.2 to record their evidence for a point of view. The teacher may also choose to provide striving readers with a prediscussion preparation session in a virtual world such as Second Life. Participating in a virtual simulation of Academic Controversy enables striving readers to prepare their thoughts on a topic and to practice using academic language.

CONSIDERING THE LANGUAGE NEEDS OF ELL STUDENTS

Source: International Reading Association and National Council of Teachers of English (1996).

IRA/NCTE Standards for the English Language Arts

10. Students whose first language is not English make use of their first language to develop competency in the English language arts and to develop understanding of content across the curriculum.

English language learners require challenging curriculum that is purposeful (Snow, 2002). Academic Controversy facilitates second language learners' discourse in the content areas. After assessing second language learners' proficiency with English, teachers can differentiate the instructional strategy through the use of technology. For students who lack oral proficiency, the teacher can pair them with a slightly advanced second language learner to create visual representations for the major ideas associated with the topic. Teachers can also use technology to aid second language learners that are orally proficient but still struggle with writing. After pairing these students with native speakers, the teacher can give them a template for recording their evidence on the selected topic or issue. Students use the template to fill in their responses for each prompt and construct their argument based on it.

AN APPLICATION FOR INSTRUCTION AND LEARNING IN THE HEALTH CLASSROOM

Eleventh graders have been placed in quads to research the question, *Should marijuana be legalized?* Students are using their laptops and note-taking sheets to record their findings on the topic. After consulting with their partners, dyads begin to construct their presentations, which vary from podcasts to streamlined video to oral presentations. After the dyads for legalizing marijuana justify their position by citing its use as a pain reliever for cancer, the opposing team discusses research pointing to a link to more serious drug addictions. When both dyads have presented, the teams flip their positions and begin persuasive arguments based on their research. Immediately after the final presentation, students reflect on the experience and record how their thinking has changed on the topic. The quad's facilitator leads the group toward consensus, which is that marijuana should be only legalized for medicinal reasons and cites the research to support their point of view.

REFERENCES

Costa, A. L., & Marzano, R. (2001). Teaching the language of thinking. In A. L. Costa (Ed.), *Developing minds: A resource book for teaching thinking* (3rd ed., pp. 379–383). Alexandria, VA: Association for Curriculum and Development.

Fisher, D., & Frey, N. (2007). Implementing a schoolwide literacy framework: Improving achievement in an urban elementary school. *The Reading Teacher, 61*, 32–43.

International Reading Association and National Council of Teachers of English. (1996). *Standards for the English language arts.* Newark, DE: International Reading Association & Urbana, IL: National Council of Teachers of English.

Johnson, D. W., & Johnson, R. T. (1995). *Creative controversy: Intellectual challenge in the classroom* (3rd ed.). Edina, MN: Interaction Book.

Lenski, S., & Lewis, J. (Eds.). (2008). *Reading success for struggling adolescent learners.* New York: Guilford Press.

Probst, R. (2007). Tom Sawyer, teaching and talking. In K. Beers, R. Probst, & L. Rief (Eds.), *Adolescent literacy: Turning promise into practice* (pp. 43–61). Portsmouth, NH: Heinemann.

Snow, C. (2002). *Intermediate and adolescent literacy: The state of research and practice.* Retrieved December 2, 2009, from http://carnegie.org/fileadmin/Media/Publications/PDF/adolescent.pdf

Zwiers, J. (2008). *Building academic language: Essential practices for content classrooms.* Newark, DE: International Reading Association.

Strategy
29

Three-Level Reading Guide

Developing Literal, Interpretive, and Applied Reading of Text

STRATEGY OVERVIEW

Reading beyond the literal meaning of a text is extremely difficult for the majority of adolescent readers. However, proficient readers use their background knowledge to infer meaning that is not explicitly stated in the text (Keene, 2008). To bridge the performance gap in regard to interpreting text, a new paradigm is necessary for teaching critical reading across the content areas. As we require adolescent learners to read information critically, then they must be given time to analyze text and explicit instruction in how to do so (Deshler, Palinscar, Biancarosa, & Nair, 2007). One method for providing this scaffold is to offer situated practice in analysis of text similar to the process used by proficient readers (O'Brien, Stewart, & Beach, 2009).

The Three-Level Reading Guide instructional strategy (Herber, 1978) provides adolescent readers with situated practice in analyzing text on literal, inferential, and interpretative levels by offering them explicit instruction in deconstructing a text to read between the lines as well as beyond them. This instructional strategy is especially important for English language learners and striving readers who may require support in interpretation of text.

IRA/NCTE Standards for the English Language Arts

1. Students read a wide range of print and nonprint texts to build an understanding of texts, of themselves, and of the cultures of the United States and the world; to acquire new information; to respond to the needs and demands of society and the workplace; and for personal fulfillment. Among these texts are fiction and nonfiction, classic, and contemporary works.

2. Students read a wide range of literature from many periods in many genres to build an understanding of the many dimensions (e.g., philosophical, ethical, aesthetic) of human experience.

3. Students apply a wide range of strategies to comprehend, interpret, evaluate, and appreciate texts. They draw on their prior experience, their interactions with other readers and writers, their knowledge of word meaning and of other texts, their word identification strategies, and their understanding of textual features (e.g., sound-letter correspondence, sentence structure, context, graphics).

STEP-BY-STEP PROCEDURE

The purpose of the Three-Level Reading Guide strategy is to facilitate adolescent learners' processing of text on literal, inferential, and interpretative levels. The teacher selects a text that is slightly challenging for students and that will provide practice in making inferences. This strategy is best implemented after a unit of study when students have acquired background knowledge on the topic.

PREPARATION

The teacher begins the session by asking students what it means to read between the lines. The teacher records their responses on chart paper and also asks students to elaborate on the strategies they already use to make inferences. Before assigning students with a partner, the teacher distributes the Three-Level Reading Guide Study Sheet illustrated in Figure 29.1 to begin the strategy.

1. Reading silently, students use two different color highlighters to underline the literal information in the selected text: What is the main idea? Supporting details?

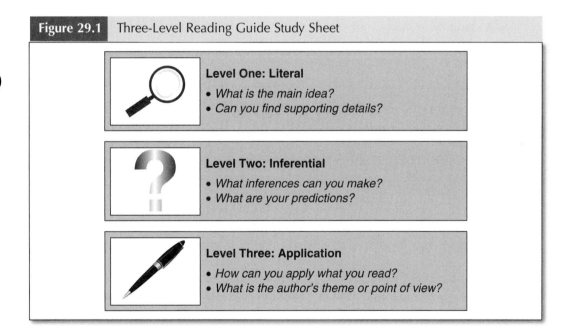

Figure 29.1 Three-Level Reading Guide Study Sheet

Level One: Literal
- *What is the main idea?*
- *Can you find supporting details?*

Level Two: Inferential
- *What inferences can you make?*
- *What are your predictions?*

Level Three: Application
- *How can you apply what you read?*
- *What is the author's theme or point of view?*

READING AND DISCUSSING

After students have underlined the information explicitly stated in the text and supporting statements, they begin to infer and interpret the author's meaning.

1. Students write down all the inferences they constructed while reading on their Three-Level Reading Guide Study Sheet.

2. Students use the second highlighter to underline text that supports their inferences.

3. When students have finished underlining their supporting evidence, they turn to their partner and begin to discuss their literal and inferential comprehension of the text. Discrepancies are resolved by examining the textual evidence. The teacher facilitates the session by walking to each dyad offering intervention if necessary.

4. After compiling their inferences, dyads discuss possible extensions of the literal meaning by answering the following questions on their study sheet:
   a. What is the author's theme or point of view?
   b. How can you apply what you read?
   c. What hypotheses have you created about the topic?

REFLECTING

After dyads complete their discussion, the teacher leads a debriefing on their situated practice.

1. Dyads report out their inferences with supporting evidence from the text. The teacher records the responses on the SMART Board or on chart paper. The class challenges dyads to clarify their rationale for each inference.

2. After reaching consensus on inferences from the text, the teacher records dyads' interpretations focusing on themes, hypotheses, and applications. The teacher also asks students to discuss any problems they had comprehending the text and how they resolved them collaboratively.

DIFFERENTIATING INSTRUCTION FOR STRIVING READERS

Striving readers often struggle with making inferences and interpreting text due to their limited background knowledge (Keene, 2008). Research indicates that striving readers make an benefit from explicit comprehension instruction in how to tap prior knowledge in order to inference (Flood & Lapp, 2000). One way to provide such support for striving readers is to use a think-aloud to explicitly demonstrate the inferential and interpretive reading of texts. The teacher may conduct the think-aloud with a small group of striving readers or assign students with a more advanced peer. After the think-aloud, the teacher asks students to record the strategies that were used to infer and interpret. Striving readers then practice the Three-Level Reading Guide strategy independently with feedback from the teacher.

CONSIDERING THE LANGUAGE NEEDS OF ELL STUDENTS

Source: International Reading Association and National Council of Teachers of English (1996).

IRA/NCTE Standards for the English Language Arts

10. Students whose first language is not English make use of their first language to develop competency in the English language arts and to develop understanding of content across the curriculum.

Similarly to striving readers, second language learners often struggle with making inferences and examining text. Visualization is a powerful strategy for English language learners to use to tap their prior knowledge while reading (Keene & Zimmerman, 1997). One adaptation for second language learners is to add a parallel activity during the first literal component of the Three-Level Reading Guide strategy. After English language learners have highlighted the main idea and supporting details in the text, they use their study sheet illustrated in Figure 29.1 to draw their visualization of the topic. The teacher then discusses the imagery with ELL students and uses the session to focus on vocabulary and to close any gaps in their knowledge base. Second language learners may also choose to illustrate their interpretations of the theme or hypotheses generated by their critical reading of the text for the final level of the strategy.

AN APPLICATION FOR INSTRUCTION AND LEARNING IN THE CAREER DEVELOPMENT CLASSROOM

Twelfth graders in an inclusion classroom are completing a unit of study on dealing with change in the workplace. Their teacher has bookmarked a series of article published by the *Wall Street Journal* that discuss the bankruptcy of General Motors and its impact on employees. The teacher begins by first asking students what they know about the General Motors Company (GM) and records their responses on a descriptive web. The class also discusses the federal government's bailout program to aid corporations at risk of failure such as GM. Students are assigned a partner and immediately begin to read the articles using an online color highlighter to focus on the main idea of the series on GM. After recording their inferences on the study sheet, students discuss their responses with their partners and reach consensus on them. Next, students use the descriptive web about GM to generate hypotheses on how its employees will cope with changes in the corporation or with layoffs. When students have completed their interpretative reading of the GM series, the teacher records their inferences and hypotheses on a SMART Board. Students also reflect on similar situations in other industries such as banking.

REFERENCES

Deshler, D., Palinscar, A. S., Biancarosa, G., & Nair, M. (2007). *Informed choices for struggling adolescent readers.* Newark, DE: International Reading Association and Carnegie Corporation.

Flood, J., & Lapp, D. (2000). Reading comprehension instruction for at-risk students: Research based practices that can make a difference. In D. Moore, D. Alvermann, & K. Hinchman (Eds.), *Struggling adolescent readers: A collection of teaching strategies* (pp. 138–148). Newark, DE: International Reading Association.

Herber, H. (1978). *Teaching reading in the content areas.* Englewood Cliffs, NJ: Prentice Hall.

International Reading Association and National Council of Teachers of English. (1996). *Standards for the English*

language arts. Newark, DE: International Reading Association & Urbana, IL: National Council of Teachers of English.

Keene, E. (2008). *To understand: New horizons in reading comprehension.* Portsmouth, NH: Heinemann.

Keene, E., & Zimmerman, S. (1997). *Mosaics of thought: Teaching comprehension in a reader's workshop.* Portsmouth, NH: Heinemann.

O'Brien, D., Stewart, R., & Beach, R. (2009). Proficient reading in school: Traditional paradigms and new textual landscapes. In L. Christenbury, R. Bomer, & P. Smagorinsky (Eds.), *Handbook of adolescent literacy* (pp. 80–98). New York: Guilford Press.

Strategy 30

Request Reciprocal Teaching

Collaborative Critical Thinking

STRATEGY OVERVIEW

In the majority of classrooms today, teachers can observe adolescent readers staring at the printed page with inadequate critical thinking skills to process the text. In particular, striving readers and second language learners need additional support to analyze text and to summarize its content. Research indicates that discussions about text are effective in promoting comprehension of difficult subject matter (Alvermann, Dillon, & O'Brien, 1987).

Palinscar and Brown (1984) documented the importance of modeling and scaffolding students' ability to predict, summarize, question, and clarify information. Recent research indicates that explicit instruction in how to process text as well as collaborative discussions on using critical thinking skills improve comprehension (McKeown, Beck, & Blake, 2009).The Request Reciprocal Teaching strategy fosters adolescent learners' critical thinking as they question, analyze, predict, and synthesize information while they read.

Source: International Reading Association and National Council of Teachers of English (1996).

IRA/NCTE Standards for the English Language Arts

3. Students apply a wide range of strategies to comprehend, interpret, evaluate, and appreciate texts. They draw on their prior experience, their interactions with other readers and writers, their knowledge of word meaning and of other texts, their word identification strategies, and their understanding of textual features (e.g., sound-letter correspondence, sentence structure, context, graphics).

9. Students participate as knowledgeable, reflective, creative, and critical members of a variety of literacy communities.

STEP-BY-STEP PROCEDURE

The purpose of the Request Reciprocal Teaching instructional strategy is to provide adolescent readers with modeling and guided practice in questioning, predicting, summarizing, and clarifying information. The strategy works best with small groups of students or in individual tutorial sessions.

BEFORE READING

Before beginning the instructional strategy, the teacher selects reading material that is slightly challenging and provides opportunities for readers to make predictions.

1. The teacher begins the session by introducing the subject of the reading through a descriptive web on chart paper. Students brainstorm concepts and vocabulary words associated with the topic.

2. The teacher distributes Figure 30.1, Request Reciprocal Teaching Guide, and explains the process of questioning the text.

3. The teacher has broken the passage into critical components for question and discussion sessions.

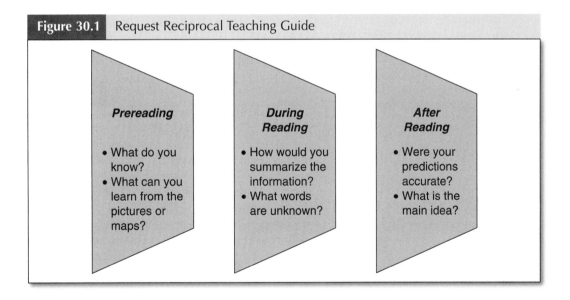

Figure 30.1   Request Reciprocal Teaching Guide

Prereading
- What do you know?
- What can you learn from the pictures or maps?

During Reading
- How would you summarize the information?
- What words are unknown?

After Reading
- Were your predictions accurate?
- What is the main idea?

DURING READING

Before students begin to read the first section silently, the teacher instructs them to jot down their questions while they read. The teacher acts as a recorder to note questions as both parties will take turns in the discussion.

1. When students have completed their reading, the teacher begins by modeling a broad inference question. The teacher explains that when a question is asked, everyone closes their book and responds. Only one answer is unacceptable: "I don't know."

2. After the teacher has modeled a few questions, students begin to query the teacher. If necessary, the teacher or students may refer back to the text or to the descriptive web to respond to a question.

3. When discussion is exhausted, the teacher demonstrates how to summarize the passage and clarifies any confusing points or unknown vocabulary words.

4. The process is repeated again for the next section of the text. At a critical point, the teacher stops and asks students to predict what they think will happen next. Students support their answers by citing evidence from the text.

AFTER READING

When all of the text passages have been queried and discussed, the teacher demonstrates how to summarize information.

1. To debrief, the teacher uses transparencies or a SMART Board to model a summary of the text. The teacher also facilitates a discussion regarding the accuracy of their predictions and how they can improve them.

2. To conclude the session, the teacher asks students to jot down their reflections on what they learned from the Request Reciprocal Teaching and how they will use it during independent reading.

Students may also choose to construct a bookmark that highlights key strategies they learned during the session for questioning, predicting, or summarizing of text.

DIFFERENTIATING INSTRUCTION FOR STRIVING READERS

Recent research indicates that striving readers need active processing of text that helps them make personal connections to prior knowledge (Blachowicz & Fisher, 1996). By engaging in collaborative discussions such as Request Reciprocal Teaching, striving adolescent readers are given the opportunity to voice their thoughts as they process information. To prepare them for this instructional strategy, the teacher may want to demonstrate the process of questioning, predicting, and summarizing of information with digital photos or paintings. As students study the photograph or painting, the teacher leads them in making inferences and predictions about the topic illustrated. After discussing their perspectives, the teacher demonstrates how to write a summary paragraph of the information they gleaned from the photo or painting.

CONSIDERING THE LANGUAGE NEEDS OF ELL STUDENTS

IRA/NCTE Standards for the English Language Arts

10. Students whose first language is not English make use of their first language to develop competency in the English language arts and to develop understanding of content across the curriculum.

Source: International Reading Association and National Council of Teachers of English (1996).

The English language learner cluster model has been shown to be effective in improving second language learners' proficiency across the curriculum (Rance-Roney, 2009). In this model, content area teachers and support personnel work collaboratively to present academic content in students' native language as well as in English. Most importantly, the team collaborates on teaching English language learners critical strategies to process and comprehend text. When the ELL cluster model is used for Request Reciprocal Teaching, the entire instructional team uses the method to model and practice questioning, predicting, and summarizing of text. Second language learners also benefit by practicing the method in their native language to understand their role as a critical reader.

AN APPLICATION FOR INSTRUCTION AND LEARNING IN THE PHYSICS CLASSROOM

Twelfth graders have just begun a chapter on waves and motion. The teacher gathers a small group of striving readers to demonstrate the Request Reciprocal Teaching strategy using the guide illustrated in figure 30.1. Using a small whiteboard, the teacher asks students to generate vocabulary and concepts for a descriptive web on the topic of waves. After this quick assessment to check prior knowledge regarding waves and their properties, the teacher explains the process of questioning, clarifying, and summarizing text. She begins by stating the purpose for her reading of the chapter with this question, "What are the different types of waves and what do they have in common?" Through a think-aloud, the teacher models how to use pictures, chapter subheadings, and graphics to generate questions. After reading aloud the next section of the chapter, the teacher demonstrates additional questions such as, "What is the difference between a longitudinal and transverse wave?" After the discussion of the passage, the teacher facilitates the writing of a summary to highlight the main ideas. The process is repeated with the next section of the text. However, now students take the lead reading the text aloud and generating questions. At the completion of the session, the teacher asks students to revisit the descriptive web that was created as a prereading activity. Students elaborate on the web by adding new concepts, supporting details, and vocabulary words. To conclude the session, the teacher asks the students to outline the main ideas regarding waves and how they transmit energy. She also asks students to reflect aloud how the Request Reciprocal Teaching strategy improved their deep processing of text.

REFERENCES

Alvermann, D., Dillon, D., & O'Brien, D. (1987). *Using discussion to promote reading comprehension.* Newark, DE: International Reading Association.

Blachowicz, C., & Fisher, P. (1996). *Teaching vocabulary in all classrooms.* Englewood Cliffs, NJ: Merrill.

International Reading Association and National Council of Teachers of English. (1996). *Standards for the English language arts.* Newark, DE: International Reading Association & Urbana, IL: National Council of Teachers of English.

McKeown, M., Beck, I., & Blake, R. (2009). Rethinking reading comprehension instruction: A comparison of instruction for strategies and content approaches. *Reading Research Quarterly, 44,* 218–256.

Palinscar, A. S., & Brown, A. L. (1984). Reciprocal teaching of comprehension fostering and comprehension monitoring activities. *Cognition and Instruction, 1,* 117–175.

Rance-Roney, J. (2009). Best practices for adolescent ELLs. *Educational Leadership, 66,* 32–37.

SECTION VII

Writing Informational Text

Developing Writing in the Content Areas

The pen is the tongue of the mind.

—Miguel de Cervantes

In 2004, the National Commission on Writing stated that writing was the most neglected area of the 3 Rs. Yet the ability to read, comprehend, and write to organize knowledge is now considered a survival skill in the digital age (Graham & Perin, 2007b). Despite its importance, teachers of middle and high school students struggle on a daily basis to engage and motivate adolescent learners to explore the process of writing. Writing informational text, or academic writing, is especially difficult for striving readers and second language learners as its structure is so different from narrative text (Johannessen & McCann, 2009). This section demonstrates the best practices in academic writing for adolescent learners of differing abilities and explores strategies across content areas.

WHAT RESEARCH HAS TO SAY ABOUT THE DEVELOPMENT OF STUDENTS' WRITING

Is the writing process similar to reading? How do I engage and motivate adolescent learners to write to learn? Across several decades, teachers have raised these questions to their peers and administrators. Although writing instruction has not received as much attention as reading, recent research has outlined "best practices" for academic writing. This section provides the research framework for the development of academic writing across modalities and content areas.

Complex Nature of Academic Writing

Approximately 7,000 adolescents *a day* are estimated to drop out of high school because they lack the necessary literacy skills required in the curriculum (Snow & Biancarosa, 2003). This disturbing fact becomes even more worrisome when business leaders report that in the digital age, writing has become a critical skill in the workplace as e-mailing, text messaging, and online conferencing becomes the norm (National Commission on Writing, 2004a). Based on these reports, we have to improve how we teach academic writing, or informational writing, in middle and high schools (Jago, 2009; Snow & Biancarosa, 2003).

According to middle and high school teachers, the major emphasis on writing instruction continues to be the five-paragraph essay structure (Graham & Perin, 2007b). Yet skilled writers use a variety of forms, strategies, and skills that they bring to each task (Graham & Perin, 2007a). Effective writing instruction recognizes that the complex nature of writing demands engagement and practice with different genres and modes of text to develop knowledge of academic discourse (Shanahan, 2008).

Before discussing effective means of instructing adolescent learners in academic writing, it is critical to understand its complex nature. Many educators view writing and reading as parallel processes. However, writing about a topic of study entails a much deeper level of processing (Fordham, Wellman, & Sandman, 2002). The writer of academic text needs to research the topic, organize ideas, provide supporting evidence, and explain other points of view (Morgan & Beaumont, 2003). It requires adolescent learners to use critical thinking skills such as analysis, causal reasoning, argumentation, and evaluation (Zwiers, 2008). Therefore, it is possible for adolescent learners to be adept at reading but still struggle with academic writing (Graham & Perin, 2007b). Proficient writers understand that each academic discipline has its own discourse and vocabulary, which has to be discussed and analyzed to process (Zwiers, 2008).

Dialogic and Collaborative Instruction

One method for engaging adolescent learners in academic discourse is through dialogic and collaborative inquiry (Chandler-Olcott, 2008). Participating in collaborative peer discussions on a topic of inquiry allows adolescent learners to cite facts, support ideas, and to "think through" ideas before writing (Morgan & Beaumont, 2003). Through discussion, adolescent learners begin to use content area vocabulary and more complex sentence structures to express their thoughts and opinions on the topic of study (Zwiers, 2008).

This dialogic approach to the teaching of academic writing is especially critical due to the "situated" nature of writing (Lesley & Matthews, 2009). For example, an adolescent learner may become proficient in writing lab reports for science but struggle with evidence-based historical critiques (Graham & Perin, 2007b). According to research, one of the most effective approaches for writing instruction is the inquiry method (Johannessen & McCann, 2009). In the inquiry method, students explore a problem or idea collaboratively and dialogue with each other during data analysis. As each student participates in the discussion, they define, explain, illustrate, and rehearse their ideas before writing them (Chandler-Olcott, 2008). As adolescent learners participate in these dialogic communities of inquiry, teachers are able to assess their background knowledge and to provide instruction to close up any gaps in vocabulary or conceptual understanding (Zwiers, 2008).

Best Practices in Academic Writing Instruction

Participation in a dialogic community of inquiry is one method for improving academic writing. According to research, it is also critical to expose adolescent learners to different types of texts or genres on any topic before students begin to write (Shanahan, 2008). When students analyze textbook chapters, magazine articles, or online video reports regarding a topic of study, they build background knowledge and also begin to notice style features of a particular academic written discourse (Zwiers, 2008).

Adolescent learners' expertise in visual text also provides teachers with another avenue of exploration regarding academic discourse (Zenkou & Harmon, 2009). As students analyze photographs or primary sources of information, they gradually react and respond to the visual image with content vocabulary and discourse through online chat rooms (Morgan & Beaumont, 2003). These online discussions become critical prewriting activities where adolescent learners transform thoughts into academic writing.

According to the research, prewriting activities such as visualization, inquiry activities, and discussion are necessary components to facilitate academic writing (Zwiers, 2008). As with reading instruction, explicit instruction in writing strategies, text features, and the process of writing have also been shown to improve adolescent learners' writing of informational text (Graham & Perin, 2007b). In addition, direct instruction on writing summaries and aspects of grammar such as sentence structure also had an impact on adolescent students' grasp of informational writing (Graham & Perin, 2007a).

A Framework for Teaching Informational Writing Skills to Adolescent Students

To develop academic writing, adolescent learners need explicit instruction in the writing process across content areas. The following suggestions provide the foundation for development of informational writing:

1. Writing for information, or academic writing, is a complex process that requires deep understanding of the topic and of the discourse community (Fordham et al., 2002).

2. Effective writers of informational text implement critical thinking skills such as analysis, causal reasoning, argumentation, and evaluation (Zwiers, 2008).

3. Explicit instructional strategies for academic writing as well as the writing process have been shown to improve adolescent learners' writing skills (Graham & Perin, 2007b).

4. Dialogic and collaborative inquiry that facilitates academic discourse enables adolescent learners to "think through ideas" before engaging in writing for information (Johannessen & McCann, 2009).

5. Analysis of multiple texts across genres and formats allows adolescent learners to develop background knowledge on a topic and to analyze text features and discourse (Morgan & Beaumont, 2003).

In this section, "Developing Students' Informational Writing Skills," five instructional strategies are presented for use in content area classrooms. The strategies are presented as guides for teachers of adolescent learners to adapt and use for their specific discipline and student profile.

Tips on Teaching Informational Writing

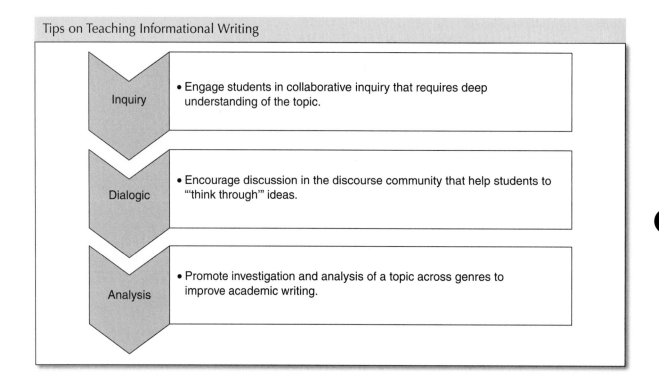

Inquiry	• Engage students in collaborative inquiry that requires deep understanding of the topic.
Dialogic	• Encourage discussion in the discourse community that help students to "'think through'" ideas.
Analysis	• Promote investigation and analysis of a topic across genres to improve academic writing.

A Strategy for Assessing the Development of Students' Writing of Informational Text

According to the National Commission on Writing (2004b), adolescent students continue to struggle with composition of academic text. Learning to write informational text has been compared to the process of acquiring a second language as students grapple with new vocabulary words and more complex sentence structures (Mota-Altman, 2006). To scaffold the acquisition of this new academic language, teachers observe and record anecdotal data on the following: (a) identification and use of academic vocabulary, (b) comprehension of academic discourse and its features, (c) use of specific style features for each academic genre, (d) summarization of ideas with citations from sources, and (e) revision and reflection of academic writing. The performance-based assessment illustrated in Figure VII.1, Assessment of Informational Writing, is designed to assist teachers

Figure VII.1	Assessment of Informational Writing			
Writing Element	*Advanced*	*Target*	*Developing*	*Below Standard*
Critical thinking	Demonstrates *advanced* critical thinking skills with analysis and creative synthesis of ideas and use of logic. [4 points]	Demonstrates *strong* critical thinking skills with analysis and synthesis of ideas and use of logic. [3 points]	Demonstrates *developing* critical thinking skills with analysis and synthesis of ideas and use of logic. [2 points]	Demonstrates *limited* critical thinking skills with little analysis or synthesis of ideas and use of logic. [1 point]
Organizational structure	Presents *sophisticated* thesis with supporting paragraphs and decisive conclusion. [4 points]	Presents *strong* thesis with supporting paragraphs and conclusion. [3 points]	Presents *adequate* thesis with supporting paragraphs and conclusion. [2 points]	Presents *limited* thesis with little support and no concluding paragraph. [1 point]
Discourse community	Engages in discourse of academic community with *advanced* vocabulary and sentence structure. [4 points]	Engages in discourse of academic community with *target* vocabulary and sentence structure. [3 points]	Engages in discourse of academic community with *adequate* vocabulary and sentence structure. [2 points]	Engages in discourse of academic community with *limited* vocabulary and sentence structure. [1 point]
Mechanics	Demonstrates *advanced* skills with no spelling or grammatical errors. [4 points]	Demonstrates *strong* skills with *one* spelling or grammatical error. [3 points]	Demonstrates *adequate* skills with *several* spelling or grammatical errors. [2 points]	Demonstrates *limited* skills with numerous spelling or grammatical errors. [1 points]

Advanced: 16–13 points

Target: 12–9 points

Developing: 8–5 points

Below standard: 4–1 points

as they scaffold students' composition of academic content. Teachers can use the rubric for the whole class, small group, or individualized instruction.

REFLECTIVE PRACTICE ON THE TEACHING OF WRITING OF INFORMATIONAL TEXT

Proficiency in academic writing varies among adolescent learners. To meet individual student needs, the teacher has to observe writing performances and record anecdotally apparent needs. The rubric illustrated in Figure VII.1 may also be used to holistically view how a class comprehends an academic genre. After analyzing performance data from the rubric, the teacher can reflect on the following questions:

- How are students acquiring vocabulary in this content area? Are certain words still problematic?
- How can their academic discourse be expanded or elaborated?
- What models of academic writing may help them with a targeted problem area?

Only through careful observation and analysis by the teacher will adolescent writers develop their academic writing. As with any language learning, adolescent writers will gradually acquire knowledge of academic discourses through immersion, modeling, guided practice, and reflection.

PROFESSIONAL RESOURCES

Foster, G. (2009). *12 sides to your story: Simple steps for turning ordinary writing into something extraordinary*. Portland, ME: Stenhouse.

Gallagher, K. (2006). *Teaching adolescent writers*. Portland, ME: Stenhouse.

Graham, S. (2005). *Writing better: Effective strategies for teaching students with learning difficulties*. Baltimore, MD: Brooks.

Graham, S., MacArthur, C., & Fitzgerald, J. (Eds.). (2007). *Best practices in writing instruction*. New York: Guilford Press.

National Writing Project, & Nagin, C. (2006). *Because writing matters: Improving student writing in our schools*. San Fransisco: Jossey-Bass.

National Writing Project Website. http://www.nwp.org.

REFERENCES

Chandler-Olcott, K. (2008). Humanities instruction for adolescent literacy learners. In K. Hinchman & H. Sheridan-Thomas (Eds.), *Best practices in adolescent literacy instruction* (pp. 212–228). New York: Guilford Press.

Fordham, N. W., Wellman, D., & Sandman, A. (2002). Taming the text: Engaging and supporting students in social studies readings. *Social Studies, 93*, 149–158.

Graham, S., & Perin, D. (2007a). A meta-analysis of writing instruction for adolescent students. *Journal of Educational Psychology, 99*, 445–476.

Graham, S., & Perin, D. (2007b). *Writing next: Effective strategies to improve writing of adolescents in middle and high schools. A report to the Carnegie Corporation of New York.* Washington, DC: Alliance for Excellent Education.

Jago, C. (2009). Writing in the 21st century: Crash! The currency crisis in American culture. Report retrieved December 9, 2009, from http://www.nwp.org/cs/public/download/nwp_file/12468/Crash!_The_Currency_Crisis_in_American_Culture.pdf?x-r=pcfile_d

Johannessen, L., & McCann, T. (2009). Adolescents who struggle with literacy. In L. Christenbury, R. Bomer, & P. Smagorinsky (Eds.), *Handbook of adolescent literacy* (pp. 65–79). New York: Guilford Press.

Lesley, M., & Matthews, M. (2009). Place-based essay writing and content area literacy instruction for preservice secondary teachers. *Journal of Adolescent and Adult Literacy, 52*, 522–533.

Morgan, W., & Beaumont, G. (2003). A dialogic approach to argumentation: Using a chat room to develop early adolescent students' argumentative writing. *Journal of Adolescent and Adult Literacy, 47,* 46–158.

Mota-Altman, N. (2006). Academic language: Everyone's second language. *California English.* Retrieved December 7, 2009, from http://www.nwp.org/cs/public/print/resource/2329

National Commission on Writing. (2004a). *The neglected R: The need for a writing revolution.* Retrieved December 7, 2009, from http://www.college board.com

National Commission on Writing. (2004b). *A ticket to work . . . or a ticket out: A survey of business leaders.* Retrieved December 7, 2009, from http://www.writing commission.org

Shanahan, C. (2008). Reading and writing across multiple texts. In K. Hinchman & H. Sheridan-Thomas (Eds.), *Best practices in adolescent literacy instruction* (pp. 57–77). New York: Guilford Press.

Snow, C., & Biancarosa, G. (2003). *Adolescent literacy and the achievement gap: Where do we go from here?* New York: Carnegie Corporation of New York.

Zenkou, K., & Harmon, J. (2009). Picturing a writing process: Photovoice and teaching writing to urban youth. *Journal of Adolescent and Adult Literacy, 52,* 575–585.

Zwiers, J. (2008). *Building academic language: Essential practices for content classrooms.* Newark, DE: International Reading Association.

Strategy

31

Concept Star

Visualization for a Prewriting Strategy

STRATEGY OVERVIEW

The new vision of literacy for the information age calls for an inquiry-based model that engages adolescent learners in collaborative dialogue across content areas and text formats (Hobbs, 2005). Visual representation of knowledge is a critical mode for processing information in the digital age (Zoss, 2009). As students translate their conceptual understandings into symbolic or visual representations, they are developing new ideas and understandings in the process (Griffin & Schwartz, 2005; Zoss, 2009). According to the research, deep understanding of content area vocabulary and topics is critical before adolescent learners can engage in academic writing (Harmon, Wood, & Hedrick, 2008).

The Concept Star strategy facilitates adolescent learners' understanding of a topic or concept. It may also be used to develop understanding of specific academic vocabulary terms before students write informational text.

Source: International Reading Association and National Council of Teachers of English (1996).

IRA/NCTE Standards for the English Language Arts

2. Students read a wide range of literature from many periods in many genres to build an understanding of the many dimensions (e.g., philosophical, ethical, aesthetic) of human experience.
4. Students adjust their use of spoken, written, and visual language (e.g., conventions, style, vocabulary) to communicate effectively with a variety of audiences and for different purposes.
5. Students employ a wide range of strategies as they write and use different writing process elements appropriately to communicate with different audiences for a variety of purposes.

STEP-BY-STEP PROCEDURE

Before beginning the instructional sequence, provide adolescent learners with readings on the topic or concept. Each group of students is provided with a menu of reading options that include the following: textbook chapters, magazine articles, Internet Web site bookmarks, YouTube or other videos, and digital photographs.

Students are grouped with a partner to peruse the materials on the menu. As students read materials, they jot down their notes on the topic or concept.

BEFORE WRITING

When students have completed their readings on the topic, the teacher distributes the Concept Star graphic organizer as illustrated in Figure 31.1.

Figure 31.1	Concept Star Graphic Organizer

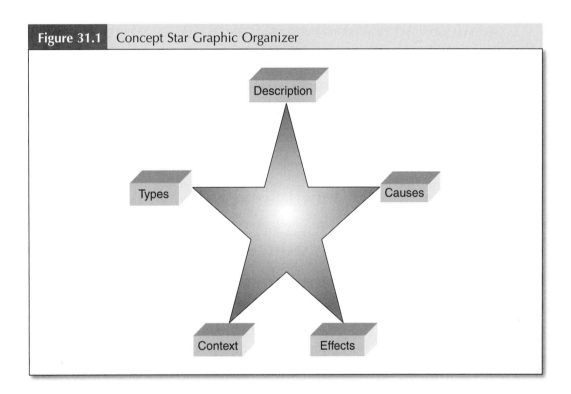

1. The teacher and students jointly construct the text for each point on the star. The categories for each star can be revised depending on the topic.

2. During the construction of the graphic organizer, the teacher requires students to cite their sources as they address each component of the concept star:

    a. *Description/definition:* How would you define or describe the topic or concept?

    b. *Causes/problem:* What are some of the causes for the current problem or situation?

    c. *Effects/solutions:* What are some possible effects/solutions?

    d. *Context:* What is the context of the problem or topic (e.g., geography, political, or cultural context)?

    e. *Types/applications:* What are some examples from your research on how solutions or applications are being implemented?

3. As students discuss and elaborate on each component, the teacher adds any additional content vocabulary words to the word wall for future reference.

DURING WRITING

The following components may take several sessions for the students to complete.

1. Students work with their partners to construct a draft of their text on the topic using the Concept Star graphic organizer. Each component of the star is used to begin a new paragraph in their text.

2. When students have completed their draft, they use the Concept Star graphic organizer as a revising tool to analyze their written work. If details or supporting evidence from the graphic organizer is missing, it is added to the text. Students also use their reading materials from the prewriting component to include content area vocabulary and further information on the topic.

3. When students have completed their informational text on the topic, they work with their partner and teacher to edit their writing for peer review. During the editing process, students compare their informational writing with the models that were shared during the prewriting component.

AFTER WRITING

To conclude the Concept Star strategy sessions, the teacher facilitates a Socratic seminar on the topic. Students use their informational writings to participate in the discussion.

1. The teacher begins the Socratic seminar by asking students to reflect on how their thinking about the topic has been transformed through the writing process.

2. After reflections are shared, the teacher turns the discussion over to students to raise questions or opinions that were formulated during the writing process.

3. To conclude the session, the teacher returns to the original Concept Star graphic organizer and asks students to add supporting facts, details, or examples from their informational writings.

DIFFERENTIATING INSTRUCTION FOR STRIVING READERS

When striving readers engage in active instruction, review multiple sources of information, and make connections to prior knowledge, they understand concepts and vocabulary words at a deeper level (Blachowicz & Fisher, 1996). The Concept Star instructional strategy provides striving adolescent readers with a dialogic discussion of concepts or content that will prepare them for academic writing. One modification to include for striving readers is a menu of podcasts on the topic or concept. This option of audio files allows striving readers to hear academic discourse and vocabulary on a higher level than their actual reading performance. When students are exposed to academic vocabulary on the receptive level, they begin to assimilate and accommodate the information.

CONSIDERING THE LANGUAGE NEEDS OF ELL STUDENTS

Source: International Reading Association and National Council of Teachers of English (1996).

> ### IRA/NCTE Standards for the English Language Arts
>
> 10. Students whose first language is not English make use of their first language to develop competency in the English language arts and to develop understanding of content across the curriculum.

English language learners require content area instruction that builds on their cultural, cognitive, and linguistic backgrounds to make personal connections (Garcia & Nagy, 1993). One adaptation of the Concept Star strategy for second language learners is to use digital photographs or illustrations as a preparation for the lesson. Students work with the teacher or a partner to create a vocabulary ring to use as a reference. As students discuss and describe the photos or illustrations, they construct academic vocabulary cards and definitions to use during their writing.

AN APPLICATION FOR INSTRUCTION AND LEARNING IN THE HISTORY CLASSROOM

Ninth graders in global history class are beginning a unit on the Crusades. Before beginning the unit, the teacher provides students with readings from the textbook, history magazines, and short movie clips on the Crusades. When students have completed their readings, the teacher facilitates a discussion on the five points of the Concept Star graphic organizer (See Figure 31.1):

- *Description/definition*: How would you define or describe the Crusades?
- *Causes/problem*: What are some of the causes for the series of wars?
- *Effects/solutions*: How did the Crusades finally end?
- *Context*: What was the cultural, religious, and political context of the day that led to the wars?
- *Types/applications*: How are we still feeling the effects of the Crusades in today's political climate?

Students use their reading materials as references during the construction of the graphic organizer. The teacher allocates additional time for each dyad to elaborate on their Concept Star with supporting details and citations. Students begin the next class session by using their Concept Star graphic organizer to draft a report on the Crusades. During the drafting period, students discuss style issues such as sentence structure and vocabulary choice. After revising their work, dyads use their Concept Star graphic organizer as a self-assessment tool to ascertain if they included key facts and supporting evidence. The teacher then facilitates a class discussion on the causes and effects of the Crusades and focuses on possible ramifications for today's global society.

REFERENCES

Blachowicz, C., & Fisher, P. (1996). *Teaching vocabulary in all classrooms.* Englewood Cliffs, NJ: Merrill.

Garcia, G., & Nagy, W. (1993). Latino students' concept of cognates. In D. Leu & C. Kinzer (Eds.), *Examining central issues in literacy, research, theory, and practice* (pp. 367–373). 42nd Yearbook of the National Reading Conference. Chicago: National Reading Conference.

Griffin, M., & Schwartz, D. (2005). Visual communication skills and media literacy. In J. Flood, S. Brice-Heath, & D. Lapp (Eds.), *Handbook of research on teaching literacy through the visual and communication arts* (pp. 40–48). Mahwah, NJ: Lawrence Erlbaum.

Harmon, J., Wood, K., & Hedrick, W. (2008). Vocabulary instruction in middle and secondary content classrooms: Understandings and direction from research. In A. E. Farstrup & S. J. Samuels (Eds.), *What research has to say about vocabulary instruction* (pp. 150–181). Newark, DE: International Reading Association.

Hobbs, R. (2005). Literacy for the information age. In J. Flood, S. Brice-Heath, & D. Lapp (Eds.), *Handbook of research on teaching literacy through the visual and communication arts* (pp. 7–14). Mahwah, NJ: Lawrence Erlbaum.

International Reading Association and National Council of Teachers of English. (1996). *Standards for the English language arts.* Newark, DE: International Reading Association & Urbana, IL: National Council of Teachers of English.

Zoss, M. (2009). Visual arts and literacy. In L. Christenbury, R. Bomer, & P. Smagorinsky (Eds.), *Handbook of adolescent literacy* (pp. 183–197). New York: Guilford Press.

Concept Mind Map

Strategy 32

Facilitating Collaborative Writing

Academic language proficiency is the ability to construct meaning from oral and written language, to analyze complex ideas and information, to identify features of different genres, and to use appropriate discourse to communicate (Cummins, 1979; Zwiers, 2008). To engage in informational writing, adolescent learners need to be immersed in content area vocabulary and discourse to become proficient in academic language. Concept Mind Maps is a prewriting instructional strategy to facilitate adolescent learners' conceptual understanding of a topic.

The purpose of the Concept Mind Map instructional strategy is to aid adolescent writers in summarizing information from multiple sources, processing complex ideas, and relating new concepts to prior knowledge. As students collaborate on constructing their mind maps, they discuss relationships between ideas and supporting evidence (Zoss, 2009). Through discussion and collaboration, adolescent learners improve their academic language proficiency and generate the conceptual knowledge base to write informational text.

As adolescent learners become adept at using Concept Mind Maps, they begin to internalize an independent strategy to prepare for academic writing. The following procedures are for whole-class discussion to introduce adolescent learners to this prewriting strategy.

IRA/NCTE Standards for the English Language Arts

2. Students read a wide range of literature from many periods in many genres to build an understanding of the many dimensions (e.g., philosophical, ethical, aesthetic) of human experience.

4. Students adjust their use of spoken, written, and visual language (e.g., conventions, style, vocabulary) to communicate effectively with a variety of audiences and for different purposes.

5. Students employ a wide range of strategies as they write and use different writing process elements appropriately to communicate with different audiences for a variety of purposes.

Source: International Reading Association and National Council of Teachers of English (1996).

STEP-BY-STEP PROCEDURE

It is important that adolescent learners approach the Concept Mind Map as a collaborative, brainstorming activity. It is not meant to be an outline for a report or presentation, but a concept association instructional strategy.

BEFORE WRITING

The session begins with the teacher asking students to define the concept or topic that is displayed on chart paper or a SMART Board.

1. After discussing initial definitions, the teacher distributes the Concept Mind Map graphic organizer (Figure 32.1).

2. Students collaborate with the teacher to generate concepts or vocabulary words they associate with the topic/idea. These associations are posted in the first circle around the concept.

3. After the initial concept association discussion, students then work with a partner to edit or elaborate on the ideas or vocabulary words within the first circle.

4. Next the teacher and students collaborate to generate a deeper layer of ideas or vocabulary words related to first conceptual circle on the graphic organizer.

5. When the class has exhausted their conceptual associations, the teacher asks students to analyze their concept map to discern relationships among the concepts. The graphic organizer is then reordered to reflect these relationships.

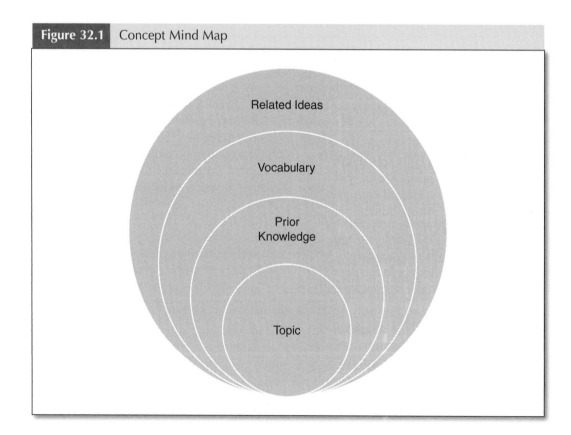

Figure 32.1   Concept Mind Map

DURING WRITING

In the next class session, the teacher distributes content materials composed of text-book chapters, magazine articles, Web sites, and videos on the topic. Students select their reference materials and meet with their partner to read and examine them.

1. Students discuss their reference materials and revisit the Concept Mind Map to add additional ideas, relationships, or vocabulary words.

2. After revisiting the graphic organizer, students begin to draft their report on the topic. With their partner, adolescent learners discuss their outline, focusing on key concepts and supporting details.

3. During the drafting component, students use their reference materials and Concept Mind Map to improve their use of academic vocabulary and sentence structure.

AFTER WRITING

The postwriting component is used to edit and revise students' informational text. The teacher facilitates the session and conferences with individual students.

1. Students work with their partners to edit and revise their informational text. Partners use their Concept Mind Map as an editing tool to elaborate or eliminate text.

2. Students meet with another dyad to switch their informational writing for analysis and review. Peers critique their text and engage one another in discussion on the topic.

DIFFERENTIATING INSTRUCTION FOR STRIVING READERS

Visual representations or symbols for more complex concepts are beneficial for adolescent striving readers to become proficient in cognitive academic language (Zwiers, 2008). An adaptation of the Concept Mind Map strategy is to provide striving readers with the option of creating a digital story on the topic or idea. Striving readers research facts, supporting details, digital photos or clips on their topic and then create a multimedia presentation that represents their thinking on the topic. The multimodal format promotes inquiry and allows striving readers to be actively engaged in constructing conceptual understanding of the topic.

CONSIDERING THE LANGUAGE NEEDS OF ELL STUDENTS

IRA/NCTE Standards for the English Language Arts

10. Students whose first language is not English make use of their first language to develop competency in the English language arts and to develop understanding of content across the curriculum.

Source: International Reading Association and National Council of Teachers of English (1996).

Developing proficiency in academic language often takes several years for second language learners. One method for expediting the process is to facilitate instruction that builds on the cultural, linguistic, and cognitive backgrounds of English language learners (Garcia & Nagy, 1993). An adaptation of the Concept Mind Map strategy for ELL students is to partner them with a slightly more advanced native speaker to construct the mind map. As their partner acts as scribe, the ELL student also writes on the map the vocabulary word in their own language. If they do not know how to write the word in their native tongue, they can illustrate it. Afterwards, the Concept Mind Map becomes a bilingual reference tool for both students to use while writing their text.

AN APPLICATION FOR INSTRUCTION AND LEARNING IN THE CHEMISTRY CLASSROOM

Chemistry students have just begun a chapter in their textbook on three types of matter: elements, compounds, and mixtures. The teacher facilitates a hands-on inquiry lesson using different materials such as metal bolts (elements), salt (compounds), and salad (mixture). Students work with their partners to categorize and describe each type of matter. After the debriefing, the teacher shows students a video on YouTube that presents the topic using music and cartoon animation.

After the introduction to the topic, the teacher distributes the Concept Mind Map illustrated in Figure 32.1. Working independently, each student jots down their first associations with the topic and ideas on the inner circle. Then they meet with their partner to elaborate on their graphic organizer with supporting evidence or related terms. At this point, students also use their textbook and other reference material to further develop their Concept Mind Map. In the next class session, students meet in dyads again to revise their graphic organizer and to begin to write down key concepts with supporting evidence. When students have completed their Concept Mind Map, the teacher facilitates a discussion on the key concepts regarding types of matter and records students' responses on the SMART Board. For homework, students use their Concept Mind Map to write their summary of categories of matter and record examples of elements, compounds, and mixtures.

REFERENCES

Cummins, J. (1979). Cognitive/academic language proficiency, linguistic interdependence, the optimum age question, and some other matters. *Working Papers on Bilingualism, 19,* 121–129.

Garcia, G., & Nagy, W. (1993). Latino students' concept of cognates. In D. Leu & C. Kinzer (Eds.), *Examining central issues in literacy, research, theory, and practice* (pp. 367–373). 42nd Yearbook of the National Reading Conference. Chicago: National Reading Conference.

International Reading Association and National Council of Teachers of English. (1996). *Standards for the English language arts.* Newark, DE: International Reading Association & Urbana, IL: National Council of Teachers of English.

Zoss, M. (2009). Visual arts and literacy. In L. Christenbury, R. Bomer, & P. Smagorinsky (Eds.), *Handbook of adolescent literacy* (pp. 183–197). New York: Guilford Press.

Zwiers, J. (2008). *Building academic language: Essential practices for content classrooms.* Newark, DE: International Reading Association.

Research for Choice

Facilitating Student Voice in Academic Writing

In today's digital revolution, daily writing consists of text messaging, chatting online, or e-mailing. Yet recent reports urge educators to engage students in tasks that prepare them to develop their writing, extend arguments that analyze ideas, or to critique complex issues (Jago, 2009). In our fast-paced culture, we rarely take the time anymore to study a topic indepth or to develop a "habit of mind" that focuses on examination or analysis (University College London CIBER Group, 2008). Research for Choice is an instructional strategy that facilitates adolescent learners' analysis of a topic from their own perspective.

Engaging and motivating adolescent learners in research on an academic topic is difficult. Yet when offered a menu of options as well as the opportunity to express their own perspective, their involvement and performance improves (Roth, 1996). In the Research for Choice instructional strategy, adolescent writers use their cumulative knowledge on a topic of study to respond to an essential question or prompt. Through their research and analysis, adolescent students construct their own perspective on the topic and prepare a logical, evidence-based argument to present their position. The Research for Choice instructional strategy engages students in note taking, research, and critical thinking thereby facilitating their development of critical "habits of mind" for the information age.

IRA/NCTE Standards for the English Language Arts

4. Students adjust their use of spoken, written, and visual language (e.g., conventions, style, vocabulary) to communicate effectively with a variety of audiences and for different purposes.

5. Students employ a wide range of strategies as they write and use different writing process elements appropriately to communicate with different audiences for a variety of purposes.

8. Students use a variety of technological and informational resources (e.g., libraries, databases, computer networks, video) to gather and synthesize information and to create and communicate knowledge.

Source: International Reading Association and National Council of Teachers of English (1996).

STEP-BY-STEP PROCEDURE

The purpose of the Research for Choice instructional strategy is to improve adolescent students' ability to research, categorize, and analyze information. It is best implemented when students are at the midpoint or end of a unit of study and have prior knowledge on the topic. This instructional strategy takes approximately three class sessions to complete.

BEFORE RESEARCH

The teacher begins the session by reviewing the key concepts for the topic of study. The essential question or prompt is then displayed on the SMART Board or overhead projector. A broad essential question that requires students to compare/contrast information works best such as: Who was the best President in the 20th century?

1. The teacher begins the session with the essential question: What is the best historical drama written by Shakespeare? The teacher asks students to generate some titles of Shakespeare's historical dramas such as *Henry V* and *Richard II*. Next, the Research for Choice Grid (Figure 33.1) is distributed to the students.

2. Students generate research subtopics for the three main columns on the grid with input from the teacher. For example, the following are recorded on the grid:

   - Impact on public or historical perception of figure
   - Influence on genre or other literary works
   - Inclusion of terms or vocabulary into our language

Figure 33.1	Research for Choice Grid	
Essential Question: What is the best historical drama by Shakespeare?		
Impact on Historical Perception of Figure	Influence on Genre or Literary Works	Inclusion of Vocabulary Into our Language

RESEARCH

The teacher presents bookmarked sites for their initial research and assigns students to groups of three.

1. The teacher demonstrates the process by reading aloud a literary critique of Henry V. She records in the first column the historian's comments on the "party image" of Henry V fueled by Shakespeare's portrayal of Prince Harry in Henry IV. Then the teacher searches online for any opposing argument of this criticism.

2. After the demonstration, students work in their groups to research each subtopic. Students assign a column to each member of the group to research and analyze. When students have exhausted their individual searches, they reassemble to share their findings. Members of the group act as critical reviewers requiring supporting evidence for each contribution.

3. When students have completed their group grid, they select the major points for each column. The scribe for the group records the summary, which outlines their response to the essential question regarding Shakespeare's historical dramas.

4. Next the teacher facilitates a debriefing session and records each group's response to the prompt on a transparency or SMART Board.

The teacher then models how to use their grid to develop a persuasive essay. Through a write-aloud, the teacher demonstrates how to convert each research subtopic into a paragraph using the research in the grid. After completing the model persuasive essay, the teacher distributes the rubric illustrated in Figure 33.2 for students to use as a self-assessment during their writing.

Figure 33.2	Self-Assessment of Persuasive Writing
Directions: Rate your writing on a scale of 5 to 1. A score of 5 indicates a strong performance and 1 the lowest.	
Writing Element	*Rating*
I choose a position and use my prior knowledge to discuss it clearly.	_____
I present the opposing position in a rational and interesting manner.	_____
I include smooth transitions between paragraphs.	_____
I use the vocabulary of the content area throughout my essay.	_____
I revise my work for spelling and grammatical errors.	_____
Overall Rating and Suggestions for Improvement:	

WRITING

In the next class session, students meet in their groups to review their grid and response to the essential question.

1. Students use their grid to outline their argument. Each column is converted into a paragraph. Members of the group discuss stylistic ways to write opening and closing remarks for the essay.

2. Individual members of the group are assigned specific paragraphs to construct based on the model provided by the teacher. Students work independently and then reconvene when they complete their task. The group uses their rubric to revise and edit their essay. The grid is also used to check facts and to elaborate on their argument. After each group has finalized their essay, students gather in a round-table format to present their essay. A designated student reads aloud the group essay and the whole class weighs the evidence for each response. To conclude the activity, the teacher leads the class on constructing an evidence-based decision chart to reach a consensus on the issue.

DIFFERENTIATING INSTRUCTION FOR STRIVING READERS

Engaging in content area discussions provides a strong foundation in vocabulary and academic discourse for striving readers (Zwiers, 2008). Striving readers especially need to rehearse their ideas orally to process complex concepts and relationships (Dashiell, Griffith, Jacobs, & Wilson, 1989). To scaffold striving readers' performance in this session, teachers can provide each student with an interactive dialogue journal. As striving readers record their thoughts on the essential question and jot down their research, their conceptual understanding is strengthened. Additionally, striving adolescent readers converse through dialogue with their teacher or more advanced peers, which provides an opportunity to use academic vocabulary and sentence structure in context of use.

CONSIDERING THE LANGUAGE NEEDS OF ELL STUDENTS

Source: International Reading Association and National Council of Teachers of English (1996).

IRA/NCTE Standards for the English Language Arts

10. Students whose first language is not English make use of their first language to develop competency in the English language arts and to develop understanding of content across the curriculum.

Effective instruction for adolescent English language learners recognizes that bilingual speakers are a resource in the classroom (Rance-Roney, 2009). To participate fully in the Research for Choice instructional strategy, second language learners need prior knowledge in the content area and a grasp of key academic vocabulary words to discuss the issue. One way to adapt this session for English language learners is to ask more proficient bilingual students to create podcasts on the topic in their native language. This modification will allow second language learners to grasp the key concepts and to engage in the group discussion of the essential question. Additionally, the podcasts become a resource for the whole class to use to improve their knowledge of another language.

AN APPLICATION FOR INSTRUCTION AND LEARNING IN THE MATHEMATICS CLASSROOM

Students in an advanced placement geometry class are at the midpoint of the semester. To review their study of prior proofs, the teacher distributes the Research for Choice grid illustrated in Figure 33.1 and asks the following essential question: Which civilization provided the earliest proof? The teacher leads the class in a brainstorming activity to record the subtopics to appear in the grid. Students generate the following three subtopics:

- Impact of the Chinese square proof
- Analysis of Greek contribution
- Inquiry on Arabic tradition

After the brainstorming component, students are assigned to a group and given specific roles such as facilitator, scribe, and editor. Students discuss their ideas regarding the essential question and begin to research their subtopic. Working independently, students use podcasts, Web sites, textbooks, video clips, and journal articles to gather information to record on their grid. In the next session, groups meet to review reports from individual members and to discuss any remaining questions or gaps of knowledge. The facilitator leads the group in creating an outline for their persuasive essay and individual members begin to draft their contributions. In the final session, the group's essay is edited based on the rubric illustrated in Figure 33.2 and members decide how to present their argument. The group decides to create a PowerPoint presentation that illustrates their choice of the Chinese impact on mathematical proofs with video clips and scanned quotes from textbooks. After each group presents, the teacher leads the class in voting on the evidence for each selection. During the discussion, the teacher uses the session to assess any problems students faced during the research and drafting components.

REFERENCES

Dashiell, M., Griffith, M., Jacobs, B., & Wilson, S. (1989). Changing the model: Working with underprepared students. *The Quarterly, 11.* Retrieved December 7, 2009, from http://www.nwp.org/cs/public/print/resource/1587

International Reading Association and National Council of Teachers of English. (1996). *Standards for the English language arts.* Newark, DE: International Reading Association & Urbana, IL: National Council of Teachers of English.

Jago, C. (2009). Writing in the 21st century: Crash! The currency crisis in American culture. Report retrieved December 9, 2009, from http://www.nwp.org/cs/public/download/nwp_file/12468/Crash!_The_Currency_Crisis_in_American_Culture.pdf?x-r=pcfile_d

Rance-Roney, J. (2009). Best practices for adolescent ELLs. *Educational Leadership, 66,* 32–37.

Roth, R. (1996). Creating work of their own: Skills and voice in an 8th grade research project. *The Quarterly, 18.* Retrieved December 7, 2009, from http://www.nwp.org/cs/public/print/resource/1203

University College London CIBER Group. (2008). *Information behavior of the researcher of the future (CIBER Briefing Paper 9).* London: Author. Retrieved December 6, 2009, from http://www.jisc.ac.uk/media/documents/programmes/reppres/gg_final_keynote_11012008.pdf

Zwiers, J. (2008). *Building academic language: Essential practices for content classrooms.* Newark, DE: International Reading Association.

Strategy
34

Shared Pen

Interactive and Collaborative Writing

STRATEGY OVERVIEW

During the past 20 years, teachers across the country have been focusing on a contextual approach to teach writing skills (McAndrews, 2008). In the writing process approach, students are provided scaffolded instruction in brainstorming, drafting, revising, editing, and publishing in the context of use (Graves, 1983). However, recent reports have also documented the need for collaborative, explicit instruction in the components of the writing process (Graham & Perin, 2007). Outside of school, adolescent writers use social networking sites to post their fanfiction or to blog about a current event (Yancey, 2009). This shift toward collaborative, interactive writing calls for a new approach to writing instruction.

The Shared Pen instructional strategy is an interactive approach to provide adolescent learners with an explicit demonstration of how to compose academic text (Rogoff, 1990). During the strategy, teacher and students collaborate to brainstorm, draft, and revise academic content through discussion and interactive writing. Through modeling and discussions, the process of tapping prior knowledge, organizing thoughts, and drafting becomes visible for students to grasp.

Source: International Reading Association and National Council of Teachers of English (1996).

IRA/NCTE Standards for the English Language Arts

4. Students adjust their use of spoken, written, and visual language (e.g., conventions, style, vocabulary) to communicate effectively with a variety of audiences and for different purposes.

5. Students employ a wide range of strategies as they write and use different writing process elements appropriately to communicate with different audiences for a variety of purposes.

9. Students develop an understanding of and respect for diversity in language use, patterns, and dialects across cultures, ethnic groups, geographic regions, and social roles.

STEP-BY-STEP PROCEDURE

The purpose of the Shared Pen strategy is to scaffold adolescent learners' composition of academic text. As the teacher guides students through the phases of the writing process, questions are addressed and problems are resolved. This instructional activity is best implemented as a small group activity or in a tutorial session.

BEFORE WRITING

The teacher begins the session by asking students to brainstorm about the topic. This can be done by generating a list of statements or words associated with the topic or by completing a descriptive web.

1. The teacher begins by asking the students to think about the purpose for writing and the intended audience. The students then draft an outline.

2. The outline is posted on a transparency or SMART Board for students to comment on.

3. Students may refer to reference material during the brainstorming session to generate more ideas and vocabulary.

DURING WRITING

After students and teacher generate the outline, the teacher begins to write the first paragraph.

1. The teacher asks students for ideas in how to begin the paragraph with a topic sentence that is engaging for the reader.

2. As the teacher writes down the sentence, he thinks aloud any ideas regarding word choice or sentence structure for students to hear.

3. The process is repeated with supporting sentences that supply details and evidence to build on the topic sentence.

4. After recording their concluding sentence, the teacher leads the students in a discussion about their writing:

   • How can we improve on this paragraph?
   • Does any information or key vocabulary words need to be added?
   • Is there a better way to express our ideas?

REFLECTION

After the group completes the revisions, the teacher leads them in a debriefing session.

1. Immediately after the Shared Pen instructional strategy, the teacher asks students to do a 2-minute quick-write to reflect on what they learned regarding academic writing.

2. When students have completed their reflections they read their reflections and the teacher records their new understandings on chart paper.

Differentiating Instruction for Striving Readers

Research indicates that creating a sense of community and support impacts adolescent writers' performance (Dashiell, Griffith, Jacobs, & Wilson, 1989). The Shared Pen instructional strategy creates a collaborative context as students work with their teacher to construct academic text. One adaptation for this strategy is to assign a partner to each striving reader for further practice. After a small group of striving readers has participated in the activity, they can work with a partner on a simulated shared pen activity as they compose academic text together.

Considering the Language Needs of ELL Students

Source: International Reading Association and National Council of Teachers of English (1996).

IRA/NCTE Standards for the English Language Arts

10. Students whose first language is not English make use of their first language to develop competency in the English language arts and to develop understanding of content across the curriculum.

The process of acquiring academic language proficiency is similar to learning another language for adolescent learners as they strive to grasp new vocabulary and sentence patterns (Cummins, 1979). For English language learners, the process is difficult as they are also grappling with a second language. One adaptation of the Shared Pen instructional strategy for English language learners is to provide students with a sample of academic prompts or sentence starters such as "According to historians, President Ford's pardon of Richard Nixon remains controversial." Academic prompts facilitate second language learner's acquisition of the complex sentence structure needed to write expository text (Mota-Altman, 2006). Teachers may also provide English language learners with an academic prompt sheet that provides samples from myriad content areas.

An Application for Instruction and Learning in the Business Education Classroom

A ninth-grade business education class is avidly watching a video from CNN in which a young girl states, "I don't understand why the prices keep going up when no one has any money." The teacher uses this statement as a springboard to review the topic of inflation, which the class has been studying. To summarize the main unit topics, the teacher will facilitate an interactive writing activity on the causes of inflation and how that impacts prices for goods. The teacher begins by asking the students to jot down their concepts regarding inflation. As students respond, the teacher creates a chart with their comments. Next the class collaborates with the teacher to determine the the purpose and audience for their piece on inflation. The teacher distributes a sheet containing some samples of academic prompts they can use to begin their writing. The teacher acts as scribe and records the topic sentence that the students created. Next she asks students to generate supporting sentences that elaborate on the main ideas and cite factual evidence. Students take turns coming up to the SMART Board and jotting down their samples. As students compose their sentences, the teacher facilitates the process by asking, "Can we use more sophisticated language here? Did we leave out any important facts? Does anyone have a better way to write it?" When students and teacher are satisfied with their work, the teacher prints it for all to read. After silently reading their text, students discuss further improvements and work in pairs to strengthen it.

REFERENCES

Cummins, J. (1979). Cognitive/academic language proficiency, linguistic interdependence, the optimum age question, and some other matters. *Working Papers on Bilingualism, 19,* 121–129.

Dashiell, M., Griffith, M., Jacobs, B., & Wilson, S. (1989). Changing the model: Working with underprepared students. *The Quarterly, 11.* Retrieved December 7, 2009, from http://www.nwp.org/cs/public/print/resource/1587

Graham, S., & Perin, D. (2007). *Writing next: Effective strategies to improve writing of adolescents in middle and high schools.* A report to the Carnegie Corporation of New York. Washington, DC: Alliance for Excellent Education.

Graves, D. (1983). *Writing: Teachers and children at work.* Portsmouth, NH: Heinemann.

International Reading Association and National Council of Teachers of English. (1996). *Standards for the English language arts.* Newark, DE: International Reading Association & Urbana, IL: National Council of Teachers of English.

McAndrews, S. (2008). *Diagnostic literacy assessments and instructional strategies.* Newark, DE: International Reading Association.

Mota-Altman, N. (2006). Academic language: Everyone's second language. *California English.* Retrieved December 7, 2009, from http://www.nwp.org/cs/public/print/resource/2329

Rogoff, B. (1990). *Apprenticeships in thinking: Cognitive development in social context.* New York: Oxford University Press.

Yancey, K. (2009). *Writing in the 21st century: A report from the National Council of Teachers of English.* Retrieved December 7, 2009, from http://www.ncte.org/library/NCTEFiles/Press/Yancey_final.pdf

Strategy 35

Targeted Text

Guided Writing of Informational Text

STRATEGY OVERVIEW

How can I help the needs of my adolescent students with writing when their skills and abilities are so varied? This query is commonly voiced by teachers of adolescents as they attempt to remediate difficulties for writing. Recent research indicates that effective writing programs for adolescent learners use a variety of teaching approaches based on students' needs (Langer, Close, Angelis, & Preller, 2000). The Targeted Text instructional strategy uses assessment data to design minilessons on specific writing skills or strategies. This small-group activity facilitates individualized instruction and helps the teacher guide students through the writing process.

One of the difficulties of academic writing is that each content area has its own vocabulary and discourse (Zwiers, 2008). Therefore, an adolescent student might have trouble writing in mathematics class but clearly expresses his thoughts in social studies. A minilesson is a short, targeted instructional episode where the teacher models the skill or strategy that the students need (Atwell, 1998). The focus of the minilesson varies according to the needs of the students. At the end of the minilesson, students report out where they are in the writing process and reflect on how they will apply the newly learned skill or strategy (Lunsford, 1997). The Targeted Text instructional strategy individualizes academic writing instruction by providing focus minilessons on the informational writing strategies or skills students need to improve their performance.

Source: International Reading Association and National Council of Teachers of English (1996).

IRA/NCTE Standards for the English Language Arts

5. Students employ a wide range of strategies as they write and use different writing process elements appropriately to communicate with different audiences for a variety of purposes.

STEP-BY-STEP PROCEDURE

The purpose of the Targeted Text instructional strategy is to focus on individual students' needs in academic writing through a minilesson. The focus of the minilesson is determined through assessment data and may be a strategy for writing or a skill.

BEFORE WRITING

To focus on targeted academic writing needs, the teacher analyzes assessment data, which consists of classroom writing samples, reports, or standardized tests. The teacher focuses on patterns in the data and groups students according to need.

1. The teacher begins the session by showing students samples of their work that pinpoint the focus area. For example, if students are plagiarizing from sources on the Internet without citing sources, the teacher would show several examples of plagiarism to the group.

2. The teacher asks the group to define the problem. What is the problem with copying and pasting information from the Internet and not citing it? How can you summarize the information in your own words?

3. The teacher records students' responses to each prompt on a whiteboard. The whiteboard chart will be used as a reference after the minilesson.

DURING TARGETED INSTRUCTION

The teacher uses the current topic of study to focus on a targeted strategy or skill.

1. After discussing the focus of the minilesson, the teacher models how to perform the strategy or skill. For example, the teacher would demonstrate how to take a paragraph of information from a Web site, summarize it, and then cite the source. The teacher may also provide models of quality writing samples for students to analyze.

2. The teacher asks members of the group to comment on the demonstration and to report on how they will apply it.

3. Time is allotted for students to practice independently the strategy or the skill. During independent practice, the teacher confers with each student to guide or extend their performance.

AFTER WRITING: REFLECTION

After each individual member has completed the targeted assignment, the teacher gathers the group again.

1. At the conclusion of the session, the teacher asks the group to report out any difficulties or new concepts developed during guided practice.

2. The teacher reviews the chart on the whiteboard from the beginning of the session and asks students to revise or elaborate on it based on their experiences.

The Targeted Text instructional strategy is a strategy to meet individual needs and therefore should be data-driven for maximum effectiveness.

DIFFERENTIATING INSTRUCTION FOR STRIVING READERS

Adolescent learners who struggle with writing often lack awareness of what constitutes good writing and do not analyze their own work (Troia & Graham, 2003). The Targeted Text instructional strategy is especially effective for striving readers and writers as it focuses on a particular need based on their own work. One modification for this population is to provide multiple models of effective academic writing for students to analyze. For example, students that excel at academic writing or have solved the particular writing problem the teacher is focusing on, may lead the group through a "write-aloud" as they share their work. Members of the group can then ask the student specific questions regarding their writing. Explicit models of quality writing help striving writers to visualize exactly what they need to do to improve their performance.

CONSIDERING THE LANGUAGE NEEDS OF ELL STUDENTS

Source: International Reading Association and National Council of Teachers of English (1996).

IRA/NCTE Standards for the English Language Arts

10. Students whose first language is not English make use of their first language to develop competency in the English language arts and to develop understanding of content across the curriculum.

English language learners often grapple with the specific writing demands of each academic genre (Mota-Altman, 2006). One adaptation of this instructional strategy for second language learners is to assign each student a slightly more advanced partner to provide additional practice. After the guided practice in the targeted writing strategy or skill, the more advanced writing partner may provide additional individualized scaffolding as they complete an academic text together. The teacher then convenes the dyad to receive feedback on their progress and to denote any behavioral problems they may be having working together.

AN APPLICATION FOR INSTRUCTION AND LEARNING IN THE HEALTH CLASSROOM

Sophomores in a health and nutrition class are required to write a brochure to be distributed in the cafeteria on healthy eating habits as a performance-based assessment.

The teacher convenes a group of struggling writers based on their writing samples from the previous week. The focus of the targeted minilesson is the format for an informational brochure. The teacher distributes samples from a nearby hospital on basic daily food groups. Students examine the brochures and the teacher asks them to note what they have in common. The teacher records the following comments on chart paper:

- Brochures use graphics and bullets

- Sentences are not very long or complex

- Readers are given examples in each bullet point

After analyzing the brochures, the teacher leads students in a minilesson on the components of their brochure. When a template is outlined, students work in pairs to construct the first section, "You Are What You Eat." During this component, the teacher meets with each dyad to answer any questions and to provide suggestions. At the end of the session, the teacher convenes the group again and asks each dyad to report out any problems or solutions they developed during their work. Students examine one another's work and also comment on ways they can be improved in a collaborative dialogue. In the next few sessions, dyads continue to work on their brochures with the teacher monitoring their progress. If students need additional support, another targeted minilesson will be implemented.

REFERENCES

Atwell, N. (1998). *In the middle: New understandings about writing, reading, and learning.* Portsmouth, NH: Heinemann.

International Reading Association and National Council of Teachers of English. (1996). *Standards for the English language arts.* Newark, DE: International Reading Association & Urbana, IL: National Council of Teachers of English.

Langer, J., Close, E., Angelis, J., & Preller, P. (2000). *Guidelines for teaching middle and high school students to read and write well: Six features of effective instruction.* Report of National Research Center on English Learning and Achievement. Retrieved December 7, 2009, from http://www.adlit.org/article/19907

Lunsford, S. H. (1997). "And they wrote happily ever after": Literature based mini-lessons in writing. *Language Arts, 74,* 42–48.

Mota-Altman, N. (2006). Academic language: Everyone's second language. *California English.* Retrieved December 7, 2009, from http://www.nwp.org/cs/public/print/resource/2329

Troia, G. A., & Graham, S. (2003). Effective writing instruction across the grades: What every educational consultant should know. *Journal of Educational and Psychological Consultation, 14,* 75–89.

Zwiers, J. (2008). *Building academic language: Essential practices for content classrooms.* Newark, DE: International Reading Association.

SECTION VIII

Independent Learning

Promoting Strategies for Independence in Learning

I am still learning.

—Michelangelo

Michelangelo, one of the greatest masters of the centuries, was a lifelong learner. Within their lifetimes, most people are satisfied with becoming good in one or maybe two areas. Michelangelo was not! He was a master painter, sculptor, poet, engineer, and more. His thirst for knowledge and independence resulted in his greatest accomplishments. As teachers, our goal is to promote and teach for life-long learning by helping students become independent in reading, writing, and learning. For most students, such independence is acquired through using the strategies that assist them to learn on their own. The purpose of Section VIII is to offer strategies that will develop students' independence in learning.

WHAT RESEARCH HAS TO SAY ABOUT DEVELOPING INDEPENDENCE IN LEARNING

Students who are on the pathway to becoming lifelong learners possess metacognitive strategies and skills. When we think about our own thinking, we are metacognitive. We have metacognitive strategies when *we know when we know, and when we don't know, we know what to do to fix it.* Students' development of metacognitive strategies is especially important in comprehending text (Snow, Griffin, & Burns, 2005). For example, to understand what is being read, students must consciously attend to print and monitor the reading processes that result in comprehension of text (Flavell, Miller, & Miller, 1993).

Attending to print and monitoring the reading processes are metacognitive skills that are taught to young children who are learning to read. However, as students approach middle and high school, the texts and the tasks change dramatically. Now students read complex texts independently and are expected to monitor their own reading as they are required to read to learn. The strategies they developed early in school are the foundation for their reading and learning but are inadequate for students in middle and high school where independent learning is central to achievement. Research shows that proficient readers have well-developed metacognitive strategies. Such strategies allow them to monitor their reading processes on complex texts, enabling them to do the following: (a) set purposes for reading, (b) skim the text to determine if it meets one's purpose, (c) make text connections, (d) identify relevant information, (e) understand the meanings of technical terms or academic vocabulary discussed in the text, (f) take notes that are meaningful, and (g) summarize the sections of the text and make applications (Pressley, 2002).

A FRAMEWORK FOR TEACHING INDEPENDENT LEARNING TO ADOLESCENT STUDENTS

The aim of all schooling is to create lifelong learners by developing the strategies, skills, and motivation for becoming independent learners. Such knowledge begins within the context of the classroom where students are encouraged to engage in talk that promotes learning, to represent their developing ideas through writing, to think about their own thinking, and to develop the specialized skills needed to learn from reading complex texts. This valued goal is achieved by teachers who do the following:

1. Demonstrate and promote academic talk as a way of knowing and encourage students to initiate and engage in such types of conversations in learning about new ideas.

2. Seek a variety of ways that help students to activate and use their prior knowledge in learning and reading about new ideas and concepts.

3. Teach skills to read for learning from text and encourage students' use of such skills as they engage in independent reading.

4. Introduce students to journaling as a way to represent, develop, and record their ideas through writing, and encourage them to use journals on their own.

ASSESSMENT OF STUDENTS' INDEPENDENCE IN LEARNING

TEACHER'S ASSESSMENT

Monitoring students in developing independence in learning allows teachers to know what and how they learn. This knowledge facilitates teachers to assist students in becoming independent learners. Determining what students know as well as how they come to know is important. What are the tools and strategies they use for learning? Classroom observation is a powerful assessment tool that will help teachers monitor students' learning habits. When this approach is used to evaluate students, teachers should focus on specific learning behaviors and record their observational data much like the scores on a test. Without a record of observations, the results will soon be forgotten. The rubric in Figure VIII.1, Rubric for Assessing Independence in Learning, may be used by teachers to focus their observations on students' learning behaviors.

Figure VIII.1	Rubric for Assessing Independence in Learning		
Criterion	Emerging (0–1 points)	Developing (2–3 points)	Proficient (4–5 points)
Academic talk Engaging in	The student rarely engages in academic talk that promotes learning and initiates such talk for learning outside of structured discussion activities.	The student sometimes engages in academic talk that promotes learning and initiates such talk for learning outside of structured discussion activities.	The student frequently engages in academic talk that promotes learning and initiates such talk for learning outside of structured discussion activities.
Questioning	The student rarely initiates appropriate questions that lead to a greater understanding of the concepts and ideas that are being studied.	The student sometimes initiates appropriate questions that lead to a greater understanding of the concepts and ideas that are being studied.	The student frequently initiates appropriate questions that lead to a greater understanding of the concepts and ideas that are being studied.
Note taking	The student rarely engages in note taking using effective strategies that result in usable notes for learning.	The student sometimes engages in note taking using effective strategies that result in usable notes for learning.	The student frequently engages in note taking using effective strategies that result in usable notes for learning.
Using prior knowledge	The student rarely demonstrates an ability to activate and use prior knowledge in comprehending text.	The student sometimes demonstrates an ability to activate and use prior knowledge in comprehending text.	The student always demonstrates an ability to activate and use prior knowledge in comprehending text.
Thinking about learning	The student rarely demonstrates through writing and discussion that he/she is thinking about learning and the learning process.	The student sometimes demonstrates through writing and discussion that he/she is thinking about learning and the learning process.	The student frequently demonstrates through writing and discussion that he/she is thinking about learning and the learning process.
Writing to learn	The student rarely engages in writing that promotes learning such as journaling, both as assigned and self-initiated activities.	The student sometimes engages in writing that promotes learning such as journaling, both as assigned and self-initiated activities.	The student frequently engages in writing that promotes learning such as journaling and note taking, both as assigned and self-initiated activities.

(Continued)

Figure VIII.1	(Continued)

Criterion	Emerging (0–1 points)	Developing (2–3 points)	Proficient (4–5 points)
Reading to learn	The student rarely demonstrates effective reading-to-learn behaviors through efficient skills in reading, skimming, using of text features, discussing, summarizing, retelling, and mapping.	The student sometimes demonstrates effective reading-to-learn behaviors through efficient skills in reading, skimming, using of text features, discussing, summarizing, retelling, and mapping.	The student frequently demonstrates effective reading-to-learn behaviors through efficient skills in reading, skimming, using of text features, discussing, summarizing, retelling, and mapping.

Scores

Proficient in independence in literacy and learning: 35–28 Points

Developing in independence in literacy and learning: 27–14 Points

Emerging in independence in literacy and learning: 13 points and below

Student's Self-Assessment

By engaging students in the self-assessment of their learning behaviors, we help them to strengthen their strategies that lead them to independence in learning. Do we take time to allow students to examine their thinking and learning processes and behaviors? Such a self-interrogation or self-assessment will help students to realize the importance of becoming independent learners as they examine their strengths and areas for improvement related to independence in learning. The self-assessment survey shown in Figure VIII.2, Survey for Self-Assessing Independence in Literacy and Learning, may be used as one approach to help students develop important practices of mind.

Figure VIII.2	Survey for Self-Assessing Independence in Literacy and Learning

Name: _____ Date: _____

Directions: Assess your independence in literacy and learning by thinking about how you learn and what you do to help you to learn on your own. Read each learning behavior. Then use the rating scale of 0 to 5 to assess your own literacy and learning behaviors by circling one number for each behavior. A rating of 0 is the lowest and a rating of 5 is the highest.

Talking and discussing to learn	I participate in discussions and talk to my friends and teachers so that I understand the topic we are studying.	0	1	2	3	4	5
Asking questions	I ask the kinds of questions to help me learn from my reading and from others.	0	1	2	3	4	5
Taking notes to learn	I take good notes while reading my text, and I review my notes to help me remember what I read.	0	1	2	3	4	5

Using what I know	When I am reading and learning about a topic, I think about what I already know about the subject and try to make connections to what I am learning.	0	1	2	3	4	5
Thinking about my learning	I think about the way I learn and whether it is helpful. I also think about what I have learned from each lesson.	0	1	2	3	4	5
Writing to learn	I know that when I write, I will learn about the ideas because I must think about them. So I write in my class journals, and I also keep my own journal to write and draw about ideas.	0	1	2	3	4	5
Reading to learn	When I read textbooks and other books, I try to understand them by using the title and subtitles, the words in bold, the diagrams, charts, pictures, and other features that will help me to understand and learn from my reading.	0	1	2	3	4	5

Scores

Proficient in independence in literacy and learning: 35–28 Points

Developing in independence in literacy and learning: 27–14 Points

Emerging in independence in literacy and learning: 13 points and below

Tips on Developing Independent Learners

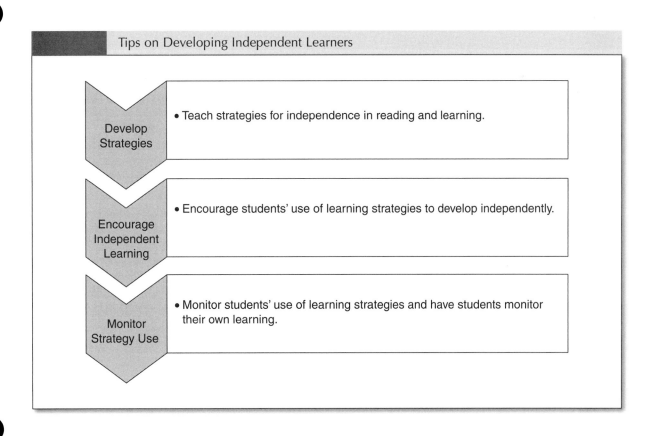

Develop Strategies
- Teach strategies for independence in reading and learning.

Encourage Independent Learning
- Encourage students' use of learning strategies to develop independently.

Monitor Strategy Use
- Monitor students' use of learning strategies and have students monitor their own learning.

Reflective Practice on Teaching Independent Learning

As teachers, we recognize the benefits of reflecting on our thinking, learning, and teaching. Sharing our appreciation with our students about "thinking about our own thinking" is not always conveyed in words but more appropriately conveyed through our own reflective practices. As we monitor our students' strategy use through observation, we begin to understand their learning strategies. Using anecdotal data from our observations, we may begin to ask questions that will support our inquiry in assisting students to become independent learners:

- When students' discussions do not result in learning, how can I help them engage in academic talk that promotes learning?

- Have student-generated questions led to inquiry and learning? Will they benefit from a lesson that models how to develop questions that promote their own learning?

- Some students struggle with note-taking and simply copy the text. Will mini-lessons that target summarization skills help these students?

Professional Resources

Allen, J. (2004). *Tools for teaching content literacy.* Portland, ME: Stenhouse.
Buckner, A. (2009). *Notebook connections: Strategies for the reader's notebook.* Portland, ME: Stenhouse.
Buehl, D. (2009). *Classroom strategies for interactive learning* (3rd ed.). Newark, DE: International Reading Association.
Israel, S. E. (2007). *Using metacognitive assessments to create individualized reading instruction.* Newark, DE: International Reading Association.

References

Flavell, J. H., Miller, P. H., & Miller, S. A. (1993). *Cognitive development* (3rd ed.). Upper Saddle River, NJ: Prentice Hall.
Pressley, M. (2002). Metacognition and self-regulated comprehension. In A. E. Farstrup & S. J. Samuels (Eds.), *What research has to say about reading instruction* (3rd ed.). Newark, DE: International Reading Association.
Snow, C. E., Griffin, P., & Burns, M. S. (Eds.). (2005). *Knowledge to support the teaching of reading: Preparing teachers for a changing world.* San Francisco: Jossey-Bass.

Talking Around the Text

Strategy 36

Using Dialogic
Reading and Writing to
Promote Independent Learners

When classroom talk is used effectively, it becomes one of the most powerful tools for academic learning. Many teachers endeavor to engage students in teacher-led discussions of their readings with their focus on determining what students have learned from the text. However, this type of question-answer discussion narrows student talk to a simple recitation of what they have read. Researchers (Alvermann & Moore, 1991; Mehan, 1979; Nystrand, 1997) have found that most questions that teachers use elicit simple responses that do not provoke thinking, facilitate students' construction of knowledge, or promote further learning. These types of questions posed by teachers simply are not effective tools that will lead students to engage in talk for academic learning.

Remember when you first used a new software program? You may have begun by reading the instructional manual. You then tried to use this new software, but this resulted in your asking questions to get started. You knew that with answers to your questions, you could be able to continue to use the program with some success. Such real-world questions result in talk-for-learning or *dialogic talk* that is used by students and teachers to co-construct meaning. Students work together to understand, define, and represent knowledge through authentic talk. Vygotsky (1978) described this type of language use as a mental tool because it facilitates students' acquisition of concepts and helps them to internalize academic discourse. Indeed, talk is a tool for learning. In other words, when students engage in a conversation about a topic, the dialogue furthers their conceptual understandings as they appropriate the language of the discipline.

The purpose of Talking Around the Text strategy is to provide students with a tool for developing academic literacy as they gain ownership of the language of the discipline. Such a tool includes student-generated discussion that includes questioning the text and leads to authentic text talk with peers. Students' comprehension of academic texts occurs through sustained discussion of readings (Torgesen et al., 2007). Further research shows that when talk is generated by students who are working to construct meaning from text, their comprehension increases (Gambrell, 1996). Dialogue allows students to negotiate meaning from text with others as they voice their opinions and listen to other ideas and interpretations of the text. In such dialogic conversations, academic language is appropriated; that is, students begin to gain ownership of the language of the discipline along with an understanding of the concepts that it represents.

Although this strategy will lead students to take responsibility for their own comprehension and learning from text, their engagement in text talk should be initially scaffolded or monitored by the teacher. Further, students come to learn that a dialogic discussion of the text does not always lead to complete or accurate interpretations of concepts or ideas. It does, however, result in literate thinking and learning (Wells & Chang-Wells, 1992). Figure 36.1, Talking Around the Text, presents a simple graphic that displays the components of the strategy.

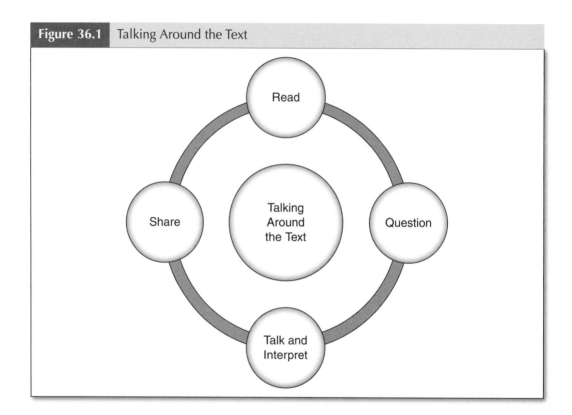

Figure 36.1 Talking Around the Text

IRA/NCTE Standards for the English Language Arts

2. Students read a wide range of literature from many periods in many genres to build an understanding of the many dimensions (e.g., philosophical, ethical, aesthetic) of human experience.

4. Students adjust their use of spoken, written, and visual language (e.g., conventions, style, vocabulary) to communicate effectively with a variety of audiences and for different purposes.

9. Students develop an understanding of and respect for diversity in language use, patterns, and dialects across cultures, ethnic groups, geographic regions, and social roles.

STEP-BY-STEP PROCEDURE

As students begin to read their texts, they focus on areas they do not understand. For such areas, they develop questions. Within small groups, students work together to construct meanings from those difficult areas of the text through questioning and conversations, known as *dialogic text talk*. Dialogism or *dialogic reading* includes talking about the text for the purpose of constructing meaning. The talk is student-generated and authentic for the purpose of constructing meanings from the text. The teacher prepares for reading by selecting concepts and academic vocabulary from the text that students will find difficult to understand. Using these concepts, the teacher plans a discussion that integrates background knowledge required for comprehending the text and allows for students to make personal connections to the topic.

BEFORE READING

1. Prepare students for reading by engaging them in a motivating discussion of the topic they will read about. Link the content of the text to students' experiences and build background knowledge when necessary.

2. One way to build students' background knowledge is by selecting the academic vocabulary they may not know but is necessary for understanding the text. Provide a lesson on the meanings of the words as they relate to the text and explain the underlying concepts and themes within the text.

3. Before students read the text, provide them with an overview of the strategy, emphasizing its role in helping students to become independent readers and learners. Tell students they will do the following:
   - Read the assigned text
   - Identify areas in the text that are difficult to comprehend
   - Write an open-ended question for discussion of the text that they do not understand
   - Work in small groups to talk about the questions that will help them to further understand and learn from the text
   - Summarize the groups' responses to the questions that lead to an answer to the question
   - Share their questions and interpretations with the class and ask the class the question(s) that could not be answered by their group

DURING READING

1. The students begin to read their assigned pages in the text.

2. The teacher reminds the students to read for meaning and understanding, and when they do not understand a part of the text, they should mark it with a Post-it.

3. Distribute Talking-Around-the-Text Guide (Figure 36.2) and briefly review the procedure.

4. Have students return to the areas in the text where they had difficulty and reread those parts. Help them to turn it into a question for discussion by the group.

5. At this point, the teacher may help students by modeling how to write questions that will promote discussion. For example, instead of the *who* and *when* questions that may elicit a single word response, encourage the *why* and *how* questions that may begin a rich discussion. In any case, the teacher encourages students to ask questions that will help them to better understand what they have read.

Figure 36.2	Talking-Around-the-Text Guide		
Difficult Text and Page	*Questioning the Text*	*Talking to the Question*	*Summarizing the Talk*
Identify the area in the text that is difficult and the page(s) that it may be found.	Think about the area of text that is difficult and change it into an open-ended question.	Lead the conversation about the text by asking the question. Engage in the talk until the text is clear. Write notes from the different responses.	Summarize the notes so there is a clear answer to the question. When there is no clear answer, ask the class.
• Text topic: • Page number:	• Question:	• Notes:	• Summary:
• Text topic: • Page number:	• Question:	• Notes:	• Summary:
• Text topic: • Page number:	• Question:	• Notes:	• Summary:
Unanswered Questions			
• Text topic: • Page number:	• Question:	• Notes:	• Summary:

AFTER READING

1. Students work in small groups of two to four.

2. Using the graphic Talking-Around-the-Text Guide in Figure 36.2 and their textbook as a reference, students engage in talking about each question to construct meaning.

3. As students talk about the question, they refer to the text to interpret it and explain it in their own words. Their responses are noted on the guide sheet.

4. After they have completed their discussion, they write a summary statement of the group's responses that focuses on the question.

5. Students also note new words they have learned from their talking around the text.

6. Some questions may be too difficult for the group. These are presented to the class for a teacher-led class discussion.

7. After the small-group discussion, students from each group present their questions and summary statements to the whole class. Clarifications to summary statements may be given by the teacher as well as other students when ideas are not clear.

8. The teacher then asks for those questions that posed a problem to all group members and uses their questions to lead the class in a discussion and help clarify meaning by returning to the text.

DIFFERENTIATING INSTRUCTION FOR STRIVING READERS

Having identified striving readers within the class, the teacher may modify the strategy instruction to meet the learning needs of the students, depending on the nature of their reading and writing disability. Because this strategy calls for small-group work, it may be easier for the teacher to support striving readers. The teacher may assist students during reading as they learn to identify and mark areas from the text they do not understand, work with them to frame questions to clarify meaning, demonstrate how to use questions to initiate the discussion, and show them how to go back to the text to construct meaning. For students who cannot read the text, reading material on their level should be provided. Numerous informational picture books written for young adults exist that provide rich discussions of the concepts and outstanding visuals for further understanding.

CONSIDERING THE LANGUAGE NEEDS OF ELL STUDENTS

IRA/NCTE Standards for the English Language Arts

10. Students whose first language is not English make use of their first language to develop competency in the English language arts and to develop understanding of content across the curriculum.

Source: International Reading Association and National Council of Teachers of English (1996).

Discussion is essential for learning content knowledge for all students but especially for those who are learning the English language. ELL students need to appropriate their new language, that is, they need to gain ownership of the language they are learning. Using new words, especially academic vocabulary, in their discussions is the most effective way of learning the language. The following are tips for helping ELL students in content area classrooms: (a) Consider placing ELL students who are reluctant to use the English language freely in a small sheltered group that will not be overwhelming and will be accepting of mispronunciations and errors in word usage. (b) Divide text into smaller segments for discussion. (c) Offer discussion prompts at first, then gradually allow the discussion to be more student-led. (d) Certain disciplines, such as social studies, English language arts, and art have numerous picture story books that have appropriate content for adolescent students. Whenever possible, consider using text supported by different types of visuals and graphics.

An Application for Instruction and Learning in the Social Studies Classroom

In one 10th-grade classroom, the students were reading and writing about the people and cultures of Africa. The teacher used a series of books that focuses on the people and cultures of Africa by region. Using a slide show, the teacher introduced the unit showing photographs of the geographical area of the region and the countries that comprise North Africa. To help students connect to their study of Africa, she displayed slides of the immense sand dunes of the Sahara Dessert, the Great Pyramid at Giza, as well as life on the Nile River and in the major cities of Casablanca, Tangier, Cairo, and Khartoum.

Before students began to read about the physical features of North Africa and its biomes, the teacher divided them into small groups and explained what they would do during and after reading. As the students read their texts, they identified areas in their readings they found difficult to understand, marked them with Post-it notes, and wrote questions that would be used by their group to talk about so they could get at the meaning for each aspect of the text that is difficult to understand. Additionally, students highlighted some vocabulary that made the text confusing and difficult to understand and needed clarification. After rereading, students used their Talking-Around-the-Text Guide: An Application to Social Studies, as shown in Figure 36.3, to think about difficult areas in the text and write questions to initiate group talk.

Figure 36.3	Talking-Around-the-Text Guide: An Application to Social Studies

Difficult Text and Page	Questioning the Text	Talking to the Question	Summarizing the Talk
Identify the area in the text that is difficult and the page(s) that it may be found.	Think about the area of text that is difficult and change it into an open-ended question.	Lead the conversation about the text by asking the question. Engage in the talk until the text is clear. Write notes from the different responses.	Summarize the notes so there is a clear answer to the question. When there is no clear answer, ask the class.

Difficult Text and Page	Questioning the Text	Talking to the Question	Summarizing the Talk
• Text topic: Physical regions of North Africa • Page number: pages 6 & 7	• Question: Why do so many people live around the Nile River? What is hinterland?	• Notes: Lots of people live around the Nile River. The land is good for growing food (fertile). Not all of the Nile River is good for planting.	• Summary: Certain parts of the land around Nile River have a large population and other parts do not. People live on this land because it is good for planting and close to the Mediterranean Sea. There are many different biomes in North Africa. One is the delta at the northern part of the Nile River located on the Mediterranean Sea. Before the Aswan Dam, the delta was a flooded grassland and papyrus swamp.
	What makes the Nubia course of the Nile harder to travel on?	The Nubia course could be harder because it looks jagged and there are different kinds of landscape.	
Page 9	How did the Aswan Dam change the Nile Delta?	Before the Aswan Dam was built, the Nile Delta was a flooded grass land. The Aswan Dam holds the waters back from the Nile Delta and they are stored in the reservoir. This has changed the ecosystem of the delta.	
Unanswered Questions			
• Text topic: • Page number: page 7	• Question: What is hinterland?	• Notes: The hinterland of the Nile is region located around the river.	• Summary:

The members of each group used their questions to talk about the text. Their primary purpose was to gain meaning from the text that they found difficult to understand. After the small groups completed their talk around the text, the teacher asked them to share one significant question and clarification with the class. For questions that were not resolved by the small group, the teacher led a class discussion around such challenging questions and students took notes.

REFERENCES

Alvermann, D. E., & Moore, D. W. (1991). Secondary school reading. In R. Barr, M. L. Kamil, P. B. Mosenthal, & P. D. Pearson (Eds.), *Handbook of reading research: Volume II* (pp. 951–983). New York: Longman.

Gambrell, L. (1996). What research reveals about discussion. In L. Gambrell & J. Almasi (Eds.), *Lively discussions! Fostering engaged reading* (pp. 25–38). Newark, DE: International Reading Association.

International Reading Association and National Council of Teachers of English. (1996). *Standards for the English language arts.* Newark, DE: International Reading Association & Urbana, IL: National Council of Teachers of English.

Mehan, H. (1979). "What time is it, Denise?" Asking known information questions in classroom discourse. *Theory into Practice, 18,* 285–294.

Nystrand, M. (1997). *Opening dialogue: Understanding the dynamics of language and learning in the English classroom.* New York: Teachers College Press.

Torgesen, J. K., Houston, D. D., Rissman, L. M., Decker, S. M., Roberts, G., Vaughn, S., et al. (2007). *Academic literacy instruction for adolescents: A guidance document from the Center on Instruction.* Portsmouth, NH: RMC Research Corporation, Center on Instruction.

Vygotsky, L. (1978). *Mind in society: The development of higher psychological processes.* Cambridge, MA: Harvard University Press.

Wells, G., & Chang-Wells, G. L. (1992). *Constructing knowledge together: Classrooms as centers of inquiry and literacy.* Portsmouth, NH: Heinemann.

Textbook Activity Guide (TAG)

Strategy 37

Developing Independence in Learning From the Textbook

A major accomplishment of students is achieving independence as they read to learn from their textbooks. However, too many middle and high school students find the textbook difficult to comprehend and even more confusing as they attempt to use it as a tool for learning. Content area teachers who show their students how to use the textbook as a tool for understanding further facilitate their independence in learning. Textbook guides offer a type of roadmap that helps students to think and learn with print (Vacca & Vacca, 2008).

Among the number of study guides that teachers may use to assist students in learning from their texts, the Textbook Activity Guide (TAG) introduced by Davey (1988) promises to develop students' competence in reading to learn (Wood & Harmon, 2001). An important aspect of achieving such independence in learning is becoming metacognitive, developing a conscious awareness of one's own learning. Using a textbook guide for reading and learning demonstrates to students how proficient readers learn from text. Such a strategy serves as a scaffold as it guides students to read with a purpose, retell what they have read, make predictions, discuss ideas from the text, write written responses, skim their texts for information, and map salient information they have read. Teachers will make use of the textbook guide to help students learn how to use titles, sub titles, and graphics as rich sources of information. As they begin to use these learning strategies during content area reading, students will organize the information in such a way that will help them to think and learn from their texts.

In short, TAG provides teachers with a structured approach to scaffold students through the text using a printed guide helping them to predict, read selected text, and reread when they do not understand. TAG also encourages students to think about their learning through the use of self-monitoring cues. When teachers offer assistance in using the guide, students learn the process of reading to learn. To ensure that the strategy is secure and students are proficient in using strategies used in TAG on their own, it is important that the teacher establishes a purpose for using TAG, provides instruction in how to use the guide, offers the appropriate assistance to students while using it, and encourages them to try out the strategies learned in TAG while reading independently. Using TAG will lead to students' development of independence in learning from their reading.

The TAG strategy facilitates the development of strategic reading and active engagement with text. Additionally, TAG includes a self-monitoring strategy to help students think about their own learning. Depending on the content of the text and its structure, the purpose set for reading, and levels of students' proficiencies in reading the textbook, the teacher selects the appropriate types of strategies and the sequence for their use.

Source: International Reading Association and National Council of Teachers of English (1996).

IRA/NCTE Standards for the English Language Arts

3. Students apply a wide range of strategies to comprehend, interpret, evaluate, and appreciate texts. They draw on their prior experience, their interactions with other readers and writers, their knowledge of word meaning and of other texts, their word identification strategies, and their understanding of textual features (e.g., sound-letter correspondence, sentence structure, context, graphics).

STEP-BY-STEP PROCEDURE

Prior to the lesson, the teacher uses the TAG sheet shown in Figure 37.1, Textbook Activity Guide, to prepare the guide for reading. Preparation for reading begins with the TAG sheet, as the teacher carefully reads the text, selects the most effective strategies to be used, and plans the text guide for the students.

Figure 37.1	Textbook Activity Guide

Textbook Activity Guide (TAG)

Name: _____ Grade:_____

Title of Text:_____

Pages:_____ Date:_____

Directions to the students: The textbook guide will help you to read and learn from your textbook. Read your text and work with your partner to complete the guide. Be sure to consult the code to help you determine the strategy you and your partner will be using.

Reading and Learning From the Text

Strategy Code	**Strategy Name**	**Direction**
R	Read	Read the assigned text silently.
RT	Retell	In your own words, retell the information that you have read to your learning partner.
W	Written response	Write a brief response to your reading.
S	Skim	Read quickly for the purpose that you were given in the directions.
P	Predict	Make a prediction about the information you will find in your readings.

Reading and Learning From the Text		
Strategy Code	**Strategy Name**	**Direction**
S	Share	Share with your partner.
C	Connect	Make a connection to the text.
M	Map	Construct a map of the ideas and information within your text.

Self-Monitoring My Reading and Learning		
Code	**Self-Monitoring Strategy**	**Direction**
√	I understand.	Continue reading, writing, or discussing; move on to the next section.
?	I am not too sure.	Reread the part of the text that you do not understand.
x	I don't understand.	Reread to determine the parts of the text you do not understand; use title and subheadings, margin notes, and glossary; work with your learning partner to get at the meaning of the text.

Strategy Code	**Pages**	**Direction**	**Self-Monitoring**

BEFORE READING

The teacher prepares students for using the TAG sheet during reading by doing the following:

1. Divide the class into groups of two learning partners.

2. Distribute a prepared TAG sheet to each student.

3. Teach students how to use the TAG sheet by showing them and talking through each of the sections including the overall directions, the strategy codes and their names, the prompts that offer directions for each strategy, and the section on self-monitoring strategies.

4. Engage students in a lively discussion of the text they will be reading. Within the discussion, activate and build prior knowledge that will help students comprehend the text.

DURING READING

The teacher shows students how to use the TAG sheet while they are reading. The students are directed to do the following:

1. Use their TAG sheet to guide them through reading the assigned pages of their textbook.

2. Note the strategy code that guides them during the use of specific strategies during reading. Under the directions, follow the prompt(s) that directs them with specific instructions while they are reading and learning from their text.

3. Work with their learning partner on each section, until all parts of the guide sheet have been completed.

4. Think about how well they understood the areas in the text they read and used the strategy for understanding and learning from the text. Evaluate their learning by marking each section using the self-monitoring codes.

After Reading

The teacher and students work through the completed TAG sheet as a guide for their discussion of the readings in the text. The teacher uses feedback from the students to help them in areas that were difficult. The teacher may also use their TAG sheets to evaluate the lesson and prepare for the next lesson that will further help students' understanding of the content, the text, and the learning process.

Differentiating Instruction for Striving Readers

The TAG will be most useful to readers who struggle with the grade-level text by modifying the guide for students' learning needs. Most students who struggle reading the text are not fluent readers. One very useful way to address a lack of reading fluency is to reduce the number of assigned pages to be read within the class time. An additional modification to the TAG sheet that would benefit striving readers would be to limit the number of strategies required of the student in one session. Teachers need to provide explicit instruction through demonstration and modeling on using the text guide and to offer students assistance while they are working through the process.

Considering the Language Needs of ELL Students

Source: International Reading Association and National Council of Teachers of English (1996).

IRA/NCTE Standards for the English Language Arts

10. Students whose first language is not English make use of their first language to develop competency in the English language arts and to develop understanding of content across the curriculum.

To increase comprehension and learning from texts for ELL students, use text talk as a major strategy on the TAG sheet. A technique with an added value effect on learning is to pair ELL students with native speakers. To promote discussion after reading, use short prompts on their TAG sheets. When discussion of ideas within content area texts is promoted, English learners will begin to appropriate the language of the discipline and concepts will be clarified.

AN APPLICATION FOR INSTRUCTION AND LEARNING IN THE GENERAL SCIENCE CLASSROOM

Students in general science were studying chemical reactions and were using the book *Essential Chemistry: Chemical Reactions* by Krisi Lew (2008) to learn about chemical reactions in nature. Prior to their lesson, the teacher developed the TAG sheet shown in Figure 37.2, Textbook Activity Guide for Readings in Chemistry.

Figure 37.2	Textbook Activity Guide for Readings in Chemistry

Name: _____ Grade: *8*

Title of Text: _*Chemical Reactions: Chapter 6*_____

Pages: _*63–71*_ Date: _*11/24/09*_

Directions to the Students: The textbook guide will help you to read and learn from your textbook. Read your text and work with your partner to complete the guide. Be sure to consult the code to help you determine the strategy you and your partner will be using.

Reading and Learning From the Text

Strategy Code	Strategy Name	Direction
R	Read	Read the assigned text silently.
RT	Retell	In your own words, retell the information that you have read to your learning partner.
W	Written response	Write a brief response to your reading.
S	Skim	Read quickly for the purpose you were given in the directions.
P	Predict	Make a prediction about the information you will find in your readings.
SH	Share	Share with your partner.
C	Connect	Make a connection to the text.
M	Map	Construct a map of the ideas and information within your text.

Self-Monitoring My Reading and Learning

Code	Self-Monitoring Strategy	Direction
√	I understand.	Continue reading, writing, or discussing; move on to the next section.
?	I am not too sure.	Reread the part of the text that you do not understand.
X	I don't understand.	Reread to determine the parts of the text you do not understand; use title and subheadings, margin notes, and glossary; work with your learning partner to get at the meaning of the text.

(Continued)

Figure 37.2	(Continued)		
Strategy Code	**Pages**	**Direction**	**Self-Monitoring**
S P	63–71	The chapter title, the subtitles with their introductory sentences, and words in italics. What chemical reactions will you read about? _____ _____ _____	
R RT	63–65	After reading about the chemical reactions—photosynthesis, respiration, and digestion—retell the process of the chemical reactions to your partner and interpret their chemical formulas.	
M SH	66–67	Study Figure 6.1. With your partner, construct three separate maps, one for each of the chemical reactions that describes the chemical formulas that tells how caves are formed.	

To prepare students for reading on "Reactions in Nature," the teacher reviewed chemical reactions and discussed some of the everyday chemical reactions by showing students some objects that have rusted as well as others that have gone through corrosion. After distributing TAG sheets, the teacher assigned learning partners and reviewed the TAG sheet. When students have completed reading and working through the activities on the text guide, the teacher asked them to think about the readings and activities by directing their attention to self-monitoring their own reading and learning processes. The teacher completed the lesson by giving individual groups an opportunity to share their responses with the whole class and identify any areas of difficulty.

REFERENCES

Davey, B. (1988). Using textbook activity guide to help students learn from textbooks. *Journal of Reading, 29,* 489–494.

International Reading Association and National Council of Teachers of English. (1996). *Standards for the English language arts.* Newark, DE: International Reading Association & Urbana, IL: National Council of Teachers of English.

Lew, K. (2008). *Essential chemistry: Chemical reactions.* New York: Chelsea House.

Vacca, R. T., & Vacca, J. L. (2008). *Content area reading: Literacy and learning across the curriculum* (9th ed.). Boston: Allyn & Bacon.

Wood, K. D., & Harmon, J. M. (2001). *Strategies for integrating reading and writing in middle and high school classrooms.* Westerville, OH: National Middle School Association.

Academic Note Taking

Supporting Students' Independence in Learning

Strategy 38

STRATEGY OVERVIEW

Most teachers understand the usefulness of taking notes in content area classrooms, yet few teach students this important skill. Upon close scrutiny of students' notebooks, teachers find a wide variation on the effectiveness of notes they produce. Many students who are not proficient readers and writers often are less successful at taking notes they can use for learning. The good news is that note taking is a skill that can be taught, and when students receive direct instruction and guidance in taking and using notes, their academic performance increases. Further, substantial research supports the divergence in note-taking strategies with some types being more effective than others, and when students know how to take appropriate notes and use them for learning, they are simply better in school than students who lack this skill (Faber, Morris, & Lieberman, 2000).

We know that reading and writing possess a close relationship where both help and nourish the other. Note taking is one form of writing that helps students to become literate as they "develop listening, synthesizing abilities, and overall language proficiency" (Zwiers, 2008, p.120). Although note taking is limited to one type of writing, it does have an important place in content area classrooms. Effective note takers attend to class discussions and are able to capture the essence of what is said, summarize the text, identify important information and dismiss nonessential details, and organize information in useful ways to show connections among ideas (Burke, 2002). Students who possess proficient note-taking skills and use them for learning have developed one of the most important traits of an independent learner.

The most effective way to help students take notes is to engage in direct instruction for this crucial skill. A three-prong explicit teaching approach of academic note taking includes modeling, practice, and evaluation (Stahl, King, & Henk, 1991). A number of structured approaches exist to benefit students in learning to take notes within content area classrooms. The one we suggest is an adaptation of the Cornell note-taking strategy that includes (a) taking notes, (b) developing questions that would answer the notes, and (c) summarizing the main ideas from the notes and questions (Pauk, 2000). The adaptation of this strategy includes an additional essential element: students' identification of the academic vocabulary that represents central concepts within their readings and notes.

Source: International Reading Association and National Council of Teachers of English (1996).

IRA/NCTE Standards for the English Language Arts

3. Students apply a wide range of strategies to comprehend, interpret, evaluate, and appreciate texts. They draw on their prior experience, their interactions with other readers and writers, their knowledge of word meaning and of other texts, their word identification strategies, and their understanding of textual features (e.g., sound-letter correspondence, sentence structure, context, graphics).

5. Students employ a wide range of strategies as they write and use different writing process elements appropriately to communicate with different audiences for a variety of purposes.

STEP-BY-STEP PROCEDURE

The teacher introduces the Academic Note Taking strategy prior to students' reading of their texts. Students then read and practice taking notes. As they take notes from their reading, the teacher offers assistance and feedback in taking notes.

BEFORE READING

The teacher will model the use of the Academic Note Taking strategy through the use of a think-aloud.

1. Prior to assigning readings from the text, the teacher engages students in a discussion to help them think about the topic and build background knowledge that will promote understanding.

2. The teacher then distributes the Academic Note-Taking Guide shown in Figure 38.1 and projects a copy on the white board.

3. Briefly, the teacher and students explore the different parts of note taking found on the guide sheet.

4. The teacher then reads a short section of the assigned reading aloud.

5. Thinking aloud, the teacher models how to take notes, writing them on the white board. She shows the students how she selected the main or central ideas from the text and why she did not include the details.

6. The teacher continues to demonstrate to the students how to (a) write a question that the notes will answer; (b) search the readings for academic vocabulary, one or two words that represent the main concepts and are important to remember; and (c) use notes, questions, and academic vocabulary to write a summary statement that captures the main idea of the reading. As the notes are displayed on the white board, the students copy them onto their guide sheet as a model to follow.

Figure 38.1   Academic Note-Taking Guide

Notes	Questions	Vocabulary
Write the most important ideas that will help you remember what you have read.	**Write a question(s) that may be answered by your notes.**	**Write the word that best represents each major idea within your notes.**

Summary: Read your notes and your questions. Write a summary of the main idea.

DURING READING

1. As the students continue with the assigned readings, they take notes using the Academic Note-Taking Guide.

2. The teacher monitors and assists students by providing them with appropriate feedback to help them in taking notes.

AFTER READING

The teacher engages students in a discussion of the readings and encourages students to refer to their notes.

1. Students work in small groups or with their learning partner to compare their notes.

2. Students engage in discussions around their notes, questions, academic vocabulary as well as their summaries recorded on their guide sheets.

3. After student discussions, the teacher provides an opportunity for the groups to share highlights from their notes and discussions with the class.

4. Students are given time to review their notes to determine if they (a) included the most important ideas, (b) can read and interpret their notes, and (c) identified the date, topic, and text for future readings.

DIFFERENTIATING INSTRUCTION FOR STRIVING READERS

For students who have difficulty in reading and writing fluency, it may be necessary to provide additional instruction and explicit tips that will help them in taking notes. Tips for taking notes should include a basic plan in simple language that students may follow. It is important to explain and review the process and provide necessary clarifications. Students may be given the set of procedures as a reminder, or it may be displayed in the classroom for all students to benefit. Some basic procedures that will promote effective note taking are shown in Figure 38.2, Simple Tips for Note Taking.

CONSIDERING THE LANGUAGE NEEDS OF ELL STUDENTS

Source: International Reading Association and National Council of Teachers of English (1996).

IRA/NCTE Standards for the English Language Arts

10. Students whose first language is not English make use of their first language to develop competency in the English language arts and to develop understanding of content across the curriculum.

Figure 38.2   Simple Tips for Successful Note Taking

Remember These Tips for Successful Note Taking

1. Record the date, topic, title of the text, and page numbers.
2. Check the titles and subtitles in the text that may assist in identifying main ideas.
3. Avoid copying from the text.
4. Write short sentences that capture the main ideas.
5. Create your own set of abbreviations and use them consistently.
6. Check out the pictures, graphs, and figures with their captions for useful information.
7. Note important vocabulary.
8. Mark ideas you do not understand with a "?"

Students who are language learners may understand the concepts and skills in their native language but are not able to comprehend those same ideas from their content area textbooks. Therefore, they will not be able to take useful notes from the same readings as their peers. Providing ELL students with reading materials on the same topic at their reading and language levels would be very beneficial. Additionally, many books contain pictures, graphs, and diagrams that ELL students would be more apt to understand. Another useful tip for ELL students engaged in note taking is to take notes in their first language and then translate their notes to English.

AN APPLICATION FOR INSTRUCTION AND LEARNING IN THE STUDIO ARTS CLASSROOM

Students in the ceramics class are learning about ceramics, the tools and materials that artists use in creating different types of ceramics, as well as the processes they use in their creations. The teacher engaged students in the topic by showing them a number of different pieces and classified them with respect to the major categories—earthenware, stoneware, and porcelain. After an introduction of the assigned reading, *The Artist's Tools* by Stuart A. Kallen (2007), "Chapter 3: Ceramics and Glass," the teacher modeled the process of Academic Note Taking. First, she distributed the Academic Note-Taking Guide (Figure 38.1) and reviewed each of the components and described how to use the guide in taking notes during reading. The teacher read the introduction of the book aloud and modeled the note-taking process by using the whiteboard to take notes, developed an essential question, and identified the important vocabulary. The students began to read and take notes while the teacher monitored them, offering assistance to students when necessary. Using their completed Academic Note-Taking Guides, the teacher engaged them in a discussion on their notes, their essential questions, and on their selected vocabulary with the meanings and uses of the words. A sample of one student's notes is shown in Figure 38.3, Sample of Academic Note-Taking Guide for Ceramics.

Figure 38.3	Sample of Academic Note-Taking Guide for Ceramics	
Notes	*Questions*	*Vocabulary*
Write the most important ideas that will help you remember what you have read.	**Write a question that may be answered by your notes.**	**Write the word that represents each idea within your notes.**
The Artist's Tools by Stuart A. Kallen Pages 46–54 Ceramics has been around for centuries. It includes earthenware, stoneware, and porcelain. They differ because of their contents. Earthenware is used as tableware and for decorations, stoneware is used for pots, and porcelain has many uses. All of the ceramics must be heated at very high temperatures, some at higher temperatures than others. The tools of sculptors who work on different types of ceramics are very similar.	Can you tell the difference between the three types of ceramics by looking at them? What are the steps in making a ceramic bowl? How do sculptors know how long each piece is fired? Do sculptors paint their pieces too?	Ceramic earthenware stoneware porcelain kiln bisque firing glaze

Summary: Read your notes and your questions. Write a summary of the main idea.

Ceramics are not new. They were around for centuries and were first made in China between AD 600 and 900. There are three categories into which ceramics fall. They are earthenware, stoneware, and porcelain. Each of the three types has different contents and is fired in the kiln at different temperatures.

All types of ceramics must be baked.

Artists who create ceramics are called sculptors and use similar tools and have similar skills. Clay is the material that artists use to create their pieces of ceramic. It must be processed before it is used and the artist must work on the clay to get it ready for using it. After preparing the clay, the sculptor will use the pottery wheel to shape it. When it is finished, the artist adds other features. Before the sculptor places it in the kiln to fire it, the piece must dry. Part of the method of creating a ceramic is glazing that takes place in a kiln during the glaze firing process.

REFERENCES

Burke, J. (2002). Making notes, making meaning. *Voices From the Middle, 9*(4), 15–21.

Faber, J. E., Morris, J. D., & Lieberman, M. G. (2000). The effect of note taking on ninth grade students' comprehension. *Reading Psychology, 21,* 257–270.

International Reading Association and National Council of Teachers of English. (1996). *Standards for the English language arts.* Newark, DE: International Reading Association & Urbana, IL: National Council of Teachers of English.

Kallen, S. A. (2007). *The artist's tools.* New York: Thomson Gale.

Pauk, W. (2000). *How to study in college* (7th ed.). Boston: Houghton Mifflin.

Stahl, N. A., King, J. R., & Henk, W. A. (1991). Enhancing students' notetaking through training and evaluation. *Journal of Reading, 34,* 614–622.

Zwiers, J. (2008). *Building academic language: Essential practices for content classrooms, Grades 5–12.* San Francisco: Jossey-Bass.

Strategy 39

Entrance and Exit Slips

Helping Students to Reflect on Their Learning

STRATEGY OVERVIEW

Entrance Slips are used prior to instruction on a specific topic in the content areas, and Exit Slips are used when the lesson has been completed. Both strategies involve thinking and writing about the content area. Entrance Slips strategy is a prereading discussion activity that helps students to reflect on what they will be learning. The benefits are numerous: students warm up "with content, thinking, and language that they will encounter in the text" (Zwiers, 2008, p. 229) or within a discussion group. With this strategy, students are required to activate prior knowledge needed for learning new content.

Similar benefits are derived from the use of Exit Slips. At the close of the lesson, students are requested to think about what they have learned or the process that they used to learn an idea or solve a problem. Such requests encourage students to become metacognitive as they begin to think about their own thinking—what they know and do not know as well as their learning processes that they used during the lesson. Exit Slips present a variety of benefits to the teacher as well. Daniels and Bizar (2005) described how Exit Slips may be used by the teacher as a diagnostic tool at the end of the lesson. The teacher reflects on how and what students learned for the purpose of informing her own teaching and modifying instruction for the next lesson. Additionally, the teacher may use Exit Slips at the beginning of the next day's lesson. By selecting a few Exit Slips and reading them aloud, the teacher helps students review yesterday's lesson and connect to the content of today's lesson.

Both Entrance and Exit Slips provide students with opportunities to think about the content they are learning and summarize their ideas. Students will learn to activate prior knowledge and take account of what they know and do not know before reading; at the end of the lesson, they will learn to reflect on what they have learned. When students are asked to write about what they have learned, the task pushes them "to use language to organize facts, concepts, and opinions in strategic ways" (Zwiers, 2008, p. 195). Using Entrance and Exit Slips is one way to help students to develop language for academic writing while thinking about their learning.

Source: International Reading Association and National Council of Teachers of English (1996).

IRA/NCTE Standards for the English Language Arts

3. Students apply a wide range of strategies to comprehend, interpret, evaluate, and appreciate texts. They draw on their prior experience, their interactions with other readers and writers, their knowledge of word meaning and of other texts, their word identification strategies, and their understanding of textual features (e.g., sound-letter correspondence, sentence structure, context, graphics).

5. Students employ a wide range of strategies as they write and use different writing process elements appropriately to communicate with different audiences for a variety of purposes.

STEP-BY-STEP PROCEDURE

Entrance Slips are used prior to a lesson, and Exit Slips are used at the end of the lesson, offering closure to the lesson. The teacher may decide to use one or both strategies within a lesson. In any case, Entrance Slips are meant to activate prior knowledge, and are therefore more appropriate to introduce students to a topic or prepare them for reading the text. Exit Slips are used at the end of the lesson for helping students to reflect on what they have learned as they summarize some of the major ideas from the lesson or from their readings.

Entrance Slips: Before the Lesson/Before Reading

The primary purpose for using Entrance Slips is to activate and build students' prior knowledge by helping them to think about what they will learn. Once students have completed the Entrance Slips, the teacher uses them to further develop the lesson, elaborate on an idea, or provide help to individual students. When asking students to use the Entrance Slips, many teachers use prompts or discussion to help them respond to a specific topic. Figure 39.1, Entrance Slip, shows a blank copy that one teacher uses. The teacher who wishes to activate and build students' knowledge may follow the steps below:

1. Begin the lesson with a motivating and engaging introduction and provide students with a hook by helping them to make a personal connection to the central theme of the lesson.

2. Ask students to think about what they already know about the ideas they will read. For students who are at the middle school level, use discussion to prod their knowledge and experiences related to the topic.

3. Give students an Entrance Slip such as the one shown in Figure 39.1. Ask them to take 3 minutes to write one or two sentences on what they already know related to the topic. If they have do not know anything about the topic or central theme, ask them to write down what they think it is about and what they wish to learn. The prompt shown on the Entrance Slip will guide them in their written response.

Figure 39.1   Entrance Slip

Entrance Slip

ENTER

Name : _____   Topic: _____

Prompt: Write two sentences telling what you already know about the topic.

EXIT SLIPS: AFTER THE LESSON/AFTER READING

Teachers use Exit Slips at the end of their lesson or after students have read an assigned passage for a number of reasons. As students are asked to write briefly about what they have learned, they are given an opportunity to think about their learning, to use the language of the discipline in summarizing the content of the lesson, and to note areas that they understood or need assistance. Teachers may simply ask students what they have learned or provide prompts for students to respond.

1. At the conclusion of the lesson, several minutes prior to the end of class, the teacher distributes the Exit Slips as shown in Figure 39.2. Depending on the teacher's purpose for using Exit Slips, the teacher prepares prompts that will focus students' responses. Prompts may be crafted to help students demonstrate through writing (a) content learning, (b) their learning processes, or (c) how instruction facilitated their learning.

2. After several minutes, students submit their completed Exit Slips.

3. The teacher may use students' responses on the Exit Slips as a diagnostic tool for preparing and modifying instruction for the class or for helping individual students who demonstrated their lack of understanding for certain areas of learning.

Figure 39.2	Exit Slip

Name _____   Topic: _____

Prompt: Write two sentences to tell what you have learned today.

DIFFERENTIATING INSTRUCTION FOR STRIVING READERS

Students who lack proficient reading skills and find it difficult to comprehend text often lack prior knowledge that is required for understanding their readings and discussions on specific topics. It is no wonder, therefore, when the teacher asks them to write what they know about a specific topic they will study on their Entrance Slips, they simply cannot. They may not know what the teacher is referring to, or they may lack background knowledge. Therefore, the teacher may begin with a brief discussion to help students connect to their own experiences that are directly related to the topic of study. For example, instead of asking the students to write what they know on the topic "Effects of Climate and Weather on Crop Production," ask students to describe the extreme weather we experienced lately. Continue the discussion leading to the topic of the "Result of Extreme Weather." After the discussion, students will be able to think deeply about what they know about the topic.

CONSIDERING THE LANGUAGE NEEDS OF ELL STUDENTS

Source: International Reading Association and National Council of Teachers of English (1996).

IRA/NCTE Standards for the English Language Arts

10. Students whose first language is not English make use of their first language to develop competency in the English language arts and to develop understanding of content across the curriculum.

ELL students may not be able to express what they know or what they have learned from a specific lesson. As a result, the teacher may assess their completed Entrance Slips and Exit Slips judging that the students did not understand the concepts and ideas. Because oral language precedes written language, have students talk through what they know and what they learned prior to their writing about the topic. Emphasize that the sentences need not be long but should be written using the language they know. If students do not know the English word for a specific idea, encourage them to use the word(s) from their native language. Students will then learn the spoken and written English word for word(s) written in their native languages.

AN APPLICATION FOR INSTRUCTION AND LEARNING IN THE AGRICULTURE SCIENCE CLASSROOM

Students in the agriculture science classroom were beginning a unit on soil and moisture conservation. The teacher commenced the unit with a set of lessons on a related topic of soil erosion and focused on the two major causes of soil erosion, factors influencing soil erosion, and the prevention and management of soil erosion. The teacher used the Entrance Slips strategy to begin the lesson to determine what students already knew about soil erosion.

To introduce students to the topic, the teacher used a slide show of photographs that illustrated how land looks as a result of erosion. After viewing the slides, the teacher engaged students in a 3-minute discussion of what they saw on the slides. The teacher then distributed the Entrance Slips to the students and asked them to respond to the written prompt in writing. For students who were reluctant to write anything, the teacher asked them to think about the slides and write down what they think they will be learning. After 5 minutes, the teacher asked students to share their responses. After some students read their responses, the teacher made comments to help the students connect to the topic. The teacher collected and reviewed the Entrance Slips to determine how much background knowledge students needed. Figure 39.3, Sample Entrance Slip on Soil Erosion, shows how the teacher helped students focus on the lesson as they were activating their background knowledge of the topic.

After the lesson, the teacher used the Exit Slip strategy to help students think about what they have learned from the lesson, to hold them accountable for learning, and to assess student learning for determining the next lesson. The teacher directed the students to take 5 minutes to write to the prompt on the Exit Slips and collected them when they

Figure 39.3 Sample Entrance Slip on Soil Erosion

Name: Peter Thomson   Topic: Soil Erosion

Prompt: What does land look like when there is soil erosion? What happens to cause soil erosion?
Land that has soil erosion has large holes and spaces.
Sometimes there is soil erosion when there is a flood.

left class. Students' Exit Slips, such as the one found in Figure 39.4, Sample Exit Slip on Soil Erosion, were read by the teacher to plan for the next lesson and determine what individual students learned from the lesson.

Figure 39.4 Sample Exit Slip on Soil Erosion

Name: Peter Thomson   Topic: Soil Erosion

Prompt: Tell what you have learned today about soil erosion.
Soil erosion happens when part of the land is removed. This happens from rain and wind.
When farmers use poor methods for growing crops, the land will have soil erosion.

REFERENCES

Daniels, H., & Bizar, M. (2005). *Teaching the best practice way: Methods that matter, K-12.* Portsmouth, NH: Heinemann.

International Reading Association and National Council of Teachers of English. (1996). *Standards for the English language arts.* Newark, DE: International Reading Association & Urbana, IL: National Council of Teachers of English.

Zwiers, J. (2008). *Building academic language: Essential practices for content classrooms, Grades 5–12.* San Francisco: Jossey-Bass.

Strategy 40

Journaling

Helping Students to Respond, Reflect, and Learn Through Informal Writing

STRATEGY OVERVIEW

Journaling in content area classrooms offers students the benefits of developing literate thinking through writing and drawing. Journal writing is unlike note taking where students are focused on summarizing and copying ideas in the text. By writing in their journals, students are encouraged to develop their ideas and concepts about topics through personalized text and illustrations. The type of writing used by students engaged in journaling is called *exploratory writing* because students use writing to represent their emerging concepts. As students explore new ideas, they construct and reconstruct their knowledge to make sense out of what they are learning (Britton, 1993). They know their writing is unfinished; it is simply a draft of what they now know. Therefore, students may go back to their journals to rework their ideas, develop statements, and add new thoughts or even draw pictures to clarify meanings. When journals are used in this way, students make visible their thinking and ideas through writing (Popp, 1997).

Much like exploratory talk that helps us understand a new idea or issue by "talking through it," exploratory writing has the same purpose and results in literate thinking and construction of knowledge (Barnes, 1976). Wells and Chang-Wells (1992) studied how writing leads to literate thinking concluding that "when writing is treated as a powerful means of thinking and communicating, . . . the development of writing ability and the acquisition of domain knowledge will both be enhanced" (p. 134). Therefore, when teachers use journals with the expectation of helping students to become literate thinkers, they will see growth in students' writing skills as well as content knowledge. It is no wonder that so many scientists, authors, illustrators, educators, historians, and others keep journals! Aside from using journals in content areas as a way of thinking through print and graphics, another goal of this strategy is to develop the habit of journaling beyond the classroom. Although there are many types of journals used by classroom teachers, each may be adapted for specific purposes in various content area classrooms. With response journals, learning journals, dialogue journals, and double-entry journals being the most widely used, the type of journal that teachers select will be determined by their purposes and the nature of the discipline they teach.

Source: International Reading Association and National Council of Teachers of English (1996).

IRA/NCTE Standards for the English Language Arts

3. Students apply a wide range of strategies to comprehend, interpret, evaluate, and appreciate texts. They draw on their prior experience, their interactions with other readers and writers, their knowledge of word meaning and of other texts, their word identification strategies, and their understanding of textual features (e.g., sound-letter correspondence, sentence structure, context, graphics).

5. Students employ a wide range of strategies as they write and use different writing process elements appropriately to communicate with different audiences for a variety of purposes.

STEP-BY-STEP PROCEDURE

As journaling becomes commonplace, teachers are experimenting with myriad types and applications across the curriculum. Procedures for journal use are dependent on the purpose for which it is used. In some instances, teachers may ask for specific types of entries, such as in mathematics classrooms; in other classrooms, journal writing may be open-ended, such as for students entering personal responses while reading a piece of literature. One important aspect of keeping a journal is promoting its systematic use while maintaining interest and relevance. When introducing students to journal writing, keep in mind the following tips:

1. Explain the value of journal writing in understanding ideas and content as well as keeping a record of some important experiences, ideas, and events for future reference.

2. Have students date each entry.

3. Show students sample entries written by students from previous years.

4. Keep a class journal for joint entries.

There is no specific time for making entries in one's journal. The teacher may request students to make predictions about their reading before opening their text. While reading, the teacher may ask students to select specific aspects from the book to which they would like to respond; for many, entries are written by students after reading the text. Below are descriptions of journals that are most commonly used across the curriculum: learning journals, response journals, double-entry/triple-entry journals, dialogue journals, and class journals.

Learning Journals

Learning journals are used by students in content area classrooms to record new ideas they have learned and explaining them by using words or sketches to represent meaning. The journal goes beyond the notebook where students may summarize ideas they have read. The primary purpose of keeping a learning journal is to use writing as a mode of inquiry and learning. Therefore, when teachers first use journaling to promote thinking and understanding, they will frequently provide a set of guidelines that directs students to reflect on ideas in new ways. For example, teachers in the art room may ask students to use a journal as a sketchbook to develop their ideas; in math classrooms, students may be requested to write or draw the process in solving a problem; in the science lab, journals provide a tool to encourage students to carefully record observations; and in English language arts, teachers may request their students to keep writing journals for entries of their ideas and experiences that they may use for writing. The learning journal has a place in every content area classroom.

Response Journals

The use of response journals encourages students to reflect on concepts learned through class discussions or readings. Students' responses include exploring ideas, asking questions, interpreting text, evaluating stories and characters, and expressing feelings. Response journals started with students responding or reflecting on literature with no formal structure or set of prompts. Many teachers observed that some students needed direction in their use of response journals and provided open-ended questions or a variety of prompts to stimulate their thinking.

Double-Entry and Triple-Entry Journals

Within these double-entry and triple-entry journals, students employ a wide range of strategies to respond to text, ideas, concepts, or issues that are at the heart of a lesson. In a double-entry journal, the teacher asks students to select a section of the text and respond in some way. Typically, the student creates two columns on the journal page. In the first column, students enter the text to which they wish to respond; in the second column, they enter their responses and interpretations next to the text. In a triple-entry journal, the student creates three columns. Similar to the double-entry journal, the first column includes entries of the text, and the second column includes the students' responses to the text. To promote a deeper understanding of the text, issues, and concepts, students may engage in further reading using other sources of literature, visiting Web sites, and engaging in discussions with classmates for the purpose of extending their thinking. They revisit their first responses, adding another in the third column that may demonstrate a change in perspective and an elaboration of meaning.

Dialogue Journals

Dialogue journals offer an opportunity for students to discuss with another about a story, an idea, or problem through writing. Students use journals as a venue to converse with other classmates by responding to their entries on a selection from the text or on a specific idea. In dialogue journals, students divide their pages into two columns. In the first column, they write their own entries responding to or interpreting the text. Students exchange journals, and in the second column, they respond to their partner's entry. In other words, a written dialogue around a text appears in the journal. Many teachers use electronic dialogue journals where students dialogue about a book or an issue with students from another school.

CLASS JOURNALS

Class journals provide all students with an opportunity to share their voice within one journal. Class journals, sometimes referred to as traveling journals, may be used by the entire class to respond to issues, literature, and ideas. Because class journals have such versatility, teachers have found different uses based on their specific purposes. For example, when cooperative groups are formed to research various aspects of a topic, each group may write an entry on the group's findings. When the whole class is discussing a piece of literature and students express a range of responses, the teacher may pass the journal around inviting each member of the class to make a separate entry.

DIFFERENTIATING INSTRUCTION FOR STRIVING READERS

One teacher first started to use journals with middle school students who were labeled as reluctant to learn, struggling readers, and students in need of discipline. After reading and discussing the first chapter in *Dear Mr. Henshaw,* the teacher asked students to write their responses in a new journal that she gave to each student. They simply looked at her. The teacher reviewed their discussions with them and gave them a written prompt to get them started. The students picked up their pens and wrote a few words. She collected the journals and took them home to read their responses and to respond to their entries—no small task. The following day, the students and teacher continued to read and discuss the story. When they opened their journals, they discovered that their teacher took time to write an individual response in each journal. The teacher was surprised by the students' reactions. Each student read her response, reread it, and reread it one more time. They even counted the words. They read their friends' journals and compared responses. So when the teacher asked them to write a response in their journals, this time they did not hesitate though they found writing difficult. By the end of the week, the teacher did not give prompts, and the undisciplined boys showed an increased engagement in reading their books. They anticipated opening their journals to read the teacher's responses and writing their own entries. Although the teacher had read about the multiple benefits for using classroom journals, she discovered the real power in journaling from her students. For students who were striving readers and writers, the teacher's response served as a model for writing as well as a caring audience for their writing.

CONSIDERING THE LANGUAGE NEEDS OF ELL STUDENTS

Source: International Reading Association and National Council of Teachers of English (1996).

IRA/NCTE Standards for the English Language Arts

10. Students whose first language is not English make use of their first language to develop competency in the English language arts and to develop understanding of content across the curriculum.

English language learners find writing exceptionally difficult. They may lack a large vocabulary or be unsure of syntax and proper word usage. To help them begin to write entries, assure them their writing will not be graded for errors. Encourage them to start small—one short sentence may capture their response. Prior to their writing use "talk" as a tool to help them think about what they will write. Let each student articulate what they would like to write, starting with one sentence. Finally, scaffold their writing by helping them to write their responses. Another effective tool that many authors use prior to their writing is a drawing. When ELL students cannot respond with words, ask them to illustrate their response and then talk to them about the drawing. Finally, one or two words may initiate a discussion. Ask the students to respond by saying and writing one or two words in their native language. Then ask, "Why did you use that word to tell how you feel?" and encourage them to answer in writing.

APPLICATIONS OF JOURNAL WRITING

An Application for Learning Journals

In every classroom, teachers may use learning journals. Their primary goal is to have students write or draw about *what* and *how* they think about ideas. The teachers may use students' journals to understand their thinking, identify misconceptions, and further develop their ideas. Listed below are applications of the learning journal in the mathematics and science classrooms.

Mathematics: In one of the first geometry classes, the teacher asked students to solve the following problem: Find the radius OC when it is the same as the radius OD; find diameter AB of that circle, when radius OC is the same or equal to OD and OD=12. Students were then asked to use their math journals to sketch and explain in words what the problem means and the procedure or process that they will use in solving the problem.

Science: Students in a biology class kept a learning journal for their scientific research. They were conducting experiments on pulse rates. They collected data from friends and members of their families engaged in different physical activities. Students recorded the data in their learning journals. The teacher asked students to describe in words the meaning of each set of data, to compare the data for each of their subjects, and write an interpretation of the comparison data.

An Application for Response Journals

In the following application of response journals in the English language arts and theater arts classroom, students enter responses in their journals. In each of the disciplines, their responses are guided by the related content.

English Language Arts: Response journal writing and English language arts are complimentary. After we read a book, it is natural to think about the characters and events and express our feelings. The teacher in an English language arts class asked students in the 8th grade who were reading *Rat* by Jan Cheripko (2005) to make entries in their response journals. They were asked to select one of the characters and follow him through the story through responses to his actions—by supporting or confronting him, suggesting a change in behavior, or expressing their feelings toward their character's behaviors and intentions.

An Application of Double-Entry and Single-Entry Journals

The purpose of these journals is to provide students with an opportunity to think deeply about their text and the concepts, ideas, and issues that they are learning.

Social Studies and English Language Arts: In one 6th-grade classroom, the students were learning about Irish Immigration in their social studies class. The teacher used their textbooks, Web sites, and podcasts to teach about the historical events, the land, and the people. As students read each day from their texts and Web sites, they used their double-entry journals to respond to and interpret their readings. In English language arts, the teacher used a text set of children's literature on the same topic. In this class, students used triple-entry journals, extending their entries to include a third. Using additional readings, a range of literature including nonfiction, fiction, and poetry, students were able to extend their responses.

An Application to Dialogue Journals

This is another type of journal that has a wide range of applications in a single content area as well as across curriculum areas. Students may respond to their partner's entries by expressing their points of view, by sharing their own similar responses, and by solving problems jointly. A number of students use electronic journals for conversing because of their convenience and accessibility. Below is an example of how a theater arts teacher used dialogue journals with students to help them develop a strong point of view on an issue that they would use for improvisation.

Theater Arts: In a theater arts classroom where students are studying improvisation, they are expected to develop a strong opinion on an issue and then use improvisation to convey their point of view to their audience. The teacher used dialogue journals asking students to write their opinions on a controversial issue, encouraging them to use drawings as well. One approach the teacher found to support students' writing was to have students begin by writing words and phrases in their journals that demonstrated a point of view or opinion and continue by drawing figures that showed body language or facial expressions to express their point of view. They wrote their entry expressing their strong opinions on an issue. They then exchanged their journals with their partners who responded to their entries by expressing their own opinions. This continued until students developed a point of view that could be articulated through improvisation on an aspect the topic.

REFERENCES

Barnes, D. (1976). *From communication to curriculum.* New York: Penguin.

Britton, J. (1993). *Language and learning.* Portsmouth, NH: Boynton/Cook.

Cheripko, J. (2005). *Rat.* Honesdale, PA: Boyds Mills Press.

International Reading Association and National Council of Teachers of English. (1996). *Standards for the English language arts.* Newark, DE: International Reading Association & Urbana, IL: National Council of Teachers of English.

Popp, M. S. (1997). *Learning journals in the K–8 classroom: Exploring ideas and information in the content areas.* Mahwah, NJ: Lawrence Erlbaum.

Wells, G., & Chang-Wells, G. L. (1992). *Constructing knowledge together: Classrooms as centers of inquiry and literacy.* Portsmouth, NH: Heinemann.

Index

About the Authors

Patricia A. Antonacci is a Professor of Education and teaches in the literacy education program at Iona College. Antonacci entered the teaching profession as a classroom teacher for the middle and elementary grades and continued as a reading specialist. Her long career in public schools brought her a range of experiences as a teacher at all grade levels including a number of years working in diverse classroom settings. As a reading specialist for K through 12, she assisted teachers in integrating literacy instruction in content areas. Working in a large urban school district afforded her rich experiences teaching striving readers and English language learners.

Antonacci has taught courses at Fordham University and Iona College including the following: reading in the content areas for middle and secondary grades, foundations of literacy, literacy across the curriculum, action research in literacy as well as mentoring doctoral students in conducting research in literacy education. Currently, she is at Iona College teaching courses in the literacy program. She has published numerous journal articles and books including (as coauthors) Antonacci & O'Callaghan, *Portraits of Literacy Development: Instruction and Assessment in a Well-Balanced Literacy Program, K–3* (2004), Antonacci & O'Callaghan, *A Handbook for Literacy Instructional & Assessment Strategies, K–8* (2006), and Antonacci & O'Callaghan, *Using Children's Literature Across The Curriculum: A Handbook of Instructional Strategies (K–8)* (2010).

Catherine M. O'Callaghan is a Professor of Education and Chair of the Education Department at Iona College. She entered the teaching profession as a classroom teacher and continued her career as a literacy specialist with teaching experiences that span across the grades. Teaching in New York City within diverse settings afforded her a wide range of teaching experiences. Her doctoral degree from Fordham University in Language and Literacy initiated her research interests in new literacies, critical literacies, teacher education, and intervention plans for helping striving readers and writers. O'Callaghan began working with preservice and inservice teachers at St. Joseph's College in the Child Study Department and as an adjunct at Fordham University in the School of Education. She currently teaches courses at the graduate and undergraduate levels in literacy education including the following: language development, action research in literacy, literacy across the curriculum, and reading in the content areas. She is also involved in supervising in-service teachers who work with struggling readers and writers in the literacy practicum course.

O'Callaghan has published numerous journal articles and books including (as coauthors) Antonacci & O'Callaghan, *Portraits of Literacy Development: Instruction and Assessment in a Well-Balanced Literacy Program, K-3* (2004), Antonacci & O'Callaghan, *A Handbook for Literacy Instructional & Assessment Strategies, K–8* (2006), and Antonacci & O'Callaghan, *Using Children's Literature Across The Curriculum: A Handbook of Instructional Strategies (K-8)* (2010).